FROM CRIME TO REHABILITATION

For Mmankudu Mopipi and Bothakga

with much love

From Crime to Rehabilitation

M. J. A. GLICKMAN
Department of Sociology,
University of Botswana

Gower

Published by
Gower Publishing Company Limited,
Gower House, Croft Road, Aldershot, Hampshire, England.

British Library Cataloguing in Publication Data

Glickman, M.J.A.
From crime to rehabilitation.
1. Rehabilitation of criminals—Great Britain
I. Title
364.8'0941 HV9345

ISBN 0-566-00539-5

Printed and Bound in Great Britain by
Robert Hartnoll Limited, Bodmin, Cornwall.

Contents

Acknowledgements

Sincere acknowledgement is due to the Home Office Research Unit and the Worshipful Company of Weavers for grants covering part of my maintenance and expenses for this study. I am also grateful to the former Steering Committee of NACRO-Education for its invitation to pry into its affairs. Dare I hope that, in return, I have contributed not only to an understanding of rehabilitative and educational problems but also to restricting the generalisation that 'there is little to be gleaned from previous attempts at evaluation, due to the lack of a conceptual framework' (Gordon and Morse 1975, p.34)?

I owe more than I can ever repay to the citizens about whom I write, caught up as so many have been in the rigmarole of crime and rehabilitation, about which topics they taught me most of what I know. They also shared with me a scepticism about conventional wisdom, an attitude without which no sociological research can properly proceed.

My appreciation is boundless for the guidance in my research of John Barnes, a sociologist whose interests and insights know no subdisciplinary boundaries. My two main critics were Meyer Fortes, whose knowledge about crime goes back more than half a century, when he studied juvenile delinquency in London, and Stan Cohen, who has worked so hard to make British sociologists aware of how much American theorists have to offer. Without the scrutinising advice of Fortes and Cohen, I would have regarded writing this monograph as out of the question. Donald West, Director of the Institute of Criminology in Cambridge, suggested that no offence would be given to readers by making more explicit the 'philosophical stance' which I have reached. I am grateful for the effect which his advice has had on my argument in general and on Chapter 7, Section G in particular. Finally, I thank Gower Press for being so patient in awaiting my manuscript, written in a year of heavy teaching and other duties at 'UB', and my colleagues, Conrad Halloran, Ken Jones and Peter Takirambudde, for their comments on the final draft.

Preface

Sociologists, anthropologists and other social scientists sometimes accuse colleagues in their profession of a fixation on the more dramatic manifestations of social life, thus disregarding the less spectacular. I doubt if such an accusation can fairly be levelled against the choice of topic of this book.

The 1970s saw the emergence in Britain and elsewhere of a number of radical groups which, totally rejecting the legitimacy of the criminal justice and prison systems, were bent on revolutionary change. The membership of these groups consisted of prisoners, ex-prisoners and their comrades. They wished to give active expression to their opposition to a society which they considered distributed life chances inequitably; which hypocritically imposed long prison sentences on petty property offenders while leaving untouched the unjust, and sometimes illegal, methods of accumulating property on the part of the rich; and which allowed against prison inmates a regular regime of physical and psychological cruelty comparable with any violence which prisoners might manifest in the outside world.

But such radical movements were by no means the first to protest against the way in which law-breakers are treated. Criticisms of the extent, methods and abuses of imprisonment as a form of punishment probably go back almost as far as the beginnings of the institution itself. Its critics, however, have usually been privileged members of society, and pressure groups for prison reform have normally been inspired by the liberal sentiments of, for instance, prison chaplains and other prison visitors, lawyers and probation officers. The aims of these more conventional associations have been to stimulate the interest of like-minded members of the public and to influence legislators and politicians.

One of the main organisations of this kind is the National Association for the Care and Resettlement of Offenders - NACRO. In the early 1970s, NACRO had a policy of establishing widely a chain of short-term 'pilot projects' whose very success, it was hoped, would lead to their speedy adoption by local authorities or other statutory bodies as soon as the experimental period ended.

One of these projects, 'NACRO-Education', was set up to assist ex-offenders to return to formal education in the outside world. The project had two components: an 'Advisory Service' and a hostel. Clients were referred to the Advisory Service by probation officers, prison welfare officers and prison education officers. There were also cases of self-referral by clients who had seen a copy of a brochure about the project on prison notice boards (see Appendix A). Clients were advised, usually by mail, of colleges to which they might apply. The Advisory Service also advised colleges on the suitability of those clients whom it recommended.

Out of the many clients from whom the Advisory Service received enquiries, a small number was selected for a place in the hostel, which was viewed as an intermediate step between being subjected to imprisonment or other form of treatment by the courts and becoming an ordinary student at a college or university. The hostel was usually referred to by NACRO, its staff and its clients as the 'Unit'. This monograph is a study of the Unit. The research on which it is based focussed on the Unit's 'experimental' three year period and on the forty-five clients who received assistance from its staff while living in the Unit or nearby mostly during that period. Most of these clients are referred to in various parts of this book and are, of course, given pseudonyms. An index of clients is provided for the purpose of cross-reference. In the body of the book, I have chosen twelve case studies for more detailed discussion. I consider them to be as 'representative' of the very diverse types of client in the total universe of forty-five as it was possible to obtain.

I hope that this study will be of concern to probation officers, social workers, criminologists, magistrates, policy makers and others with a professional or lay interest in offenders, in rehabilitation and in the uses of education. But my aim is also to make a contribution to sociological theory.

In developing my theoretical analysis, I considered that the most serviceable explanation of the process of rehabilitation could be derived from Becker's commitment hypothesis, which the Unit seemed to offer a useful opportunity to test. According to Becker, a person stifles any deviant impulses he may possess because of the adverse effects which acting on them might have on 'lines of behaviour', such as schooling (1963, p.27), which he may be committed to. But, as will become clear, the theory falls short of a completely satisfying explanation of our data. Yet I do not regard it as completely false. Rather, I found it useful to modify it, as well as situate it within a wider body of theory. Such may be the fate of many sociological hypotheses after they have been tested on the ground.

An earlier draft of this book has been read by people who have worked with offenders and in rehabilitation projects, and they have found that the account has a familiar ring. I hope that the theoretical analysis may help to provide such practitioners with a means of intellectually organising their experience. I hope also that the descriptive account will give some grounding to sociological generalisations.

Please note that, in this monograph, a cursive script is used for quotations from handwritten letters, in order to distinguish them from quotations from speech, official letters and other documents, fieldnotes and literature. Quotations from all sources are reproduced faithfully: I have neither corrected statements which do not conform to the standards of 'standard' English nor been pedantic by repeatedly using '[sic]' whenever such conformity is lacking.

Foreword for the Non-British Reader

This monograph, though by no means intended for readers in Britain only, inevitably refers to educational and criminal justice institutions peculiar to that country. Attached to such institutions are terms which are also insular, although, in some cases, there is the opposite problem: transnational terms, such as 'parole', do not correspond to precisely the same phenomena in Britain as, for example, in the United States. I have made an effort in this book to make the meaning of terms clear from the contexts in which they occur, as far as this is possible, without burdening the reader by diverging from the main theme. However, I considered it might also be useful to include at this early stage a special foreword devoted to removing obstacles to international understanding before they occur.

The oddest example of parochial usage is 'public school', which, in Britain, means a school which is private and, far from offering access to the public, is mainly reserved for the children of the upper and upper middle class, as well as the children of the élite of third world, and other, countries.

Especially treacherous are words which have a variety of meanings even in Britain. Thus, 'tutor' can refer to a person who teaches a small group or just one individual. In a university setting, such a tutor provides educational guidance to students additional to what they derive from lectures. The term, however, can also refer to a university teacher with nonacademic duties, as in 'moral (counselling) tutor' or 'admissions tutor'. In the older universities of Britain, such as the University of London, a tutor, of either kind, even nowadays, may see his students for lengthy discussion every week or fortnight. With the fast expansion of university education in the 1960s, however, contacts between tutors and students have become much briefer and more occasional.

'College' is another term which has various meanings, which, however, do not include, as is frequently the case in the United States, an alternative term or title for a university. In Britain, it may refer to an academic division, sometimes specialising in particular subjects, of a university, so that, for example, the London School of Economics is a constituent (social science) college of the University of London. However, in the Universities of Oxford and, even more so, Cambridge, academic activity is mainly the work of university faculties or departments. Membership of one of the many constituent colleges of these universities is based mainly on rights to the use by university students and teachers (usually of sundry academic disciplines) of its residential, dining and recreation facilities.

But the word 'college' can also refer to a teaching institution above secondary school level but below university level or status, such as the Cambridgeshire College of Arts and Technology - shortened in this book to the 'Tech'. In regard to this particular study, it is important to emphasise that, although the Unit was situated in Cambridge, and although its founder was a University of Cambridge graduate, neither it nor the Tech, which many of the Unit's clients went to, had much significant connection with the University, except that I, the researcher, was a member of one of the University of Cambridge colleges.

Adult residential colleges, few in number, are places of education designed for working people who wish to take a break in order to advance their formal education. Students from such colleges who successfully obtain a certificate or diploma after one or two years are usually regarded as having suitable qualifications to apply for a university place if they so wish. These colleges enjoyed expansion in that almost unique period in modern British history, 1945-51, when many government ministers had had little formal education.

Among the many other educational institutions to which 'college' may refer are 'correspondence colleges', which teach by mail, and 'village colleges', mainly confined to the rural areas around Cambridge, which were founded on the idea of providing centres of culture by combining schools for young people with evening courses of study and recreation for adults. Other schools in Britain are utilised in a similar hybrid way but do not use the title 'college' in most cases.

The term 'higher education' includes both universities and polytechnics. At one time, there was a sharp distinction between the two, insofar as the latter tended to specialise in applied science. But in the 1960s many polytechnics developed degree programmes in such 'humanities' as psychology and sociology. Just as 'secondary education' refers to the stage after 'primary education', so the term 'tertiary education' refers to the stage after secondary education. Tertiary education, therefore, includes places of higher education as well as 'further education', such as the Tech, which is as much concerned with courses leading to the General Certificate of Education (GCE) and such professional qualifications as the Higher National Diploma (HND) as with courses leading to a degree.

The following may be consulted for further details about British education: Halls (1971, pp.305-12) for a general synopsis; Douglas (1964) on the 'eleven plus'; Jackson and Marsden (1962), who deal not only with the eleven plus but also with the GCE Ordinary (O) and Advanced (A) levels, which are qualifications usually obtained at secondary schools; and Locke and Pratt (1979) for such diverse statuses and qualifications as 'mature student', HND and the certificate of the Royal Society of Arts (RSA).

The British term 'postgraduate student' corresponds to the American 'graduate student' except that in the U.S.A. such a student is usually obliged to take examinations as well as present a dissertation based on research, whereas in Britain he is still frequently expected to present a (usually lengthy) dissertation without also having to take examinations.

The Open University was established in 1971. It is open to people of any background with or without previous academic qualifications. Graduation takes place on completion of a certain number of credits and the period in which these may be obtained is not limited. The OU produces its own texts linked with special radio and television programmes, and students submit their written work by mail for marking. There is usually a long waiting list for enrolment with the OU. A considerable minority of students are prisoners, usually longterm prisoners. A standard work on the history and operation of the OU is Tunstall ed. (1974).

For further details about the treatment of offenders, such as Approved Schools, Detention Centres, Borstal, bail, social enquiry reports, conditional discharge, deferred sentences, community service orders, probation, the prison welfare service, prison education, remission, parole and after-care, the most serviceable sources are probably Bean (1976), Briggs (1975), Davies (1974a), Fitzgerald and Sim (1979), Hood and Sparks (1970), Mays ed. (1975), Thomas (1979), Tutt ed. (1978), Walker (1968) and Wootton (1978).

The New Encyclopaedia Britannica (15th edition) provides a good, up to date, coverage of most items concerned with British education and criminal justice.

Terms from the criminal underworld will be few, and I trust that their meaning too will normally be apparent from the contexts in which they occur.

PART I

APPROACHING A STUDY OF REHABILITATION

> Today, the central problem is commitment. To what past, present, or future can the idealistic young commit themselves? (Mead 1972, p.9).

1 Introduction

A. EX-OFFENDERS AND THEIR REHABILITATION

Since 'ex-offender' and 'rehabilitation' do not have any generally accepted definition it is necessary from the start to state how I shall be using these terms.

I shall use 'ex-offender' ambiguously, for most of the Unit's clients did not refrain from continuing to break the law. Similar liberality will be given to the term 'student'. Of another project Millham et al. (1978, p.143) say, 'The hostel ... filled with young offenders who, thanks to the application of labelling theory, were graced with the title "student"'. I too shall employ this title, and regardless of whether its recipients did much studying.

'Rehabilitation', however, must be given more precise meaning for the term has such ambiguity that only confusion can result from loose definition in our analysis. It may be that 'rehabilitation', rather like 'community' (Scull 1977, p.60; Croft 1979, p.1), is such a positively charged emotive word that its meaning has never been clarified. Contexts, however, reveal three main senses of the term.

The first occurs in statements like, 'the aims of the court in imposing custodial sentences include ... the reformation or improvement of the offender' (HMSO 1978, p.29).

'Rehabilitation', however, is also commonly used in the sense of reinstatement in society. Reform and reinstatement, however, are different processes. For example, as we shall see, Leo achieved a measure of reinstatement in society but none of the reform which the court apparently wished for him. There are surely many people of outward virtue in the outside world who continue to commit offences for which they were once sentenced to prison or other form of punishment.

Confusion is further confounded when 'rehabilitation'

is defined in a third sense of being 'concerned with overcoming the effects of incarceration' (Davies 1974a, p.5). For ever since the Gladstone Report (HMSO 1895, vol.2, pp.8 and 18), if not before, it has been declared about imprisonment that the 'regime should be the individual rehabilitation of each inmate. This should be the conscious aim of the whole of the institution's staff' (HMSO 1963, p.22). To add yet further to the confusion, one of the effects of incarceration seems to be that some ex-offenders sometimes come to see it not so much as a debility from which they will later have to recover, but as a means of overcoming the effects of society. As Ian once wrote to the judge in his usual candid way:

> *While people try to form some kind of defence on my behalf ... Sir, since coming out of prison, I have found life unbarable ... the only thing left for a person like myself is inprisonment ... remove me from torment of soal ...*

Or, as a probationer told his officer, 'in many ways it would be easier to be back inside; you haven't got the frustrations of living' (Davies 1974a, p.71).

To avoid not only these difficulties but also the common tendency for anything done to or for offenders to be called rehabilitation, I shall keep to the first denotation of 'rehabilitation' which we have discussed, thus following Bean (1976, p.6) in using the word in the sense of reforming - becoming more law-abiding. Thus, a client such as Leo, who became less law-abiding but succeeded in avoiding further arrest, will not, strictly speaking, be considered to have rehabilitated.

B. STUDYING A REHABILITATION HOSTEL

The majority of the clients who were attached to the Unit had applied for a place voluntarily. It was hoped that they would use it as a base from which to further their academic education and, after passing examinations at the end of a few months of study, gain admission to universities and colleges in the role of ordinary students. Members of staff, though living not far away, were never themselves resident in the hostel. They normally worked a nine to five day, five day week. One of their main tasks was to provide places for new residents when the latter were discharged from prison or when vacancies occurred.

Characteristics mentioned above, such as voluntary referral and nonresidential staff, were among various features which appeared to make the hostel distinctive. When, therefore, in 1976, the Unit's Steering Committee appointed me as a research officer to study the Unit and its performance I was intrigued by these distinctive features. Some of them, however, turned out to be less unusual than they had seemed at first. The chapters of this book concerned with the history of the Unit indicate that elements of compulsion rather than voluntary motivation and participation developed, which suggested that the impression of free involvement in the programme (see Appendix A) was more of an ideal representation than an actual one. It will be seen, for instance, that the fact that the staff did not sleep on the premises did not mean that little control was exercised over the clients. It seemed, therefore, that tools of analysis which could help to account for rehabilitation - and continued recidivism - among the Unit's small number of residents might also be adaptable to other rehabilitative settings.

C. REHABILITATION AND COMMITMENT

An explanatory model has particular merit when it can be applied to a wide range of situations. Becker's concept of commitment was originally developed to address the sociological topic of careers (Becker 1952; Becker and Carper 1956; Becker and Strauss 1956; Becker et al. 1961). In the course of working on this subject, Becker discerned that the concept of commitment could also be relevant to the sociology of deviance. In his 'notes' on commitment, Becker (1960, p.40) says that 'the conception of commitment I have sketched gives us the theoretical tools for assimilating the common-sense notion that people often follow lines of activity for reasons extraneous to the activity itself'. Now, rehabilitation does not have any intrinsic or direct connection with an academic programme; the process of rehabilitation may, therefore, be regarded as 'extraneous' to an academic programme. But if we regard 'leading a more law-abiding life' as an example of a 'line of activity', and if we regard 'motives for working for academic qualifications' as an example of 'reasons extraneous to the activity itself', then we have a testable theory applicable to the Unit's 'students'.

Becker (1963, pp.27-8) incorporates his thinking on the theme of commitment into a discussion of deviance and normality in a most useful way:

> the normal development of people in our society (and probably in any society) can be seen as a series of progressively increasing commitments to conventional norms and institutions. The "normal" person, when he discovers a deviant impulse in himself, is able to check that impulse in thinking of the manifold consequences acting on it would produce for him. He has staked too much on con-

> tinuing to be normal to allow himself to be swayed by unconventional impulses.

The applicability of this hypothesis can be judged from the following statement, again by Ian:

> there's lots of cars in Cambridge, what's got suitcases and God knows what in 'em, wallets stuck in the dash, etc., it's unbelievable. I don't know why I 'ave'nt jumped to the job of taking 'em. P'raps it's 'cos I'm older than what I was ... I'm aiming at something I want'a do which plays a big part in it. I've an aim to get at, and I can only get at that aim by keeping my nose clean and 'ard at work. I've got a choice. I can either keep straight, and 'ave the possibility of being accepted, or I can get the wrong side of the law again and 'ave a good rest at Strangeways Prison or somewhere. It's as simple as that.

In his notes on commitment, however, Becker continuously indicates an awareness that the concept can form a part only of any explanation of a human lifestyle. Accordingly, in Part II, I shall introduce additional variables to be examined in relation to our data: the <u>functions</u> which the Unit performed for its clients and the <u>meanings</u> which the Unit had for them. It will also be necessary to discuss different <u>levels</u> of commitment.

In my theoretical analysis, it would have been possible to have disproved Becker's pristine commitment hypothesis by marshalling negative evidence. Instead, I have preserved it from demolition not only by modifying it, but also by invoking additional causal variables. There may be some methodologists, perhaps with an understanding of the writings of Karl Popper which is too simplistic, who might object to such complex conservation measures. I consider, however, that using a combination of several theoretical principles is sometimes unavoidable. Colleagues in chemistry, fluid dynamics and other fields tell me that much of their research consists of finding the best fit between the data they have collected and ideas taken from whatever assorted theories are available. These researchers refer to this procedure as 'interpretation' of data, a term which will be well-known to sociologists.

If such theoretical eclecticism pervades experimental science it is even more in evidence in sciences which are historical. Writing about the cosmos Calder (1968, p.98) says:

> In weighing arguments about the nature of the universe (and other theories which will come along) it should be remembered that all of them are speculative. They are based, however, on other well-tested theories like the Theory of Relativity; the absolute constant of the velocity of light; Hubble's constant (recession velocity

= distance), the Doppler Effect, with its red-shift significance; and many, many more. Those insights have suggested observations, and observations have provided insights. All go into the stockpot from which cosmological chefs prepare their recipes.

In sociology, we have very few 'well-tested' theories. This study, however, attempts to test a theory. In the next sections of this chapter, therefore, I will discuss the way I shall present my data for testing theory.

D. THE CASE-STUDY METHOD

Much of the data gathered during my research are presented in this book in the form of case studies. It may be useful, therefore, to discuss the place which the case-study method has occupied in sociology in general and in the sociology of deviance in particular.

The classic case study in this branch of sociology is The Jack-Roller (Shaw 1930), a biography of the early life of an American delinquent. Significantly, one of the most prominent factors in bringing about the rehabilitation of the subject of the book is his progressive commitment to 'lines of activity' which would have been in jeopardy if he had continued in his recidivism.

An important merit of the case-study method is that it can often provide detailed information about a person's motivations which may elude methods of investigation which collect more superficial facts on a large sample of individuals. It may well remain the case that 'there are many aspects of delinquency which are not, for the present at least, susceptible to treatment by formal statistical methods. While quantitative methods are applicable to a wide range of the more formal aspects of delinquent conduct, some more discerning, though perhaps less exact, method is necessary to disclose the underlying processes involved in the formation of delinquent behavior trends' (ibid., p.31).

The popularity of the case-study method has, in the course of the century, developed in waves. When it powerfully emerged in Chicago sociology in the 1920s it came as a strong reaction against the excessively speculative and ungrounded theories of the previous decades. The mighty study, more than 2000 pages long, by Thomas and Znaniecki (1918-20) of Polish immigrants set a style which influenced sociology for more than a generation. Among the most notable examples of such influence are Reckless (1929), Shaw (1930, 1931, 1938), Sutherland (1937) and Riesman (1952).

In the 1950s and 1960s, however, the method received less favour, becoming replaced again by ungrounded theory. If we peruse some of the main works in the sociology of deviance during this period we find that case studies are often totally lacking. Thus, Cohen's Delinquent Boys (1955) contains no case study of any delinquent boy, Cloward and Ohlin's Delinquency and Opportunity (1960) contains none on any opportunistic delinquent. Becker's Outsiders (1963) contains none on any outsider, and Matza's Becoming Deviant (1969) contains no case study of any individual undergoing the transition announced in the title. In Britain, Parker (e.g. 1963, 1969) wrote an excellent series of life histories, but they quickly went out of print; a possible index of the neglect which they undeservedly received.

1965 seems to have been a year of presentiment for the revival of the case-study method. Riesman's case studies of the American character were republished. Mannheim (1965, pp.1953-60) provided a compendium of literature on the study of crime (mainly from the Chicago School) using the case-study method, and listed its merits, having earlier (National Association for Mental Health 1949 , p.17) despaired of its decline. Yablonsky (1965, p.73) urged that:

> live and significant data collected by the "Chicago School" researchers in the 1920-30 period were mainly relevant to that time and place. Many recent theorists on social problems have overdrawn on this sociological bank account. The time is long overdue for a resurgence of field-study and case-history methodology to replenish our sociological storehouse ... Such contemporary data would aid the long-distance sociological theorists and statisticians to build the speculative theories about social problems on a firmer base of actual human behaviour.

In 1966, The Jack-Roller was republished, with an introduction by Becker which contained compelling arguments for the reinstatement of the case-study method. The book was reprinted six times within a year. Moreover, by the 1970s, further sociological life histories (e.g. Spradley 1970, Chambliss (ed) 1972) began to appear. (It is, therefore, unfortunate, that a recent 'guide to the major literature'(Wright ed. 1974) by the former librarian of the Institute of Criminology in Cambridge, and later director of the Howard League for Penal Reform, contains no reference to 'case study', 'case history', 'life history', etc. There are three references in the index to 'biography', but the first is a mistake for bibliography, and the other two refer to material on eminent people, in particular, penal reformers and criminologists.) Another important trend in recent years has been a series of sociologically informed autobiographies by ex-prisoners (e.g. Curtis 1973a,

Boyle 1977, Probyn 1977 and McVicar 1979).

Case-study sociology can be classified into two main types. The first consists of biographies primarily concerned with exploration. Such exploration may be of new concepts (e.g., Thomas and Znaniecki 1918-20), of refinements of the case-study method (e.g., Cressey 1953), of a new field (e.g., Bogdan 1974) or of new data in an established field (e.g., Chambliss ed. 1972).

A second genre is concerned with comparative biography aimed at illustrating similarities and differences in a common situation. The common situation may range from being gainfully employed in the United States of America (Terkel 1975) to the experience of pupils in a multiracial English primary school (Jackson 1979).

The two genres overlap and, indeed, both are used in this monograph. In addition, our case studies will be presented, as far as space allows, on 'detailed and on uniform lines' (Mannheim 1967, p.303). They will be detailed enough to allow the reader to draw other, and perhaps better, conclusions than my own. The way in which the case studies will be presented 'on uniform lines' is discussed in the final section of this chapter.

E. THE TABULATION OF CASE-STUDY DATA

Case-study material can be abused. For example, Becker (1963, p.34) theorises that:

> treating a person as though he were generally rather than specifically deviant produces a self-fulfilling prophecy. It sets in motion several mechanisms which conspire to shape the person in the image people have of him.

Instead of tying this theory to facts, however, Becker merely footnotes a reference to Ray (1961).

Now Ray's article consists of several interesting case fragments. One of them is detailed and almost a page long. Its facts, however, seem to run counter to Becker's theory. The account is of a moralistic and apparently middle class boy whose mother tells him he is a bum. There can be few terms as connotative of general deviance than that. The boy, however, determined to win approval, puts examples of his behaviour through self-examination and takes measures to correct them. He thus belies the 'prophecy' and changes the image which his mother and her neighbours have of him.

Ray's other examples are concerned with individuals who appear to be treated as specifically deviant only; they are not, therefore, significant to Becker's hypothesis about the effects of the imputation of general deviance. Their outcomes are various. Ray's final example concerns a man who gives up heroin while living with his wife. They quarrel, and he leaves for another city, where he returns to heroin. She urges him to come back to her. He does so, and he renounces the habit again. The account is an excellent one of rehabilitation.

My argument here is not primarily concerned with refuting Becker's hypothesis about labelling a person as generally deviant. My point is possibly more fundamental. It is easy to misinterpret one or two case examples. But the effects of doing so can be pernicious. An important theory can take on the appearance of being supported by facts, whereas the relationship may actually be spurious. To guard against such a danger it is necessary to present cases in great detail so that readers are provided with plenty of information, neither abbreviated nor obscure, from which they can extract explicit statements for the purposes of theoretical argument.

But, in addition, it should also be possible to compare and contrast the information from each case study, for without the comparative method no discipline can claim to be an empirical science. It has to be admitted, however, that deriving distinctive features from lengthy descriptive material can be a burdensome task. I shall, therefore, codify twelve case studies into a table representing the main factors arguably making for rehabilitation or continued recidivism on the part of the clients involved. In this way, the significant factors can, by inspection, be evaluated. Needless to say, nothing is intended to prevent the fastidious reader from wading through the descriptive material if he so wishes. The purpose of this table is his convenience. Such tabulation actually entails the simplest form of statistical scaling, where 'numerals are used only as labels or type numbers and words or letters would serve as well ... once classes containing several individuals have been formed ... we can determine the most numerous class (the mode), and under certain conditions we can test ... hypotheses regarding the distribution of cases among classes' (Stevens 1971, p.5).

Thus, by presenting a number of detailed case studies, I intend to reduce the ambiguity of interpretation which can take place when only a few brief accounts are adduced. By codifying the case studies with numbers, letters or other symbols I shall present for the convenience of the reader a schematic table such as he himself might wish to devise in order to check the fit between my data and my theoretical interpretations.

2 Background to the Unit

A. HOW IT ALL BEGAN

Douglas Curtis, after studying at Cambridge University, having previously spent twelve years in prison, graduated in 1973. Dartmoor to Cambridge (1973a) is his autobiography. Many ex-prisoners have probably followed similar careers from custody to college. He alone turned the transition into a cause célèbre, attacking, in Union Society debates and elsewhere, the mindlessness of prison and the stereotype of prisoners as stupid or sub-human (for the extent to which a prisoner can be conscious of this stereotype see Parker and Allerton 1962, p.111). Curtis sought out leading educational reformers who were trying to extend their work beyond that small part of the population which does not regard pedagogy merely as unpleasant schooling which everybody has to go through. Despite involvement in activist movements for prisoners' rights (Fitzgerald 1977, passim) seen by the Establishment as disreputable, he was also prepared to press executives of NACRO to influence in new directions politicians with a special interest in penal reform.

Doug told me that it was in Dartmoor that he first thought of the idea of an educational rehabilitation project. His own plans to go to university had been realised through fortuitous contact with a Cambridge graduate in the prison education service and other patrons with a network of associates on the outside. Doug saw the need for a more rationalised system for guiding the passage of ex-offenders into tertiary education. In particular, a hostel might be needed for those ex-offenders who had neither advice, complete entry qualifications, money nor home.

An early charter by Doug for an educational rehabilitation project called for the appointment of a director with a criminal background and a degree. After interesting NACRO in the scheme, meeting its chairman, Lord Donaldson, in the House of Lords to discuss Home Office blessing and finance, however, he obtained the position of Organiser of 'LASER' (London and South East Region) in NACRO's map.

In that capacity, he maintained in Cambridge a Steering Committee for the intended project. The committee's core comprised people with whom he had already had contact: his former university tutor, a local probation officer with whom he had participated in university symposia, and a director of a correspondence college which at one time had considered administering the project. Others co-opted included a detective inspector and Ron Noble, a former education officer at Pentonville prison. Ron served as the chairman, until the project leader post was advertised in the Cambridge Evening News. He applied and was appointed in May 1974. He immediately worked with NACRO in designing an explanatory leaflet, which stated that 'the education project ... is a pilot scheme set up to provide educational opportunities for offenders who might otherwise be denied access to the educational system. The initial three-year experimental period will be closely monitored and evaluated by independent research'. (As we shall see later, the existence of the Unit was, in fact, extended by Home Office finance year by year up to three further years.) Throughout the period covered by this study Ron was the pivot of all administrative decisions in the Unit, whereas, not long after its first residents arrived, Doug's connections with NACRO were severed and he became involved in activities outside the ex-offender field.

The story so far, and as it will further unfold later, well matches Tutt's (1978, pp.15-17) schema for phases which rehabilitation projects tend to pass through:

> The first phase ... is the appearance of a crusader ... to change and challenge the prevailing system ... polarizing opinion around himself ... The development of a sympathetic stereotype of the offender is crucial to the next stage ... He misses few opportunities to promote his ideas by public debate and articles in the popular press [two articles in a prison newsletter (Curtis 1973b; 1974) were misleadingly headed 'Curtis Suggests College' and 'New College'] ... The crusader normally avoids protracted professional debate in the learned journals, thereby avoiding ... any academic argument ... a new phase is entered ... The sympathetic myths will attract ... professional workers with a high motivation to develop different ways of working with their clients ... If the project is to be taken through the invariable crises which arise, the staff must have a committed belief in the project to maintain morale.
>
> After a limited period many of the core staff will move on to new posts ... (emphasis his).

Time elapsed between crusading presentation of the Unit as a sympathetic stereotype and the advent of academic argument. Not until January 1976 did the Unit obtain a researcher. Various factors account for the delay: the desire to wait till NACRO had appointed its own permanent national research officer, the fear that research funding might compete with money from the Home Office for a full time assistant for Ron, and negotiations with the Home Office Research Unit - HORU - for research sponsorship. I thus arrived as a researcher towards the middle of the 'experiment', and during one of the crises that had arisen, when crime was far outstripping rehabilitation or education as the order of the day. However, in spite of my arrival date, I was able to gather information from clients and former clients of the Unit for a considerable period after all its core staff had moved on to new posts.

B. AFTER-CARE

The early proposals for the project did not foresee a sharp division between the work of the Unit and that of the Advisory Service. The unexpectedly large number of applicants to the project when it started, however, and the lack of personal contact that could be offered to those not invited to be candidates for residence in the hostel, soon differentiated the two components of the project, even though clients of the Unit and of the Advisory Service were referred through the same channels, did the same initial form-filling (including stating whether they wished to join the Unit) and were assisted by the same personnel in the same building in Cambridge (It was not till the summer of 1979 that the Advisory Service was placed in a separate national NACRO office in London.) The Advisory Service had much in common with such 'people processing' agencies as APEX (Soothill 1974; Lumkin 1976), a body concerned with the placement of ex-offenders in employment. The Unit, by contrast, sociologically resembled what is often referred to as a hostel for 'after-care' - but this is another criminological term which needs further scrutiny.

Ideally, an after-care hostel is a voluntary establishment for people wishing to use its services after imprisonment or other form of punishment. In practice, however, the punished tend rapidly to commit offences which make them punishable again, and the younger that offenders are the more do they tend to do so (West 1967, pp.24-5). Moreover, imprisonment for offenders has been used for so long that it has come to be recognised increasingly widely how costly and, on the whole, ineffective (for purposes beyond the expression of moral outrage) it is. Any ongoing form of after-care, therefore, soon comes to be regarded by sentencers as an alternative to conventional punishment, additional to the various other alternatives to prison which are frequently devised.

The reasons sentencers have for applying alternative 'strategies' (Tutt (ed) 1978), including imprisonment, tend both to vary and to be multiple (Radzinowicz and King 1977, p.323). The variety and number of motivations, some mutually incompatible, for sentencing a person to one of the present alternatives to prison - community service - have recently been explored by Young (1978).

With the Unit there was a prominent factor making for its taking on the character of an alternative to prison. It provided ex-prisoners with somewhere to live. 'The availability of suitable accommodation to receive the prisoner on release is a prerequisite of suitability for parole' (West 1972, p.19).

Because the Unit was frequently utilised as somewhere to send or return clients to be rehabilitated after they had been convicted or reconvicted it always contained two client categories, though it never made the distinction explicit. The first may be called 'volunteers'; the second consisted of those on parole, Borstal licence, deferred sentence, suspended sentence, probation or some other form of duress, who may be referred to as 'detainees'.

Sometimes, an ex-offender becomes an offender again very quickly. For example, Vere, released on parole, made a snatch at a till on his journey between the prison gates and the Unit. After his arrest, however, he was permitted to continue to the Unit - unlike other expected newcomers who failed to arrive because of reincarceration. Vere was thus an example of one of the Unit's detainees who, as we shall see, lived there as one of the conditions of his parole licence.

It is impossible to be categorical about the reasons Vere was treated liberally. Reasons for parole in particular cases are confidential to the Parole Board. He may have obtained it because in the past 'his school conduct was good' (social enquiry report) or because 'in custody he has behaved himself in every way and he has accepted a Prison Visitor and the Assistant Chaplain' (prison welfare officer's report). But an equally probable factor may have been homelessness and the offer of a place in the Unit.

By thieving on his way to the Unit Vere endangered his parole. But Parole Board rules are not as severe as they at first glance seem: 'The licence conditions mean what they say and if ... your behaviour on parole gives cause for concern your licence may be revoked' (Home Office 1976, p.10; emphasis mine). Instead, Vere was issued with a 'warning':

> You were convicted at [...] Magistrates' Court ... of theft ... the Home Secretary has decided that provided you remain at the NACRO Education Unit in Cambridge, you should not be recalled to prison but you are warned that if you do not ... remain

> at the hostel your licence will <u>almost</u> certainly be cancelled (emphases mine).

Thus, while for some clients the Unit was an after-care hostel in a fairly literal sense, for others it was a provision made after offending and an alternative to prison. Furthermore, for many clients the boundaries between volunteering and detaineeship were not watertight. One way of crossing from one category to the other entailed what might be referred to as 'judicial passage' (though, in Vere's case, an administrative, as well as a juridical, decision was involved). The significance and extent of judicial passage which clients at the Unit enjoyed will be briefly discussed further in the next section.

C. <u>JUDICIAL PASSAGE FROM VOLUNTEER TO DETAINEE</u>

Dartmoor to Cambridge was, for Douglas Curtis, a passage from confinement to freedom. Many clients at the Cambridge Unit, by contrast, underwent the opposite transition. They came as volunteers but later continued as detainees, thus acquiring a status similar to that with which Vere arrived.

'A person who commits a delinquent act and ... conforms to a delinquent stereotype ... is more likely to be arrested than another person committing the same delinquent act but with a different appearance' (Farrington 1974, p.27). But when a volunteer came to the Unit such discrimination was likely to be subsequently tempered by a reverse effect. Towards the end of 1977, Ron reported:

> Thirteen students who committed imprisonable offences either just before, during or just after their time in Cambridge were given non-custodial sentences in sixteen courts in order that they could take up or <u>keep</u> their place in the Unit (emphasis mine). [1]

Judges' sentences are affected not only by the offender's present and past convictions but also by the offender's social and cultural standing (Hood 1962, pp.119-20; Walker 1968, p.219; 1969, pp.165-6; Devlin 1970, pp.43-6). When its clients were brought before the court the Unit presented educational progress as evidence of 'character'. [2] In many countries, educators operate similarly. In the USA, for example, of a youth who had committed numerous assaults:

> a guidance counselor had written the Rivertown court a glowing letter stating how well John was doing in school (although high school officials later said the counselor was mistaken) ... the Rivertown judge dismissed the case asked how could he ... incarcerate a youth ... making such

good progress in school (Fersch et al. 1978, p.72; see also Gath, Tennent and Pidduck 1971, p.278).

But a rehabilitator who thus decarcerates a delinquent is likely to make him into a detainee, since the latter's freedom may be contingent on judicial provisions governing his habitat, his lifestyle, his attitude to his probation officer, etc. We shall later see, moreover, that in addition to such externally derived status passages much of the history of the Unit consisted of the development of its own internal forms of social pressure for transforming volunteers into detainees.

D. THE INFLUENCE OF THE WIDER SOCIAL STRUCTURE

In considering in this chapter some of the significant characteristics of the Unit, I have indicated various ways in which such an outfit is likely to depart from its original charter as it comes under the constraints, values and contradictions of the wider social structure. Thus, the Unit is conceived of as an 'experiment', but the 'apparatus' is set in motion before a scientist is appointed because of a shortage of resources which might be needed for further apparatus; a predicament which perhaps besets many small organisations in an inflationary and stagnant economy. The strong educational and rehabilitative commitment of the culture hero who founds the Unit informs its ideology, but the operation of parole and other aspects of the penal system produce clients of dubious educational and rehabilitative pretensions. As a criterion for the selection of eligible candidates for the Unit, not only estimated educational capability but also homelessness, at a time of chronic housing shortage, has to be taken into account. Because recidivism rather than rehabilitation of ex-prisoners is the norm, clients originally seen as volunteers needing guidance are returned as detainees, though released from their customary restraints. As we shall see later, the rigid timetabling of the academic year necessitates a too hasty selection of candidates for the Unit right from the start; and so on.

The extent to which social processes in any group or organisation can be explained in isolation from the effects of activity in the wider society is not easy to determine. How much of one's study of an entity like the Unit should, therefore, be devoted to the impingement on it of influences from its social environment is, consequently, a matter of controversy. I have not backed away from such controversy by following those writers (e.g. Goffman 1961) who, in order to give emphasis to their argument, disregard historical and geographical context and treat their data as if collected from a small island in the ocean. [3] Indeed, if my discussion of the background of the

Unit has so far been brief my reason or excuse is that I must now focus more closely on the 'students', for their background too can scarcely be ignored.

NOTES

[1] A London magistrate told Ellis in November 1976, 'I'm letting you off because someone is prepared to come down from Cambridge and say there is some good in you, though I'm not convinced by that'. By contrast, such leniency was almost invariably absent in the Crown court in Cambridge (except for offenders who informed on others). In February 1976, the judge, before sentencing Jack and Wayne to lengthy terms of imprisonment, commented, 'It disturbs me to know that Cambridgeshire Technical College is being used to rehabilitate people with records like this when there are all these other young people trying to get in'. When Horace appeared in the same court in January 1978, the judge, upon learning that he had received a local authority grant, remarked, 'I'm absolutely astounded'. In passing sentence he said, 'I cannot see that this sort of thing is of the slightest use to you whatever ... I accept that it is well-intentioned but I consider it totally misguided'. In August 1979, two fifth year students and one former fifth year student appeared in the court on charges of burglary. The counsel for the former student stated that his client had become disillusioned with NACRO and had obtained a job [with an employer with a criminal record], though, the barrister added, he realised that such a change could not be regarded as any basis for mitigation. The judge interrupted at this point and asserted that, on the contrary, taking a job seemed to him a very powerful plea for mitigation. The judge sentenced the students to severe custodial sentences, but suspended a sentence on the former student (who, however, was re-arrested for burglary in October 1979).

[2] In a court case which is, perhaps, extreme, and which received much publicity, Judge Griffith-Jones, in suspending a sentence on an army officer convicted of planting a dummy bomb in a bank and clubbing the bank manager, stated that what he did was wholly out of keeping with his known character, his normal behaviour [he had committed a similar crime two years previously] and his military record' (Evening Standard [London] 4/4/77, p.1; emphasis mine).

[3] Coincidentally I am writing at the time of the 'Falkland Crisis' in the south Atlantic.

3 Background to the Clients

The most striking impression which greeted my first acquaintanceship with a group of ex-offenders at the Unit was how similar they seemed to be to any other working class young people one might meet. They seemed introvert, but this could be interpreted as a product of recent prison experience as well as wariness towards an unknown researcher. This trait seemed a variation rather than a deviation. Yet most of them had long criminal records. These records, of course, represented only offences for which they had been caught. Into what depths of evil had they immersed themselves for which they had not been caught?

In fact, however, the situation in most cases was actually very different. Crime was one of their activities in which they indulged only occasionally. But when they committed offences they had the surprising knack of frequently getting caught. This turned out to be their most striking deviance. When they went against the legal mores they rarely took precautions. In a short space of time, they found themselves with indictments pregnant with criminal charges, including, quite often, a number 'taken into account' which they had not committed but which they helped the police to clear in exchange for lenient treatment.

In order to emphasise the significance of this pattern it may be useful to postulate a population of offenders in Cambridge with <u>opposite</u> criminological characteristics from those of the clients living in the Unit. This other population might have been offending far more frequently than the one at the Unit, but almost invariably avoiding arrest. Many young people who persistently offend may get caught at some point. Nevertheless, 'the majority of even the most delinquent boys are unknown to the police and the courts' (Gold 1966, p.40). Indeed, I know one delinquent (not part of my sample) who regularly uses sophisticated ways of stealing. Her brushes with the law have been few and give her no more qualms than any minor hazard in any other activity in which a person might take pride.

Thus, the clients at the Unit may be regarded as what Polsky (1963, p.171) calls 'a skewed sample who over-represent the non-professionals and the bunglers'. 'In my opinion', says Radzinowicz (1964, p.917), 'what is fully brought out into the open and punished represents no more than fifteen per cent of crime actually committed'. It seems to me possible, therefore, to argue that it is people with criminological characteristics like those of the Unit's clients who may account for much of the low figure of fifteen per cent.

If the Unit's clients were, indeed 'a skewed sample' we must try to identify the skewing factors and see which ones could be responsible for these unusual ex-offenders repeatedly getting into trouble.

The rationale is straightforward. If these ex-offenders had not become known to the police, the courts, the prisons and the probation service then they would not have become known to the Unit. But it is not only this circumstance which distinguished them from offenders without criminal records. It is also the very fact of having obtained so many convictions for their offences. Since this may have been a habit which many clients brought to the Unit it is important to discuss some of the factors which may account for their repeated failure when they offended to avoid being entangled again in the criminal 'justice' system.

A. DRUNKENNESS

The vast majority of the students' convictions were for offences which took place while they were inebriated. The offender either drank in order to fortify himself for the act or conceived of it while under the influence of alcohol (cf. Holborn 1975, p.71). The chances of arrest for offending are normally substantially overestimated by non-offenders, but rather less so by offenders (Willcock 1974, p.103). Alcohol telescopes these chances. Thus, Joan, a fifth year student, was frequently arrested for smashing shop windows, alcoholically oblivious to the people around her. Willcock (ibid, p.46) found that the chances of arrest for such misbehaviour are normally very slim. The mean number of offences per court appearance (for males between fifteen and twenty) for 'smashing and slashing in public places' is at least 131.

The point at which alcohol entered the picture varied. With Arthur, still in his teens, it had been a factor from the start. Heavy drinking, it is often reported, has become increasingly popular among teenagers, even replacing other types of drug. Mott and Hope state that 'the magnitude of the increase in drunkenness convictions amongst the younger age group of both sexes suggests that real changes in public drinking behaviour are occurring. In 1973 as compared with 1964 the rate per 10,000 of the population for males between 15 and 17 increased about three times ... It seems obvious that serious property offences are unlikely to be successfully accomplished if the behaviour of the offenders is impaired by recent alcohol consumption ... The studies reviewed here have established the indirect relationship between excessive drinking, however defined, and crime in samples already known to be offenders, usually serving prison sentences' (1976, pp.28-9).

Ellis, by contrast, said that before he came to the Unit all his crimes had been sober: they had been necessary for 'survival', particularly in times of unemployment. But his subsequent offences happened while he was drunk, and he presented them as events of which he did not have the slightest recollection in the morning. This phenomenon is not confined to ex-offenders. Ron said that when he gets drunk his wife tells him the following morning of actions his memory of which remains forever drowned in beer and sleep. These actions are apparently derived from a behavioural repertoire built up during an earlier stage of life (see also Cressey 1953, p.89).

Alcohol can stimulate aggression, and, consequently, where the offender takes his leisure is significant in discovering the causes of criminal convictions. Horace's father was a heavy drinker, but all his aggression was confined to home, and never led to arrest. Horace, however, lived at the Unit, though only when he was on bad terms with his girlfriend, who lived in another part of Cambridge. His violence tended to take place in pubs or on the street, where the police could easily be summoned. Holborn (1975, pp.71-3) refers to alienation from sexual partner and living in lodging houses as factors in the lives of men with convictions connected with heavy drinking whom she interviewed.

B. THE COMPENSATIONS AND CONSOLATIONS OF PRISON

Despite the extreme unpleasantness of prison, its inmates can form various attachments to it. In any state in which oppression has lost its legitimacy, a multitude of prisoners cannot be kept in conditions far worse than those prevailing outside (HMSO 1969, pp.7-8). Last century prisons attracted some inmates because they provided basic amenities of life (Tobias 1967, p.243). These days also, prisons may have distinctive features not always obtainable elsewhere. Authors write variously about the desire to be kept under constant control (Miller 1958, pp.12-13), the desire for power based on exploiting others wanting scarce commodities (Irwin and Cressey 1962, p.149), a very regular and ordered routine (Curtis 1973a, p.62), escape from life in a boring neighbourhood (Burroughs 1977, p.xii), symbolism as a place of protest (Bottomley 1974, p.194), and so on. For some inmates, therefore, various styles of action and thought can be given emphatic expression in prison which may be more diffusely distributed in the outside world.

Many offenders achieve greater academic success in prison than outside, a fact which was never considered before the Unit was set up. Prison intellectuals are a recognised type, of whom one of the most well-known to the students was 'O Level Jones', as yet, after many years of effort, still only just behind his competitors for a place in The Guinness Book of Records for number of subjects passed at the General Certificate of Education. Stafford, Ron's deputy after the Unit's second year, taking the academic interests of one of his clients very much to heart, endorsed his proclivity for prison:

> Mortie seemed very keen to go back. I talked to him ... and became convinced that the best way of getting down to them [his examinations] was to get inside prison for two years, and have nothing better to do, like drugs. He needed to reoffend for academic reasons almost.

Most of the students at the Unit had been affected to a greater or lesser extent by 'convict culture' (Irwin and Cressey 1962) and its alternative status system, about which, from his long experience as a former prisoner, McVicar (1979, pp.165-9) writes:

> The ultimate madness of all these places is that the inmates are allowed to interact with each other in accordance with the same anti-social values which provide the motive power for crime outside prison. With no rational outlet available, such as thieving or gangsterism they find expression in the cult of toughness for its own sake. This is not to say that modified forms of thieving or gangsterism do not operate; they do, but they are attenuated by the high level of surveillance ... The natural power struggle for social dominance which any group or society exhibits is intensified in prison - mainly, I suppose, because prisoners are deprived of other distractions.

Similarly, during a recent sentence, Jack wrote:

> *The 3 years prior to my arrival in the Unit had been spent in the intensified world of P/Head Prison, where a person's capacity for violence determines his position in the social structure. Never content to be a "nobody" and accept all the "shit" handed down by would-be "gangsters" I made certain that I was "at the top". Suddenly I left there and found myself in an environment*

where nothing I had learnt in the past was of any use to me ... X [girlfriend] *once insightfully asked me if I thought I had "come down" in the world. I replied in the negative. But had the truth been known, that was exactly what I did feel: I had exchanged a position of social prominence in a criminal subculture for one of anonymity and uncertainty in a social project.*

C. FEELINGS OF GUILT AND SHAME

'Unconscious guilt, masochism, the hidden desire to be punished or do yourself down - these feelings can beckon men and women on to commit crime and to get themselves locked up in prison' (Klare 1973, p.25). Such hidden feelings were extremely common among the Unit's clients. During one of his sentences, Ben wrote:

> *I have no great love of prison, quite the reverse but at least the suffering incurred here gives me absolution to the soul for the crimes committed by the mind* (emphasis mine).

In many cases, the tendency to be one's own judge and sentencer derived from early family circumstances. As a Social Enquiry Report on Ellis in 1975 stated:

> It appears significant that he has often described himself as a person of no real worth, expressing also a belief that no-one would want any close relationship with him. It is now obvious that these feelings of rejection and self-deprecation relate to the very disturbed family situation and especially the serious problems he has encountered in his relationship with his mother. In effect, he now has considerable doubts about his own personal worth and, to this extent, he seems to have a vested interest in subjecting himself to all the humiliation and degradation which crime and its consequences entail.

In the short term, Ellis was one of the Unit's successes, in the sense that he was able to use his period of residence there to study for examinations and obtain a place in a polytechnic. But his vulnerability to self-punishment remained with him. While at polytechnic he received a letter from a younger brother accusing his recidivism of affecting the reputation and life chances of younger members of the family. Soon afterwards, Ellis reoffended and returned to prison.

One of the most disturbing aspects of the desire for punishment was the frequency with which it tended to manifest itself when so many things in the offender's life seemed to be going right. For example, Horace's entanglements with the law were too frequent, and his personal problems too disturbing, to allow for any continuity in his academic studies while he was at the Unit. But, by 1980, he had obtained a highly paid job. He also seemed enthusiastic about a prospective job-training programme in which he would be receiving what he considered a reasonable grant. For many months he had been living with an attractive girl in what seemed to be the most stable relationship which he had enjoyed in his life. In April 1980, however, he informed me that he had recently been charged with burglary. As on all previous occasions, he had been drunk at the time. I asked him why he had committed the crime. He frankly replied that deep down he felt the need for punishment. Although Horace was an introspective person he could not, however, account for this compulsive impulse.

The sense of unworthiness among the Unit's clients sometimes manifested itself in apparently contradictory drives. Daryl, who had served a number of sentences, tried to assuage his free-floating guilt with saintly acts. He spent much time in voluntary work in a Cambridge hostel for homeless alcoholics. During this period, however, he said that he felt the need to return to prison. With baffling logic he said that in the short period he had been in the outside world he had discovered that it was not a place where it was possible effectively to put into practice the ideal of genuinely loving one's fellow man.

The same strangely yoked traits of recidivism and Christian idealism were also present in Daryl's friend, Archie. The latter was very much like his father: highly moralistic, belonging to a 'hell-fire' sect, and highly criminal. He was a consummate artist, and many of his themes were of the 'Jesus in passion' kind. He had married early, but the many years of his marriage have been covered by alternating episodes in which (a) he engages in adulterous affairs, until his sense of guilt overwhelms him and he commits a crime in a way which makes him easily arrested (as at the time of his residence at the Unit, when he raided a bookmaker's shop when it opened on a Monday morning) and (b) from prison he writes numerous letters of remorse to his wife, who lives with his parents. These episodes have followed each other in an apparently unending sequence. [1]

The intention of this chapter has been to discuss factors which had led clients who came to the Unit to distinguish themselves from their many lawbreaking peers by acquiring criminal records, and in not a few cases more than one of the factors discussed had conspired against the client. We should not be unmindful of such predisposing factors when we consider cases in which students did in fact recidivise after coming to the Unit. But the task of concentrating on the significant part, if any, which the <u>Unit</u> played in the lives of its clients calls for other tools of analysis.

NOTE

[1] The project leader who succeeded Ron at the Unit for the final academic year 1979-80 read the previous draft of this book. After this chapter, she said that in the light of her experience she was interested in the punishment drive and wondered if she could add a short note. I reproduce it here without additional comment:

I was particularly interested in the suggestion that guilt feelings lead to crime. This seemed to apply to many of the clients I have dealt with in the past year. Most of my clients have seemed to be guilt ridden and at first I put this down to feeling guilty about the crimes which they had committed. On reflection, the discussions I have had with them always centred on their feelings of worthlessness. The way in which some of them went about re-offending made me seriously believe on a number of occasions that they wanted to be caught. As burglary is the most prominent crime of the past year I will use that as an example. Client A, for instance, has spent the last 5 out of 7 years in prison for burglary. The longest period he has spent out of prison is 4 months. On release he immediately returns to committing burglaries, taking no precautions, such as using gloves to stop finger-prints, in fact, he even returns to the same two streets for his crimes. He only ever takes small amounts of cash and says quite firmly that he hates doing it but has no answer as to why he does. I've visited him in police custody and he said that he was glad he was caught but couldn't really explain why. He wants to lead a 'good' life he says and indeed makes great effort to do this. The last time he was released from prison he obtained employment, studied for an 'O' level which he passed, then when everything appeared to be going well he committed two more burglaries, which he was arrested for in a matter of days. At the time of the offences he had plenty of money of his own and the total amount which he stole was very small, just 3 or 4 pounds. The only explanation can be that life was going too well and he felt uncomfortable with it. When talking about the chance of a non-custodial sentence, he remarked that he didn't deserve another chance at the hostel. My explanations that he did because of the great efforts he had made in other directions did not seem to convince him. He thought he should be sent back to prison and I believe wanted the punishment of prison. This is only one example of the many clients I've had who believe they are bad and deserve to be punished, even though they may be showing in many ways that they are not.

PART II

ANALYSING THE RESEARCH MATERIAL

> The most persistent difficulty in the scientific study of deviant behaviour is a lack of solid data on which to base our theories. I think it is a truism to say that a theory that is not closely tied to a wealth of facts about the subject it proposes to explain is not likely to be very useful (Becker 1963, p.165).

4 Analytical Constructs

Important questions seem to emerge from our discussion of the background of the Unit and of its clients.

Firstly, there is the problem of commitment. To what extent were the clients able or willing to adopt an attitude of commitment to rehabilitation by keeping to their academic programme and avoiding any distracting impulses? As we have seen, we may have to take into consideration, in dealing with this question, that, for many individuals, such impulses, like heavy drinking or a compulsive wish for punishment, were very pressing and longstanding.

Secondly, the Unit was intended as an agency for the rehabilitation of ex-offenders and for assisting them to continue in formal education after they left the Unit. We cannot be guaranteed from the start, however, that all its clients conceived of the Unit primarily in these terms, or that they all wished to move in the direction which the Unit was constituted to take them. To take an analogy: perhaps most students going to university see the latter mainly as a means of obtaining an academic qualification, but to some students the most significant aspect of university life may, for example, be the congenial environment which it provides for obtaining a suitable marriage partner. Similarly, it is important to try to ascertain what the Unit actually meant to its clients. Did it have any alternative significance beyond that of its status as an educational rehabilitation centre?

Thirdly, in evaluating the achievements of the Unit, we need to find out what exactly the Unit did for its clients, bearing in mind that it may have performed different functions for different clients, or for the same client at different times. As we have seen, for example, the Unit seems to have been instrumental in enabling reoffenders to avoid reimprisonment, a function unlikely to have been regarded as central by the founders of the project.

It may be interesting to note that the question about the functions of the Unit can be seen as complementary to the question about its meanings to its clients. For, just as the rehabilitative organisation may be regarded as the raw material out of which its clients could produce different meanings, so the clients may be viewed as the raw material with which the Unit produced certain results.

Before addressing ourselves, therefore, to an analysis of the development of the Unit and to the case studies it may be useful to consider the ways in which the concepts of attitude, meaning and function will be used, for all of them may be variables in any explanation of rehabilitation or continued recidivism in a rehabilitation hostel.

A. ATTITUDES: COMMITMENT THEORY

The investigation of commitment to programmes seems to me an indispensable method of analysis in numerous areas of social life. For example, one of the most common programmes in society is marriage and childraising. Now it seems clear that in western and other societies people have become, in some ways, less committed to the marriages into which they have entered, while, in other ways, they have become more committed. If, therefore, we wish to understand the institution of marriage we need to examine changes which have taken place in the commitments which it entails. For example, the rate of marital dissolution has increased, and a commonplace explanation is conflict between spouses. But I do not know of evidence that marital conflicts have increased; they may, indeed, have decreased. What seems much clearer is that marital conflicts, the definition of which is sometimes stretched to include incompatibility of leisure pursuits, have increasingly come to be expected to lessen commitment. Likewise, we do not know - and perhaps can never know - if marriage partners love each other either more or less than they used to. But, again, what is most striking is that love has come to be expected to augment commitment to marriage more than in the past. [1]

In the case of the behaviour of the Unit's clients, by studying the level of commitment to the academic programme which the Unit arranged, we should be able to see whether such commitment coincided with rehabilitation. Thus, if we find that clients who were committed to their academic programme avoided committing offences and the consequences which committing offences could have for their academic commitment, and if we find, contrariwise, that clients who were not committed to their academic programme were prepared to take the risks involved in committing offences, Becker's commitment hypothesis about deviance and normality would then receive 'manifold' support. (It must be noted, however, that Becker is not always entirely clear if by commitment he means repetitive checking of deviant impulses or being involved in conventional institutions (1963, p.27). I shall apply the term to both and examine their relationship.)

Unfortunately, however, the matter is even more complicated. When we examine our data on the commitment of the Unit's students to their studies we find that some were highly committed, while others were undercommitted. But there were yet other students whom we would have to categorise as 'overcommitted'. Now this is a term which may need some elucidation. If, by commitment, we mean keeping to a programme, such as one of study leading to qualifications regardless of obstacles which may occur, such as deviant impulses, then we may conceive of overcommitment as keeping to a programme to such an extreme that the stress engendered by the perceived demands and obstacles, and the efforts to cope with such stress, overshadow, distort and can even frustrate practical activity directed towards accomplishment of the programme. Thus, commitment manifests itself in effort, undercommitment in insufficient effort, and overcommitment in excessive effort, to overcome obstacles to reach a goal.

It may be noted that, in his work on commitment, Becker was mainly concerned with conventional young people whose type of career had been destined before they entered an educational programme leading by gradations towards their aims. In his analysis of the processes leading towards qualifications and settled careers, he seems to have been rarely confronted with the inertia of undercommitment or with the volatility of overcommitment. By contrast, when I put to Ken the notion of resisting deviant impulses because of commitment to such 'extraneous' lines of activity as a course of study, he reflectively retorted that 'it presupposes an awareness and discovery of the impulse and time to think it out - what, may I ask, happens in extreme stress or under duress or coercion?'.

Such overcommitment, it must be emphasised, is not restricted to people who are ex-offenders. For, as talented but unconventional students enter the higher education system, overcommitment becomes a pervasive, rather than a very abnormal, phenomenon. Hutt (1964, p.55), for example, in discussing the problems of undergraduates in one of the new British universities of the 1960s, writes of 'the pupil who "over-drives" with the consequence that he finds himself, to his horror (which only makes it worse), unable to master the work at hand'.

Moreover, as college gates have opened to, for example, the lower classes as well as to the upper, and to parentally pressured social climbers as well as to intellectuals seeking knowledge for its own sake, there has been a need to develop counselling services to help the insecure and overcommitted to cope with stress and uncertainty. In the USA, where the 'diploma disease' was pandemic earlier than in Britain, counselling services have long been established even at the high school level:

> A friend may report to a teacher or counselor that a student is 'real worried' about passing

> a course. If such a student has been typed previously as an 'over-achiever', he may be referred to a counselor, or the teacher may consult his superior about transferring the student to a 'less competitive' section (Cicourel and Kitsuse 1968, p.130).

In a paper which appeared soon after his ideas about the relationship between commitment and resisting deviant impulses, Becker (1964 pp.44-50) takes pains to distinguish commitment from 'situational adjustment'. This is a most important distinction because attitudes do not mechanically translate themselves into behaviour. In any social situation the individual is faced with the expectations of others, and, unless he adjusts to them in some measure, he may need to be prepared either to change his attitude or to have it rebuffed.

As we shall indeed see, clients of the Unit who were overcommitted to succeed academically, when faced with difficulties which they perceived as undermining their hopes of success, sometimes reacted by changing their attitude from overcommitment to undercommitment. They joined the ranks of the undercommitted because they perceived signs apparently confirming their anxieties, uncertainties and low opinion of their own potential, and accepted that a long academic struggle would not be crowned with success.

But other students, by contrast, maintained their attitude of overcommitment by making <u>situational adjustments</u>. They repeatedly offered examples of their notes and essays to staff members out of a deeply felt need for reassurance in the immediate term.

Again, such a pattern of conduct is by no means confined to ex-offenders. Consider, for example, the predicament of a large number of students in the USA, a country which has gone far in providing college places to large numbers of people from families without college backgrounds. Often lacking the self-assurance of students in the past such newcomers tend to adopt an attitude of overcommitment. When the unfamiliar environment and cultural style of a university threatens them with possible failure they are then reduced either to undercommitment or to modes of situational adjustment which they hope will sustain their flagging stamina:

> One reason why people are prone to over-commitment, i.e. commitment created by the actor which is not actually demanded by the system, is for the purpose of satisfying their own need for assurity and predictability. Thus, for example, graduate students may actually force professors into giving an examination ... Though students may gain in security, they can only lose as far as concerns time, effort, and even the possible reduction of their course grade (Vanfossen 1960, p.234).

Situational adjustment, however, is in no way a necessity for only the overcommitted. The undercommitted often also have to make situational adjustments, sometimes, indeed, very astutely. Thus, undercommitted clients at the Unit were very adept at, for example, whittling down the number of subjects they were expected to study by convincing staff that the remaining subjects, unburdened with being combined with ones in which they discovered they had little interest, afforded a sense of commitment never previously experienced; that such remnants formed a basis on which they would be able to organise their future; that they could not study too hard because they had to attend to matters as equally rehabilitative as education, etc.

A curious feature, however, of the situational adjustment of the academically undercommitted members of the Unit is that it often resembled that of the overcommitted, even though the situational adjustment of the former was pragmatic whereas that of the latter was compulsive. Thus, an overcommitted student's boasts, in unusual moments of buoyant self-assurance, of the amount of study he was accomplishing did not sound very different from the exaggerated claims by an undercommitted student of the amount he was accomplishing. In consequence, the Unit was shot through with a double irony. Staff frequently interpreted the situational adjustment of both groups as commitment, in a plain, ordinary, unqualified sense. That was not, however, the end of the matter: students who were committed but showed little situational adjustment to the expectations of staff - and I shall adduce Adam as one of the more extreme examples - were sometimes, for that reason, defined as undercommitted!

As we shall see, in the first two years of the Unit's existence, the adjustment of its students was, indeed, mainly situational, being confined to the short, and often fleeting, contacts between clients and staff. By the third year, however, student adjustment became institutionalised. For the Unit turned itself into a 'school', in which the staff could daily supervise, mark and monitor the work of the students. But such a development brought a new difficulty. An individual who is led by the hand may become over-adjusted (Becker 1960, p.37), and thus develop patterns of behaviour that are inappropriate when carried over to later situations. Ken, as we shall see, was one of the school's products who was supremely successful in obtaining a place in university, but, once there, knew of no way of obtaining continuous 'assurity'. Unable to adjust to this unfamiliar academic environment he suddenly plunged from overcommitment to undercommitment, as had so many earlier clients of the Unit long before they came anywhere near to university entry. Ken was just one of a number of scholars at the Unit whose staff was able to take to membership of a university campus, but no further.

To people running a hostel, such as the Unit, its official goals have to be of primary significance. But to other participants this need not be so. To members undercommitted to official goals an organisation may carry alternative meanings, to which they may be highly committed. To a typology of the different meanings of which an organisation such as the Unit can be a cognitive representation we now turn our attention.

B. MEANINGS: ORGANISATIONS AS SYMBOLIC PRODUCTS

As Merton (1968, pp.475-6) emphasises, 'men respond not only to the objective features of a situation, but also, and at times primarily, to the meaning this situation has for them. And once they have assigned some meaning to the situation, their consequent behaviour and some of the consequences of their behaviour are determined by the ascribed meaning'.

A situation such a rehabilitation hostel seems to have three possible meanings for the participants variously aggregated into it, which I label 'staging post', 'resort' and 'colony'.

A staging post is a place one goes to in order to continue on a journey to one's destination. Ron once described the Unit to me as a 'bridge' between crime and punishment on one side and university or college qualifications on the other side, and, indeed, a number of his clients saw the Unit in the same way.

A resort is where one goes when matters in one's ordinary routine have become intolerable, or are likely to become so. In ordinary life, there are numerous places to which a person may be able to resort, from a country holiday to a marriage guidance office. One does not wish to stay too long at a resort, lest it becomes one's ordinary routine. If a staging post is a point, A, which enables one to get from point B to point C then a resort is a point, A, which enables one to return to point B. The significance which a place of 'treatment' can possess as a resort is particularly important because people may go there to remove themselves from a troubled situation, only to return whence they came when they consider that the trouble has blown over. For example, Sampson et al. (1961) write of mental hospitals being perceived as places (for the wife as patient) to sojourn when a marital relationship runs into temporary difficulties. The notion of the Unit being a resort to its residents is captured in a letter to Ron which Ken wrote after he had got into trouble while at university and the Unit had ceased to be a staging post for him: '*You ought to run a shelter, where people can retreat from the world when they feel threatened by its seeming insanity, and find a little oasis of sanity'.*

If a resort brings respite from, or refreshment for, one's ordinary routine then a colony is where one takes one's ordinary routine, whether the latter consists of 'western civilisation' or a store setting up a new branch in a new district.

The type of person for whom a prison or a hospital or a unit can mean little more than a colony is one who passed his formative years in institutions which had strong authority and many rules, but little love, psychological security or individual adventure. As Parker (1963, pp.138-9) sums up the world view of Charlie Smith:

> As a child his only security lay in the unreal world of orderly and impersonal institutional life, and his Army service provided merely an extension of this. Since then imprisonment has reinforced his superficial adaptation to life in an institution ... "outside" was difficult and dangerous, "inside" was relatively safe.

And as Parker (ibid., p.150) expresses it for Charles in the first person: 'Ever since I can remember, in orphanages, foster-homes, the Army, and prison, I have had drilled into me the virtue of obedience, of doing as I was told'.

As we peruse our case studies we will find that the Unit was variously perceived as a staging post, resort or colony, or a combination of these, varying from one client to another, or within the same client at different times.

C. FUNCTIONS: PEOPLE PRODUCT ORGANISATIONS

In sociology, there is considerable bewilderment about what functions organisations concerned with 'working with people' actually perform:

> It may well be that organisations designed to create lasting personal change are not the ideal mechanisms. It seems possible that the modal response among recruits to all such settings is outward compliance with the aims and goals of the setting, coupled with a variety of secondary adjustments differing in form, strength and character, depending on the individual's personal needs, his particular position within the socialization setting, and the nature of his attachments outside it ...
> We may be sure, however, that organizations whose products are people will play an increasingly significant role in modern societies. As formal organizations they provide an important reference

> point for the study of other types of bureaucratic structure. As socialization settings they may have much impact on the later careers of those who pass through them. Detailed study of their forms and consequences would appear to be a strategically important task for social science (Wheeler 1966, p.113).

The above passage recognises the theoretical and practical importance of people product organizations. It is concerned about how the study of such institutions might be related to the more developed theories of other organisations (with their models of productive efficiency). There is also an earnest hope that research on organisations whose products are people will not only bring enlightenment in itself but also contribute to a greater understanding of other types of bureaucracies.

A typological advance in the study of people product organisations is that of Hasenfeld (1972, p.256), who makes a distinction between <u>changing</u> people and <u>processing</u> people in the following way:

> Scant theoretical attention has been paid ... to the emerging importance of those organizations whose ... function is not to change the behavior of people directly but to process them and confer public statuses on them. Examples of such organizations are a diagnostic clinic, a university admissions office, an employment placement office ... We shall denote these as "people-processing" in contrast to "people-changing" organizations. These organizations shape a person's life ... through the public status they confer; and they may define and confirm the individual's social position when his current status is questioned. Moreover, processing functions ... are an integral part of people-changing organizations.

There are, however, <u>further</u> functions performed by people product organisations. I would, therefore, extend Hasenfeld's typology to include <u>controlling</u> people, a feature given prominence by Weber (1947, p.337); <u>serving</u> people and <u>mobilising</u> people - the last being concerned with moving people to make changes in society.

A typology possesses a certain virtue if it can be used in the analysis of developments within an institution. For example, Zald and Denton (1963, p.216) refer to 'the transformation of the YMCA from an evangelistic social movement [changing people] to a general service organization'. Another example is that of Eckstein (1976), who shows how organizations set up for serving the housing needs of poor people in Mexico became transformed into instruments for controlling people.

In the course of discussing the development of the

Unit and case studies of its clients, and in the final chapters, we will examine the extent to which the Unit performed the functions listed in this section. We will also analyse data on the Unit and its clients with the aid of the other conceptual tools which have been presented in this chapter.

NOTE

[1] Consider, for instance, the case of a man who repeatedly turns up at a VD clinic as the result of intercourse with his wife, whom he himself originally infected:

> Clearly the man is in a dilemma. He wants his wife to be treated, but he will rarely want her to know that he has had sex outside marriage. The health worker may now try to persuade the man that he has to come clean, so to speak, reveal all and hope that adversity strengthens their love for each other (Jacobs 1978, p.425).

The reasoning here is that love can now be confidently expected to maintain commitment to the man's marriage. It overcomes obstacles to the traditional marriage programme, such as sex outside marriage.

5 The Unit's First Academic Year, 1974–5: the Policy Validation Stage

In the next three chapters, I shall record the journey of the Unit during its first three 'experimental' years. These chapters will map out the social geography within which the twelve case studies, the subjects of which arrived at the Unit in different years, can be better understood.

Instead of merely describing the changes in direction of the Unit year by year I have attached a theme to each of the three chapters. I have borrowed these themes from an important analysis of implementation of American legislation in the 1970s which decriminalised public drunkenness and established detoxification units to treat it as a disease. Regier (1979, p.4), discerning three main policy stages which the units passed through, says that 'it appears the clients and caretakers commence as idealists, intent upon implementing the policy's manifest goals (policy validation stage); should these efforts fail, they test successive models (policy critique stage) until, finally, as pragmatists, they converge on a workable solution (policy rationalization stage)'. In other words, and not elaborating on her thesis at this juncture, implementors begin with a supreme faith that they will succeed in achieving the aims for which the project was set up. When they find that their aims are not being achieved they try to locate the obstacles and formulate one policy change after another to overcome them. When these policies also fail to ameliorate the situation, policy implementors, dejected and running out of ideas, modify not only the original goals to a more modest level but also their claims about what they can actually achieve.

Regier's schema does not fit the evolution of the Unit perfectly. For example, the Unit's staff, and the wider NACRO organisation, did not neatly terminate one stage before moving on to the next: in particular, as they moved towards the 'policy rationalisation' stage, they did not forsake the possibility of returning to the original high ideals by making fresh, 'policy critique', attempts to realise them. Nevertheless, as we shall see in more detail, the fit between Regier's schema and phases in the Unit's history is remarkably close. Policy changes in the Unit tended to be concentrated at the end of each academic year, and they approximated in character to that of Regier's stages.

I began my research more than half a year after the end of the first academic year. Funds were far too small to travel in quest of students of the first year who had already left Cambridge; nor did I want to sacrifice time from recording observations on what was left of the second year. As will be seen, the former student from whom I gathered most of my information about the first year was Ben, who had been the first resident in the Unit, who had reflected a great deal about his experience in the Unit, and who revisited the Unit from time to time.

A. THE OPENING OF THE UNIT

One of Douglas Curtis's final contributions to the Unit was conducting negotiations to obtain a house for it, and one was purchased in October 1974. Ron described it as 'a somewhat shabby, rambling house'. It had neither the dignity nor the modernity of many student hostels. With its run down physical condition (and with its reserved atmosphere which was to prevail between residents) it was, perhaps, fittingly described later by Harry as a 'passing through place'.

Only a short time elapsed between Ron's appointment as project leader in May 1974 and the opening of the Unit. From a room in his home, Ron sent out leaflets advertising the project to all prison and Borstal governors and all chief probation officers. Judged by responses some of the leaflets did not go much further than their recipients' wastepaper baskets, whereas others were prominently displayed on notice boards or personally brought to the attention of potential clients. For prisoners and probation officers who wrote with enquiries Ron prepared standard application forms, and by early October there were 132 official applications, with many more coming in; far more than anyone had expected.

Nobody alone could attend to them all immediately. Nevertheless, Ron, assisted by his wife, Mary, as secretary, managed to obtain references for a large number of the applicants, helping them to obtain places in colleges or on correspondence courses. From other applicants he interviewed eight to come to the Unit and, in most cases, to attend the Cambridgeshire College of Arts and Technology (hereafter, the 'Tech'). By 10 October, however, there was still a backlog of eighty-nine applicants. According to the criterion of demonstrating a 'need' - a prominent principle in NACRO's attitude to its projects at the time - NACRO-Education had already proved itself a success.

The Unit was officially opened on 22 October 1974 by

Sir Louis Petch, Chairman of the Parole Board, and received wide newspaper coverage.

B. SETTLING INTO THE COMMUNITY

When property for the Unit was purchased the reactions of local residents were conspicuously few (cf. Sinclair 1971, p.44). By comparison, when plans were drawn up about the same time for an approved probation hostel in the neighbouring town of Peterborough, in the words of the Unit's liaison probation officer, 'all hell was let loose up there: public meetings, banner headlines, etc.'. The contrast requires explanation.

The Unit was situated where neighbourliness had been despoiled. A massive bridge (by Cambridge standards) was built in 1971, flying over riverside roads. The gardened and quiet street which it met, and of which the hostel had been the end house, was developed into an arterial highway, with heavy traffic day and night. Apart from other pollution, the noise was 3½ times the officially acceptable level according to local journalists (Gaskell and Utting 1977), who found that of the sixty-one families living in the street in 1971 only nineteen still lived there in 1977. The biggest emigrations and declines had been in the period's first and last years, the latter drop largely being accounted for by the deaths of old people. One resident said, 'I used to know quite a lot of people on the other side of the road ... these days you get killed if you try to cross it' (ibid.). Thus, although the local people might not have been very happy about the establishment of the Unit they could not easily and quickly form cohesive opposition.

On the opposite side to the Unit, by the bridge, a police car was often seen waiting, operating a speed trap. Sometimes, after departure, it returned a short time later. Perhaps, like some of the residents of the Unit, other residents of the highway believed it to be covering the Unit.

As the Unit was a corner house it had neighbours on one side only. Next door lived an elderly spinster. She had had experience in social work, and sympathised with the aims of the Unit, though not with the stereophonic noise late at night. After one of her complaints, which was accompanied by a request for residential staff, she was sent a letter saying that 'ex-offenders are at an after-care project on a voluntary basis having served their sentence. Committees, therefore, have to provide a setting which ex-offenders want to come to; secondly, a closely supervised situation which is so structured that there is no freedom of choice is very little different from a prison ...'.

The old lady in a house after that had a small sewing machine business. She said that when she first heard about the proposed hostel she thought it would be for teenagers on probation. By the time she discovered that it would include ex-prisoners she had also learnt that NACRO was patronised by Her Majesty the Queen, so that it was pointless to make a protest. Nevertheless, she said, there were a few local people at the opening ceremony who, from the back of the room, created a hubbub. But it failed to gather momentum in the face of the presiding dignitaries. In a letter from Douglas Curtis to one of the charities supporting NACRO and the project, 'Sir Louis Petch ... gave a most encouraging speech which seems to have gone down well with representatives of various statutory and voluntary agencies and some local residents who were present'.

This lady started earning money from the students soon after they moved in. Her message to them was: 'If there's any kind of breaking in here don't expect me to repair your trouser zips'. One of her regular customers was Brian in 1977-8, who frequently gave her garments for alteration, stolen in London, so that they would not fit descriptions in routine police enquiries.

The students benefitted not only the 'hidden' (Henry 1978), but also the open, economy. The publican of The Nearby Inn summed up his attitude to the Unit by saying: 'It brings in trade, doesn't it, mate?'. He said this not long after The Nearby Inn had been broken into in 1978, when money had been stolen from the fruit machine. The culprit was believed to be Stan, who, about the same time, was arrested for burglaries in Cambridge.

But what about the 'resettlement' of the students among themselves, in their own 'community'? The following is an account by Ben. I have shortened it, but I reproduce it in the order in which it was given rather than strictly chronologically. Points of particular interest include the expression of a desire for the kind of individual autonomy observed in later years and the idealisation of a lost hero even by his greatest antagonist:

> In the beginning, there was very much of a community atmosphere. This was because each student came at a different time, and knew nobody in Cambridge. It was only natural for them to hang together. This consisted in going together to The Nearby Inn. The only person who didn't join us was Denzil, who stayed in his room tippling. I supported the idea of the Unit, and when people were talking about plans for crime I would tell them I would tell Ron.
>
> But when Conrad came to the Unit tension started between him and me. I got along with him regarding the evils of the social system, but unlike him I felt that the proper path was to change things from

within rather than attacking policemen.

When George had some money pinched Conrad mentioned to Mary that I had stolen it. Mary replied that she did not believe him. Denzil reckoned Conrad did this because he resented me supporting the system. Ron said that he was going to get to the bottom of this. He called everyone into his room individually and asked their opinion of who they thought had been stealing. In the end, Ron said to Conrad, 'We haven't got to the bottom of this, but you will have to go'. When this happened the morale of the students went down.

The conflict with Conrad arose because he wanted to form a prisoners' union and get university students to go on strike so as to improve prisoners' conditions. He even went to speak to the principal of the Tech. But I went to see her first, and advised her not to see him, but she didn't agree. I had a pure ideology at that time and I thought that the Unit was good, and I saw Conrad as a threat to that. Percy was on my side and thought that Conrad was wrong. He thought I was being realistic. What caused the expulsion was that the house was split, either on Conrad's side or mine.

Ron had a go at me too - said I'd been leading a campaign against Conrad from the beginning, which was basically true ... I believed in those days that I had the interests of the students at heart. I was protecting them against Conrad ... Ron told me I was the most objective of all the students at the time. But when Conrad left, an us/them relationship developed. The main anti-authority liners were Percy, Denzil and Ena. But before he left the house was divided. Everyday someone would go to the office and say Conrad said this, or Ben said that - all this backstabbing going on.

I didn't know who was doing the nicking in the house. Ena came to my room and said, 'I've just been in Conrad's room and something funny happened. I said, "Have you got 20p you can lend me?" and he said he hadn't any money. Then his chick came and he put his hand in his pocket, drew out £2 and went to have a drink with her. Where did he get the £2 from?'. But later I thought to myself, maybe he just wants to keep the money to himself. Errol is not the most honest person in the world. He might have spent his money and told everyone it had been stolen to get money off Ron. In fact, Denzil said to Errol, 'If I find out that it's you who are fiddling all of us you'll have a sore face'.

It was bad, because if the house had split up into separate units with everyone doing their own thing without anyone else that would have been a good thing. It would have meant people breaking away from the need to be together. But it wasn't like that. They were breaking into groups and digging into other groups. Errol might say to George, 'Ben spent quite a bit of money in the pub tonight'. That's probably all he meant. Errol and I didn't get on particularly well, but we weren't exactly enemies. George might mention that to Conrad, and he would probably take that to mean I had been screwing some money. He might mention it to Ena, and she would come to me and say, 'I've been told that you've got a lot more money than you should have'. Then I would have to justify where I got the money from.

I would fall into the same trap everyone else would. I would see Conrad out with his chick and a £10 note in his pocket, while he was in The Nearby Inn. I'd tell Percy, who might mention it to Ena. Ena would go up to Conrad and say, 'I heard you had a lot of money in the pub last night'. That was just Ena - neither on my side or Conrad's side but probably more on Conrad's side because she'd been to bed with him, and she saw Denzil and me as a threat because we were the oldest guys in the Unit - we weren't as easily led by her as Errol and George. They would let her lead them on, but we would say, 'Fuck off, Ena, either you want us or you don't, we'd rather know '.

At times, I quite liked Conrad. He thought he was opening the minds of the students, being progressive. I thought political agitation could be good at times, but sometimes it was no good whatsoever. If we were both in the Unit <u>now</u> I'd probably be more objective about his arguments. I don't think Conrad could have done much damage to the Unit. His political activities he was doing legally, not illegally.

One night Dulcie, Percy and I spent all night - someone had just had their room broken into - George - and we were trying to find out who it could be. We didn't think it could be Denzil. He would rob a bank if he wanted to but he wouldn't steal from anyone in the same house. Dulcie said she thought it was Conrad, and I thought she was probably influenced by what she heard Percy say, just jumping on the bandwagon. When all this stealing began I never knew who it was, but when he started putting the blame on me I started to look at him with more suspicion.

He said it was me because I was always in the house, and my room was always open. With most people, if you wanted something from someone's room you just went in and took it, and told them when they

> came in. Anyway, it wasn't strictly true that I was in everyone's room. I was always in and out of certain people's rooms. I was always in Denzil and Percy's rooms. Ena, Errol, George and Conrad never bothered much, but they lived downstairs. Denzil lived at the bottom of the stairs. He washed upstairs rather than downstairs. Denzil was cut off from the other rooms downstairs by the length of the passage.

In the above account, the women seem to have been comparatively immune from suspicion and circulating slurs, perhaps because, being only two, they were treated as too precious to have accusations directed against them. Rivalry for the position of opinion leader, however, seems to have taken place between two males. The tension seems to have been partly the result of the strain of an intense, insecure togetherness. What solidarity remained after early fissure separated itself into the two zones of the hostel. Frictions between them brought about the expulsion of one of the two protagonists. His opponent was not able, however, to take advantage of the situation. For, though students may now have felt insecure not only towards the outside world but also in their internal relationship towards Ron, they could hardly rally around the student who had identified himself with authority. In fact, insofar as the students ever renewed a collective spirit, it was, indeed, to express opposition to authority whenever the exercise of it threatened. Moreover, as we shall presently see, whenever such opposition formed, it was not Ben but Denzil, the oldest student, who was turned to for leadership.

C. NEGLECT OF STUDENTS' EDUCATIONAL NEEDS

At the opening ceremony, the director of NACRO, Nicholas Hinton, told an audience which included dignitaries, press and neighbours that 'lack of educational opportunity could be a cause of crime'. Evidence in this study lends some support to this generalisation. There may be many people like, for example, Adam and Geoff whose criminality seems to have been associated with boredom with factory work, from which there may be few well established routes back into the educational system. But the present study provides evidence equally as strong that ex-offenders can feel considerable circumspection and trepidation in established educational environments, such as the Tech. It was not long before Ron became aware of such difficulties and of the possibility that they could be a cause of a return to crime. Ron turned to NACRO head office, but he repeatedly failed to obtain any sympathetic interest in ways and means of providing additional staff which he considered was needed to help the students to succeed in their study programmes.

Ben told of how he absented himself from classes at the Tech because of difficulty in relating to people of a different age group and social background:

> I was twenty-seven and some of them kids were only sixteen. The questions they would ask were so naive. They knew nothing of the world. Also, I couldn't get on with the lecturer. They had a rule that if you missed three lectures in a run you would be expelled. I used to miss ten in a trot. The kids in the class were talking about sociological theories, but I never see it work, Denzil never see it work, Conrad never see it work, and we were all working class. The kids didn't know what they were talking about in terms of practicalities.

A section of a memorandum which residents of the first year received reads:

> 26. Tutorials. I will be seeing you individually roughly once every three weeks, to discuss your work and anything else that you may want to talk about. You can see me at any other time, of course - you don't have to knock.

In terms of practicalities, however, it was not easy for Ben, who had been told so often in the past that he was a problem to people, straightforwardly to enter a busy office and inform Ron that he had problems, new ones.

Even in tutorials, the fear of loss of face, on the one side, and pressures of time, on the other, did not facilitate the revelation of problems and the working out of a suitable solution. Ben pointed out that:

> In the first year, Ron would never have enough time. He would just come in, ask about the work we were doing, look at it superficially, say it looked fine and then be off.

On an average of at least every two months, Ron requested NACRO for more staff, in memoranda, discussion papers, interim reports, the annual report, etc. He pointed out that applications were continuing to come into the Advisory Service at a rapid rate, that this demonstration of need required a proper response and that he and Mary were being overworked. I was able to find only one reply to these appeals. On 11 June 1975, Nicholas Hinton wrote saying that, 'It seems totally inappropriate ... that a whole section of your report should be given up ... to an expression of grievance ... There are several channels for airing grievances, of which the Newsheet is not one'. It is possible that, despite his sociological generalisation at the launching ceremony, Nicholas Hinton was not committed to bolstering a project which, as he indicated to me when I started my research, he regarded as short term and essentially experimental. A possible reason for his low commitment is suggested in a letter from Douglas Curtis, on 26 October 1973, to the criminologist, Pauline Morris:

> *Nick Hinton has mentioned to me that you have some reservations about the labelling and isolating effects of establishing an Educational Unit for ex-offenders. I did take some preliminary soundings about the possibility of providing accommodation in ordinary student quarters in co-operation with an existing college and I also raised the question of mixed sex accommodation. Both suggestions met with some initial resistance and the feeling was that, for the sake of expediency, we should set it up on the proposed basis as one way of breaking down existing prejudices ...*

Nick's attitude to the project, therefore, may have been influenced by current criminological theory.

D. A CRISIS OF UNDERCOMMITMENT

One of Doug's earliest ideas about the project was that 'the Parole Board should be asked to take possible future admission into account' (Curtis 1973b, p.7). This suggestion seems to have been responded to with alacrity, for, reporting on the Unit's opening ceremony, The Guardian of 23 October 1974 stated that:

> Sir Louis Petch, the Chairman of the Parole Board, committed himself yesterday to giving more parole to inmates who ... had been offered a place in a school or college.

The consequence of Sir Louis's commitment now seems predictable in retrospect. The presence of students with little commitment to the Unit's programme, but desiring release from custody on licence, was evident throughout the time I was studying the Unit.

The Unit, however, was not prepared for undercommitted students, as can be seen in the crisis precipitated by Percy's arrival.

Percy, seventeen years old, came to the Unit from Borstal, and was enrolled several days later at the York Street College of Further Education to study four O level subjects. Two weeks later, he dropped out, saying that college did not interest him. Instead, he used his new freedom to stay up late at night, sleeping during the day and doing no homework. Ron tried an alternative tactic by putting Percy on a correspondence course, as well as obtaining private tuition for him. But these devices were no more successful in eliciting a positive response from Percy. He felt that he was being subjected to unwanted pressure by these new expectations, and he threatened to leave the Unit. When Percy's Borstal telephoned on 5 November, Ron happened to mention the threat. Borstal officers immediately came to the Unit to arrest Percy on the grounds that he was still technically under their control. There was an outcry among the students, who blamed Ron, and at the Steering Committee meeting the following day, 'it was decided that Ron Noble would go and see the Governor on Friday 8 November to ask that Percy should be allowed back to continue his studies'.

Back at the Unit, Percy spent a lot of time with Dulcie, and by the Christmas vacation he had moved into her room. At the Steering Committee meeting of 27 January 1975, Ron stated that 'some Correspondence Course Students are not working well. I have asked them to show me written work each week. In Percy and Denzil's cases, I have said that I will review their progress in three weeks' time, and if no improvement has come about there will be a risk of their studentships being ended'. (On 6 January, Percy was formally discharged from his Borstal sentence.) In the third week in February, Percy refused to pay any rent on the grounds that he was no longer using his own room. On 24 February his studentship was ended. Ron said that 'I wanted to move Percy out because he was being a drag on us'. Again, the students protested, arguing that Percy was Dulcie's boyfriend and was not taking up any extra room. Ron consented to allow Percy to remain as Dulcie's guest. However, he increased Dulcie's rent, in a letter to her, by the cost of Percy's usual rent. The students were affronted by this manoeuvre, and, in a further Steering Committee meeting, Denzil acted as an aggressive advocate on behalf of the couple. In the discussion, a financial compromise was worked out.

Once Percy, in concert with other students, had shaken off Ron's authority over him he adopted his own way of life in the Unit. Of considerable interest in this respect is that senior members of the Steering Committee came to recognise his self-motivated activities as having their own validity, even in terms of education, in the broader sense of the term. Thus, Ron remarked that Percy 'refused to be organised into education while here. I don't think he did anything [to gain academic qualifications] in Borstal. But he made progress in himself in that he did quite a lot of reading, writing poems and songs and learning to play the guitar. In his own way, he did something about educating himself'. Similarly, the chairman of the Steering Committee (at that time, a director of the correspondence college), reflecting on the period of Percy's residence in the Unit, said, 'we soon discovered ... that what people coming out of custody wanted was often not a qualification at all but surviving as a normal human being and keeping out of crime'. As we shall see, however, this discovery was rarely to be applied. When, in the second year, many students were reimprisoned, the Committee's reaction to such official recidivism was to exercise greater control over potential recidivists, especially as the Home Office was assumed to be increasingly urgent in its expectation that the Unit show 'results'. Percy's case, however, shows us a brief interlude in which the function of the Unit changed from controlling one of the students - or trying to - to serving him, in the sense of providing him with a place where, living with others on whom there was little pressure to find a job, he was able to express himself indulgently, using the Unit for a few months as a resort from his usual lifestyle of uninteresting jobs interrupted every so often by crime and punishment.

E. OUTCOMES OF THE UNIT'S PERFORMANCE BY THE END OF THE FIRST YEAR

In the first year, there were never more than eight students residing in the Unit at any given time. Larry left after a week, Conrad was expelled after two weeks, George found his own room in town after three months, and Ena left after four months, when she married an airman from a nearby American base. These four were replaced in the course of the year by Izzie, Josh, Gene and Harvey. The last two continued into the second year and, in fact, most of their period of residence falls into that academic year. For convenience, therefore, if, at this juncture, we examine the outcomes, in terms of rehabilitation and education, for those students who ended their residence by the end of the first year then we have eleven students to consider, of whom only nine resided for more than two weeks.

Of this number, only Ena is not definitely known to have reoffended while at the Unit. Nobody, however, was reimprisoned. The most serious offences were probably those of Errol and Denzil, who broke into the Unit's office during the Christmas vacation and stole the cash. The incident was not brought to the attention of the police.

Most students attended college very irregularly and dropped out before long. Correspondence courses and private tutors, including Ron himself, were turned to for alternative methods of education, which were also applied to students who joined the Unit too late in the academic year for college enrollment. Thus, what was soon called 'liberal studies, a forerunner of the Unit's third year 'school', started to become a normal substitute for college. As it did so, money which the Unit received from charities was redirected from college fees to remuneration for private teachers employed by the Unit, while clients now 'signed on' at the local office of the Department of Health and Social Security as 'available for work' and collected social security benefit.

In terms of paper qualifications, only two gains were made. Dulcie passed O level English Language, a subject for which she had received practically no formal education, a few weeks after coming to the Unit. George passed an A level at the end of the academic year. He was a middle class boy with several O levels and also one A level already behind him when his normal middle class career was temporarily interrupted by a Borstal sentence for using cannabis. He attended the Tech regularly and, at the end of the year, gained a place in a polytechnic, from which he later graduated.

Although they had made no noticeable academic progress during their academic year in Cambridge, three other students obtained places in colleges in other parts of Britain, Ben and Denzil at an adult residential college, and Errol at the Further Education College in Cheltenham.

F. CHANGE OF POLICY

In surveying the students of the Unit's first year who left to enter colleges in different parts of the country as a result of his sponsorship, Ron observed a certain correlation between this 'success' and students' academic qualifications before coming to the Unit. On the basis of this observation, Ron decided that 'we could do better in our admissions policy. We decided to select people who had had a successful record of courses of education in prison ... some, in fact, with very little cooperation from prison staff'.

Before making this policy change, Ron might have been made more cautious by considering the experience of Conrad. After expulsion from the Unit, Conrad entered a Birmingham further education college on the merit of three O levels obtained in prison. However, he was very soon reconvicted and returned to prison, ending his formal education in the outside world. But Ron considered that a substantial period of residence in the Unit, 'of surviving as a normal human being', provided a preparation for college life. It was, indeed, in these terms that he recommended Ben, Denzil and Errol to the colleges which they went to when they left the Unit. Conrad, therefore, was considered to have had too little of such alleged preparation in the Unit.

In Regier's terms, therefore, the Unit's first year saw change from a policy validation stage to a policy critique stage. Between the opening of the Unit and the end of 1974, Ron and some of his clients seem to have been bubbling over with enthusiasm. In the Unit's files, I found memoranda to Ron's chiefs in London in which 'rehabilitation' is used unsparingly and discerned in every new activity of his clients, however commonplace, such as 'settling in' or 'getting to know the staff'.

But 1975 brought disenchantment. The students did not give the Unit inordinately bad publicity, but neither did they give it much credit in terms either of rehabilitation or of academic progress. In the detoxification study, the first model attempted in the policy critique stage was that of 'improving functional rationality' (Regier 1979, p.70). Similarly, Ron considered that his work could be made more efficient by recruiting mainly 'bright young guys', as he called them, regardless, if not inspite, of their criminal records so that the Unit would clearly achieve what it had set out to do.

G. REVIEW AND ASSESSMENT OF THE UNIT'S FIRST YEAR

1. Absence of community The mode of interaction between students in the Unit's first year provides little basis for any naive or utopian ideas that, by placing ex-offenders together in the same dwelling with official blessing, they necessarily become a 'community' with positive goals. Whatever solidarity existed among students at the beginning rested on such weak foundations as belonging to a group of pioneers whose pious sentiments were recorded in the national press when the Unit had its official opening ceremony. Even these weak foundations crumbled with the first signs of poor performance and progress in academic work or rehabilitation. The salience of the notion of community which officialdom and press fostered may even have been counterproductive, for it gave prominence to the latent ambiguity about whether what fellow clients had in common was a genuine commitment to the Unit's goals and programme or merely an official criminal background. This ambiguity soon led to a leadership conflict, with one client posing as the project leader's right hand man and the other client, by current words and action, offering legitimacy to the kind of behaviour for which all clients had been stigmatised in the past. This conflict, moreover, was not attended by firm cohesion even on a factional level. For the factional division was largely manufactured out of tensions and distrust between individuals who knew little more about each other than that they were 'ex-cons'; indeed, one of the female students was easily able to assist such manufacture by manipulating the provision of sexual gratification, from which most

clients had been officially deprived before coming to the Unit. After the project leader took drastic action to try to remedy a situation where crime seemed to be the motif of clients' disunity they became a collectivity again only for the purpose of opposing Ron's actions or policies. This new conflict, however, was inevitably perceived to a large extent in terms of the 'us/them' relationship to which official offenders are accustomed. An us/them relationship, once reactivated, could even find expression in crime against 'them' as seems to have been the case in the office raid, which, carried out by two clients who, from Ben's account, tended normally to distrust or avoid one another, also gives support to the familiar criminological observation (e.g. Shaw 1930, p.86; Sutherland 1937, pp.28, 154) that persons who commit crimes together may have no cooperative ties at all in any other respect.

2. Distorted understanding of clients' educational needs

In the educational area the wish for one kind of improvement was so determined that it tended to cloud a recognition of a different and more fundamental kind of needed improvement. There is no dispute that the unexpectedly heavy pressure on the Advisory Service, as well as the work of administering a hostel, demanded more staff manpower than the project had initially been allotted, even if this demand tended to be expressed in terms which could be interpreted as putting too much weight on the educational assistance which Ron, as a teacher, wished to give to the small number of students who lived in the hostel.

What was masked by the staff undermanning problem, however, were indications that the primary educational requirement for anyone whom the Unit intended eventually to place in college or university as an ordinary student was not so much the ability to learn, say, Shakespeare or sociology but the ability to 'survive' in a college or university environment. Such survival, as for any college or university student, requires skills in coping or coming to terms with middle class culture and/or study skills for working autonomously within the syllabuses operating in tertiary education. The need for acquiring such skills may have been partly hidden by what was felt to be a more pressing need for increase in staff - but it was not obscured completely. 'Difficulty in relating to the Tech', in fact, quickly became a standard phrase. Dismaying, therefore, is that this difficulty was never directly confronted. Informal knowledge about how to master a college environment was never considered a form of education. The latter meant a laid down syllabus only, and if quadratic equations or whatever could not be learnt at the Tech then the remedy was perceived as finding private teachers. Such a remedy, however, quite apart from creating even heavier administrative work, involved continuation of an exclusive emphasis, albeit in a less formal setting, on education in subjects rather than in learning or coping skills. Strikingly, one of the letters of appeal to NACRO actually glorifies in the flexibility of the Unit in making other teaching provisions for students unable to settle at the Tech so that they pass whatever subjects they were taking. Such alternative arrangements, however, not only isolated clients from ordinary students, about which Pauline Morris had expressed foreboding; it also isolated the Unit's students from the future educational routines for which the Unit was set up to prepare them.

In the field of after-care, NACRO has devised 'sheltered workshops' for habitual offenders who steal from employers, cannot keep to factory timetables, quickly get the sack, etc. (Many offenders work in such shelters for an indefinite period, and, indeed, the former administrator of one of them (McKinnon 1976) sees them as models of industrial life for most citizens.) Similarly, the Unit increasingly specialised, as we shall see, in what might accurately be called 'sheltered education'. But being sheltered does not necessarily teach one how to brave the cold storms which may occur outside. Withdrawing clients from the Tech could hardly be considered a move which prepared them, on leaving the Unit, to continue their education in college, university or other place of tertiary education with many elements in common with the Tech.

We thus encounter a basic irony. Prison education tends to be criticised for teaching skills which are not of value to prisoners when they are summarily discharged. After-care is seen as a solution to this problem, and the Unit was perceived as a form of after-care. The research, however, did not find evidence that students were provided with skills helpful to them when they left the Unit.

3. Processing people versus changing them; the short term versus the long term 'Education' was not the only concept about which there was confusion. Little distinction was recognised between processing clients and changing them. For this the Unit can hardly deserve blame. Hasenfeld also, in the learned journal in which he makes the distinction, writes as if the two functions are neatly articulated, with processing being an ancillary to the change which an organisation is established to achieve for people. If an organisation, however, processes people into social situations where they cannot cope, so that they revert to conduct which the organisation was designed to change then 'processing' and 'changing' may even be in conflict.

That the Unit could obtain places for them to go to after they left it for Ben, Errol and Denzil, despite the fact that they made no academic progress while in Cambridge, testifies to the extent of the Unit's success as a processing agency. It is possible that the staff of the Unit could have achieved an equal measure of success if it had from the start processed them via the Advisory Service. The necessity for the Unit to show, however, that it had achieved something for its clients may have influenced

Ron to write more glowing recommendations on their behalf than if they had merely been strangers writing from prison. Moreover, it is possible that just as the 'student' label enabled the Unit's clients in many cases to obtain lenient treatment from law courts so the word 'resettlement' on the Unit's stationery may have played a part in smoothing away any doubts which college admissions staff may have entertained about the Unit's clients, in consideration of the fact that they had had 'a fixed abode' since coming out of prison.

The distinction between processing and changing is closely associated with the distinction, also little considered by the Unit, between the short term and the long. In many cases, the long term was in fact not too long. For example, Denzil dropped out of the college he went to from the Unit after a few weeks, and Ben after a few months.

Errol's downfall took longer, but was no less disastrous. In Cambridge, Errol did little academic work. Ron considered, however, that Errol was being 'held together' by an older, divorced woman with whom he was having an affair. Indeed, Ron praised her contribution in a letter which he wrote on Errol's behalf to a college admissions officer. Errol left the Unit to live with his friend in her comfortable Cheltenham home. Reports from the Further Education College there spoke of substantial progress in Errol's academic work and of his being accepted to go on to take an HND in mathematics. It seemed that despite a small grant and other infantalising effects of being a student Errol's personal relationship held the promise of developing into a mature partnership based on matching economic and cultural resources. In fact, however, Errol had an enormous and, perhaps at times, intolerable amount of catching up to do to reach his partner's social level. His relationship, indeed, in his own words, deteriorated into one of a dependent child/mother kind, unsatisfactory and painful to her. When she told him that she wished him to leave her, he fell apart, instead of being 'held together'. 2½ years after his previous conviction (while resident in the Unit) Errol was arrested for burglary, arson and assault, the last two charges being ones for which he had no previous convictions, and he was imprisoned again. The case seems to give support to the principle, increasingly recognised in criminology (e.g. Hood and Sparks 1970, pp.178-9) that some years must pass before a treatment can properly be evaluated as having achieved a positive, negative or neutral effect. Details of the case also strongly suggest that, if Errol had not aspired for upward social mobility through education, then his relationship would probably not have lasted long and that its ending would probably not have had such a large and sudden outburst of public reoffending as its sequel. On the importance of <u>long term</u> evaluation more will be said in later chapters.

6 The Unit's Second Academic Year, 1975–6: the Policy Critique Stage

At the end of the first academic year, Ron temporarily closed the Unit, and placed the students who were remaining at the Unit for the second year in rooms provided by the Tech. He felt some sense of satisfaction. No student, other than Conrad, had been reimprisoned in the course of the year - Ben, Denzil and Errol were reimprisoned a considerable time later. Moreover, he had high hopes for the outcome of his policy change. He would be selecting clients who had shown great promise academically by gaining impressive qualifications in prison. By extending to them the opportunity to continue their education as soon as they emerged from prison, so that they would capably be addressing themselves to an activity other than crime, he would be demonstrating the success of the Unit in mere months. In the following statement, Ron expresses both his faith at the time - as well as the disappointment which soon followed:

> I decided we must have people who show more promise academically, who will be able to put more into the Tech, whom also we could get grants for. So we got people who had GCEs etc. We also selected people of about the same age - thus several bright young guys. I had grants organised for all of them. I thought we had the nucleus of something quite strong here. But it didn't work out at all.

It started not to work out at all not long after the reopening of the Unit for the second academic year and the arrival of the 'bright young guys'. Within a few weeks, Neil was reimprisoned, and a similar fate befell other students throughout the second year. Each time a student was sent down his place in the Unit was filled from the portfolio of other bright young guys, many of whom were in their turn quickly reimprisoned. As a result, there were as many as twenty second year students (in the sense that all or most of their residence fell into that period). No less than twelve of that number were reimprisoned while still living at the Unit, or within weeks of leaving because of pressure to move out or of going on the run. (It is fair to point out, however, that one student was reimprisoned, for five years, for an offence prior to his previous sentence.

On the other hand, there was at least one other student who was not reimprisoned at the time of his residence in the Unit but almost certainly would have been had he not informed the police about other students.)

This turn of events caused staff and Steering Committee members considerable alarm and mental confusion. Of a group of students who had singularly failed to avoid arrest the chairman of the Steering Committee remarked that 'our admissions policy proved no more successful - probably less - than our policy in the first year. If anything they were more able to use their wits to get into crime than in the first year'.

I think it unlikely that differences, if any, in the wits of the two groups account for the difference in their short term penological outcomes. I shall, therefore, offer two other explanations. The first simply entails looking at statistical probabilities. The second involves causal explanation. During this period, I directly noted the processes which were sending students back to prison. I also established personal relationships with many of them and received information from them not only while they were in Cambridge, but also later, in prison visits and through correspondence.

A. THE PROBABILITY OF REIMPRISONMENT FOR PRODUCTS OF THE PRISON EDUCATION SYSTEM

The likelihood of the type of client recruited for the Unit in the second year returning to prison would seem to follow from the following empirically supported axioms:

1. The probability of obtaining academic qualifications in prison is largely contingent on the length of one's sentence(s). This holds for GCE courses, as well as for Open University courses. In the case of the latter, inmates often have to wait more than a year to be enrolled, though, once enrolled, prisoners who are in custody long enough to take OU examinations show a pass rate of eighty-nine per cent (NACRO Information #5, p.2).

2. People with long sentences tend to have been convicted of more serious and/or more frequent crimes. In the Unit's first year, there were only three students resident for more than two weeks who had had more than one conviction for robbery, burglary or violence: Denzil, Errol and Josh. In the second year, there were twelve. Moreover, few of them had previously been out of prison for long without being returned there.

3. *If* the Unit's students reoffended they tended to repeat the same kind of offence, particularly during the period of their stay in the Unit.

4. More serious offences are more likely to result in conviction (and, therefore, in punishment) than less serious ones (West and Farrington 1977, p.27).

The likelihood of the type of client recruited in the second year returning to prison, if he offended, having been established, it is now necessary to pinpoint the cause which seemed to be operating in the Unit leading such clients to reoffend, for it was, indeed, during the period in which they resided in the Unit that most second year clients were reimprisoned.

B. CRISES OF UNSTABLE COMMITMENT

More than any other period, the second year of the Unit demonstrated in a most dramatic way a fundamental flaw in its theory of rehabilitation.

Regardless of the reasons which had led repeatedly to the arrest and imprisonment of most of the clients who came to the Unit in its second year, such clients had been denounced as exceptionally unlikeable individuals by the criminal justice system. If they did not already possess a poor conception of themselves they had, in most cases, responded to punishment by acquiring one. Segregated from friends outside who may have been equally lawless, they had not been able to avoid a definition of themselves as incompetent, on a similar level perhaps with that large proportion of the older prison population described by NACRO and other penal reform organisations as 'inadequates' (Crow 1979). In some cases, students had met in prison famous gangsters, and later boasted of the fact, but very few could match the skill of such men in either obtaining 'a big haul' for their pains or in attracting a following from some men because of their effective ability to threaten others with violence.

Any self-esteem which second year students may have once possessed seemed to have been knocked out of them by their long episodes in prison. As in the game of Monopoly, failure does not reach its limit in jail. Prison society is no less status conscious than the outside world, and wherever status is highly valued there are opportunities for repeated failure. One of the main sources of status in prison society is violence or a reputation for violence, and many of those who stand nowhere in that art or league gravitate to prison education classes in an alterative attempt to gain status. Such an attempt, however, is a pathetic one. Students told of repeatedly being looked down on by other prisoners and of being taunted by prison officers. A newspaper advertisement for trainee prison officers declares: 'Character is more important than anything else, and you can't swot that up - you either have it or you haven't' (News of the World 20/3/77).

Among students who made the transition from this social environment of education in prison to the education of ex-prisoners in Cambridge, the continuing sense of failure as human beings could be very intense. In the first year, when Ron went to Denzil's room during one of the latter's periods of alcoholic despair, Denzil said, 'Don't come near me. I'm not worth talking to. I'm just a load of shit'. Similar heartcries were heard from other clients. '"I'm no good" is freqently expressed by many prisoners ... It is not often that one finds self-confidence among offenders' (Klare 1973, p.16). In relation to the ex-prisoners in the Unit, this observation would be an understatement.

In order to visualise the predicament of former prison intellectuals in the Unit, some theoretical speculations of Cloward and Ohlin (1960, p.181) about offenders who are unsuccessful are worth quoting:

> There are differentials in access both to illegitimate and to legitimate means; not all who seek to obtain success-goals by prohibited routes are permitted to proceed. There are probably many lower-class adolescents oriented towards success in the criminal world who fail; similarly, many who would like to acquire proficiency in the use of violence also fail. We might ask, therefore, what the response would be among those faced with failure in both legitimate and illegitimate means. We suggest that persons who experience this "double failure" are likely to move into a retreatist pattern of behavior ... (emphasis theirs).[1]

This notion of Cloward and Ohlin that 'retreatists' have failed in both the legitimate and illegitimate 'opportunity structures' can be extended. A rehabilitation project offers the opportunity of treble failure, by adding the possibility of failure in a rehabilitative opportunity structure.

Before becoming retreatists from the Tech and the Unit's programme, however, many clients approached the possibility of treble failure with intense overcommitment. The period between such overcommitment and retreat, however, could be extremely short, as the case study of Jack, for example, shows; so short, in fact, that the Unit's staff failed to remark on the overcommitment phase. The shortness of this phase was directly proportional to the size of the gap between the clients' self-esteem and what they perceived as expected of them. They had been degraded by the criminal justice system as people unworthy of society, yet they were now told that, if they came to the Unit, they had the possibility of middle class status in society. The news tended to be received with incredulity and assimilated with anxiety and stress; states of mind which are regarded by the Home Office as one of the four main causes of persistent offending (Davies 1974b, p.31).

The Unit's programme was offered to its clients as a means of achieving success. Few, however, had previously ever been regarded as having any capacity for success, either for themselves or for any organisation, experimental or otherwise. They were also expected to achieve this success in a matter of months, and inspite of competing attractions available outside prison. They were no longer expected to use education to fill time; they were now expected to make up for lost time.

The Unit's academic programme tended to be presented to the students as a privilege. One close neighbour invariably reminded them of that whenever she saw them. Yet never in their lives had most of them appropriated privilege as a matter of course. They learnt that the project was dealing with hundreds of 'applicants' and that there were always others ready to take their place. Some felt that they had been selected by mistake and that their inadequacies would soon be found out. Another feeling was that, if they did not fulfil the expectations of the donor of the privilege, they would be guilty of letting him down badly. Indeed, numerous were letters expressing remorse sent to Ron by clients who became ex-ex-prisoners (whereas no such letters were received from ex-clients who had been consistently undercommitted to the Unit's programme). Most of the students were thus in a similar position to that of the Boston schoolchildren studied by Holt (1964, p.9):

> They are afraid, above all else, of failing, of disappointing or displeasing the many anxious adults around them, whose limitless hopes and expectations for them hang over their heads like a cloud.

To the Unit's second year clients not only its programme, with the possibility of failing in it, but also committing crime, involved stress (hence the offender's turn to alcohol). The exciting risk involved in crime, however, may have repressed the more painful and continual stress of the Unit's expectations. But even without whatever excitement there may have been in plunder and assault another psychological principle seemed to be involved, which, though it may be paradoxical, may nevertheless be fairly common. Many people consider that the <u>certain</u>, or near certain, risk of failure (such as returning to prison) is less stressful - and, therefore, preferable - than <u>uncertain</u> potential failure (such as failing examinations and letting down one's sponsor). This order of preference was noted, for example, in the 1975 Parole Board's Report, which states that 'sometimes a prisoner will "opt out" of parole rather than put himself or his family on tenterhooks' (HMSO 1976, p.5). As a result, many prisoners remain longer in prison than they would otherwise need to. Moreover, a further common element in a prisoner's disinclination to apply for parole and the client of the Unit's recidivism is that both forms of retreat can be seen as an expedient way of relieving the pressure of others' expectations. Reoffending by an 'ex-offender' seems to have been considered by him as less overtly ungrateful than simply walking out of the Unit as a poorly performing 'student'. Referring to the dive back into prison by second year students, the liaison probation officer accurately observed that 'crime of that kind is a way of withdrawing commitment to the Unit and to Ron'.

We shall note, in our case studies, various manifestations of overcommitment and of the ways in which it was sooner or later cast aside in favour of going back to crime. Such reversion was tragic and ironic, for it took place in a context in which the individual reoffended because of the frustrations of mentally trying so hard (and frequently, therefore, so ineffectively) to fulfil requirements designed to rehabilitate him and help him to conform to society's norms. This ironic twist, however, may in no way be confined to the particular setting of the Unit but may be widespread in society. As Cloward and Ohlin (1960, pp.38-9) argue:

> Efforts to conform, to live up to social expectations, often entail profound strain and frustration, For example, a boy of fourteen may desperately wish to be a man, and certainly we should agree that this is a proper goal for him. Yet the very fact that he wants so much what society at large wants for him produces problems of adjustment ... conformity, <u>taking cultural mandates seriously</u>, is thus a crucial step in the process by which deviance is generated ... it is our contention that problems of adjustment are engendered by acts of social conformity performed under adverse circumstances (emphasis mine).

It would be an exaggeration, however, to say that the strains of overcommitment to formal education always led directly to retreat to prison. There is evidence of clients settling their minds by changing their attitude from one of overcommitment to the kind of undercommitment which Percy in the first year brought with him to the Unit. Again, there is nothing unusual about such a development in a competitive society. In his study of Boston schoolchildren (Holt 1964, p.67), found that it was not uncommon for them to adopt the principle of least stress, choosing immediate failure rather than uncertain future failure, so that 'failure, unrelieved and total, may seem to some students to be a promising strategy for school and even for life'. Among older pupils, many drop out, and, indeed, Elliott (1966, p.308) finds that 'the probability of engaging in delinquent behaviour is less for out-of-school youth than for in-school youth'. He goes on to urge that, as a measure for delinquency prevention, dropping out 'should reduce school-related frustration and alienation and lead to decreasing involvement in delinquency' (Elliott and Voss 1974, p.5).

The second year students, however, were not easily allowed to switch to undercommitment. Clients could only be regarded as feckless if, labelled as 'bright', they did not manifest that quality in the prescibed way. The 'normative' sanctions which theoretically bound staff and students together at the Unit's foundation were now firmly replaced by 'utilitarian' and 'coercive' sanctions (Etzioni 1964, pp.68-70) of one kind or another, as in the following (undated) note:

> Wayne,
>
> The grant I shall pay you this week will be reduced by 1/10 for each morning or afternoon session that you miss at college. So you have lost 1/5 for yesterday morning and this morning ...

I am by now familiar with Wayne's frame of mind in the first weeks after he comes out of prison. He seems in a haze, irritable, pessimistic, unable to make decisions, and totally lacking in self-confidence. It seems to me likely that, like Charles Smith (Parker 1963, p.148), he felt up against 'standards I am incapable of attaining, and then punished for not attaining them ... Is it any surprise that I regard myself as a failure before I even try, that I do not think it worth while to make much effort, knowing I cannot succeed?'. Wayne supplemented his grant by illegal means and soon found himself back in prison. On his return there, he found that, like Holt's Boston schoolchildren, he had learnt to fail so well that his stress in attempting to study for examinations had become chronic. In letters which he wrote during this sentence, he repeatedly complained of being unable to study. In seeking relief, he turned to private reading of his own choice, and absorbed, among other volumes, most of the novels of Hardy and of the great Russian writers. His experience of the outside world had changed him from a prison intellectual to a prison literatus, with competitive examinations and qualifications left behind.

Cressey (1953) argues that having a problem which is not shareable is an important factor behind the offence of embezzlement. In fact, this factor may not be confined to people who have the opportunity to embezzle. Anxiety in a competitive situation is, perhaps, among the main problems in our society felt to be not shareable. Moreover, attempts by a person with low self-esteem to share his problem can lead to the possibility of losing prestige, which, as Van Den Haag (1956, p.214) points out, can produce even further anxiety. In a letter to me (16/8/78), Jack discusses the way in which anxiety among his fellow students in the second year led to all manner of peculiar behaviour, except a willingness to reveal one's self-doubt:

> *Instead of the solidarity and confidence of co-operation there was the suspicion and anxiety of competition, with each person afraid to reveal his or her needs through fear that they would stand exposed as inferior types. Of the few I became intimate with ... the main problem appeared to be anxiety ... Each exhibited tremendous anxiety: Ollie to the point of paranoia ... Wayne to boasting of his intelligence and disinclination to display it, to protracted somnambulance and eventual apathy; Bert increasingly to "hash"; myself to confusion and imprisonment ... In his desire to see the project succeed, Ron unknowingly terrified me with his expectation that I would secure two "A" and one "O" level in the space of a few months - a feat which I knew was beyond me ...*

The Unit's clients, living along the same corridor, had plenty of opportunity to discuss their educational programmes with each other. They did not avail themselves of such opportunity because of anxiety about loss of face. With members of staff the students, as we shall now see, did not even have much <u>opportunity</u> to discuss problems in their educational programme.

C. CONTINUED NEGLECT OF STUDENTS' EDUCATIONAL NEEDS

In the previous chapter, we saw how the work of implementing the Cambridge project as a whole, including the Advisory Service and the general running of the hostel, left little time over for advising clients with their educational problems. The situation did not improve. For, by the time the Unit was reopened for the second year, the Advisory Service's backlog of applicants had mounted to 300. Ron said, 'We began to feel the fatigue by evening of running a place like this - the Advisory Service side had built up and there were more things to do'. In notes to incoming students, the promise of sessions of study help, and the intervals between them, became much vaguer than in the first year:

> 23. Tutorials: I shall try to talk to you from time to time about your studies.

Yet there were many activities of a non-educational but paternalistic nature which Ron involved himself in on behalf of the students. He 'found so many silly things to clear up, for example, X hadn't returned his library books, Y hadn't paid his rent for the tenancy of the Tech's house during the summer, etc.'. It is hard, however, to avoid regarding these duties as displaced forms of behaviour. Helping people with their educational problems involves patience and creative thought. Such qualities are too easily dissipated by pressure and stress, being replaced by compulsive and irrelevant pettifogging concerns, which may be regarded, on a smaller scale, as similar to the 'numerous examples of accompanying clients in their leisure time pursuits, providing driving lessons, arranging holidays ...' (Folkard et al. 1976, p.7) and other (extensive) activity remote from normal probation duties engaged in by probation officers recruited to the Home Office 'IMPACT' experiment in 'intensive' treatment. Here it was found that such nursing had no effect on reconviction rates, save that 'the type of offender with moderate or high criminal tendencies and average or few personal problems did significantly worse (in terms of one-year reconviction rates) under intensive treatment than under normal supervision' (ibid., p.23).

An unfortunate irony, however, is that, though paternalism was extended to the students in irrelevant respects, it was taken away from them in particularly relevant respects. Because of Ron's exhaustion by the evening 'by the second year, we made our telephone number private ... but this did create a distance between staff and students'. Indeed, if the clients were to be put in the role of middle class youths taking GCE subjects at a technical college, they surely deserved other parts of the middle class package, perhaps especially <u>because</u> they were not middle class, such as help from an educational adviser prepared to adopt the role of a parent or older sibling in assisting his wards with notes, essays, embarrassments with the Tech and the whole area of teaching students how to learn in the mysterious middle class ways to which students themselves seemed tremulously to attach so much importance. It appears, however, perhaps because of the demands of the comparatively less problematic Advisory Service work, never to have occurred to the education officer, to use a title which Ron began to use during this period, to apply the principle of flexitime, relaxing with his young family in the afternoon and being available to his clients in the evening. Had he been prepared to adopt such a principle yet a further, far from obscure, need might also have been catered for. As the safe-breaker, Harry King, in his autobiography, complains of another rehabilitation scheme:

> The assistant director ... said, "I have regular office hours" and he said "I keep 'em ... anybody that wants to consult me has to consult me during these working hours." Well that's silly. When you're a counsellor of a bunch of people, like these potential criminals and things like that, they don't get into trouble eight hours a day. They're potentially in trouble twenty-four hours a day. They have to have a phone where they can contact you and see you and talk to you, when times get rough ... (Chambliss (ed) 1972, pp.148-9).

Indeed, the lack of availability of an education officer at a time when he was likely to be most needed poignantly brings one back again to related contradictions with which the social structure and organisation of the Unit was beset on all sides. On the one hand, there was no staff in residence lest the clients see an analogy with another familiar place. On the other hand, clients who did not march back and forth to the Tech had sanctions applied to them which were probably not less severe than any sanctions which might be applied to uncompliant prison inmates enrolled in education classes. On the one hand, clients attended the Tech in the company of middle class adolescents. On the other hand, they had neither parent, sibling nor education officer to talk to when they needed help with, or reassurance about, any homework which they brought back from the Tech. On the one hand, they were supposed to be learning history, English literature or whatever in the evening. On the other hand, there was nobody to guide them to unlearn those activities in the past which in the evening they had done from time to time and which they had come to the Unit to begin to stop doing. Yet a further observable contradiction which was closely connected with the others was that staff completely disappeared in the evening on the grounds that the Unit would otherwise be perceived as a prison; <u>however</u>, it only required something going wrong of a comparatively low order of magnitude, such as a student missing a few pounds, for every client to be liable to be interrogated in the morning. Not surprisingly, a number of students tried by all means to avoid not only the Tech but also the office and the Unit during daylight hours, particularly with the early arrival of that extraordinarily hot, cloudless, and perhaps unprecedented, British summer of 1976, which transformed so many clients into the status of virtual absconders, even if, with abnormal thirst quenched, they happened (which was by no means always the case) to be still physically present in the Unit in morning's early hours.

D. CHANGES IN POLICY AND ADMINISTRATION

At the end of the second year, as at the end of the first, Ron's plans for the Unit were strongly influenced by recent events. The most recent significant events at the end of the second year were considered to be the many reincarcerations of students. Only one more year remained for the termination of the three year experiment. Ron said:

> We reached a crisis point in which, explicitly and otherwise, the police and NACRO were asking us, 'What are you going to do about it?'. The liaison probation officer expressed concern; and I myself got very depressed and exhausted.

A management committee was set up, normally consisting

of Ron, the liaison probation officer and NACRO's regional organiser. (The Steering Committee was disbanded in the third year on the grounds that, except for allowing clients to attend, it was merely duplicating the membership and decisions of the Management Committee.) The main tasks of the Management Committee were to initiate the following new developments, and monitor them.

1. Selection policy The Management Committee now decided to tighten up on selection procedure. In previous years, interviewees had been sent to see the liaison probation officer and the Steering Committee's chairman separately. The final decision, however, had rested on Ron, and the telephone conversations which he had with his colleagues did not usually exert a countervailing sway. For the third year it was decided that the Management Committee would meet together to interview candidates and discuss its impressions more lengthily and searchingly. Ron was to face more pressure not to make hasty decisions. Candidates were interrogated about the seriousness of their past offences and about the length of time they had been able to stay out of prison if they were not at the time still there but temporarily released for the interview. On the basis of such information, candidates were classified under 'estimated risk of reoffending' as 'low', 'medium' and 'high'. Of the students coming to the Unit in the third year as newcomers four were 'low', four were 'medium' and none was 'high'. When I asked Ron what he actually meant by 'estimated risk of reoffending' he, in fact, replied, 'the amount of trouble a chap was likely to cause us, in terms of bad publicity, going back to prison, etc.'.

The implications of this definition in relation to the rationale of the Unit were disturbing. The 'experiment' now seemed to be embarking on defeating its own purpose, being used as much to rehabilitate ex-offenders through education as to try to restore (rehabilitate?) the good name of the Unit! Moreover, if the Unit were to succeed in keeping offenders out of prison whom the Unit itself had classed as having a low risk of reoffending what would the 'experiment' be demonstrating? I gently put this point to Ron, which he granted, while adding that 'one day' (the date being undefined, although Ron at this juncture was beginning to negotiate with the Home Office to extend the life of the Unit) he would really like to work with 'hard core' offenders, a sentiment which could only be applauded. The fact of the matter, however, was that the Unit was being carried along by its own dynamics, which by now had moved away from its initial direction. The point had been reached where it was the Unit as much as the clients that had to be low risk, in terms of bad publicity, keeping out of trouble, etc.

Comparison with Regier's research is once again invited. In her study, a policy implementor, having tried various solutions without success in the 'policy critique stage', tended to sigh, 'I have battle fatigue. I feel that I have been on the front line too long' (Regier 1979, p.108). The policy maker may well have been exhausted, but he was not willing to be a defeatist. He rallied and allowed his efforts to move in the direction of Regier's 'policy rationalisation stage', which, we may recall, is characterised by settling on workable rather than optimal solutions' (ibid., p.106), a process, which in the case of the detoxification units, consisted of rejecting the veteran public drunks for whom the units had been originally intended and welcoming private, respectable alcoholics who would normally never go anywhere near Skid Row. In the case of the Unit, the target clientele became a group of low and medium risk ex-offenders. 'No solution manifested such simplicity, familiarity or prominence' (ibid., p.109).

2. <u>Staff increase</u> In the middle of the second year, Ron's wife resigned because of pregnancy. Her role as secretary, bookkeeper and informal counsellor was taken by Martha, who had been the secretary of the village college where Ron had once taught. In addition to this change, a new member of staff arrived in August 1976. A master, Stafford Wise, from a well known public school was granted sabbatical leave for the academic year 1976-7. He approached NACRO head office and offered his services. He was appointed to NACRO-Education, which thus now had the benefit of an assistant project leader. He was put in charge of the Advisory Service, to deal with its large backlog of applicants, as well as the general management of the hostel, while Ron decided to specialise as 'headmaster' of the 'school' (see next subsection). Stafford also joined the Management Committee, which thus now usually needed the visit to the Unit of only one other member, normally the liaison probation officer, for an effective interviewing quorum.

Stafford's attitudes were consistent with the pervasive student anxiety discussed in this chapter. In particular, he emphasised each student's assigned privilege and his potential dispensability if he did not justify it:

> When I get to the stage of inviting a chap to Cambridge, I say, 'Of course, you do realise that you are now only at the starting point - it is only a fifty/fifty chance that you will be taken. We've got lots of applicants and very few places'.
>
> Insofar as we are trying to steer students into what's best for them, we can say, 'If you are only going to do two O level subjects you are wasting your place in the Unit and there are other people who might be able to use it better'.

In more explicit terms than ever before each new ex-prisoner was thus told that there were spectres ready to dispossess him as soon as he displayed signs of faltering or failing in the academic race designed for competitors of sterling qualities. What the student did not need to have spelled out was where else he might go if he wished to have his 'place' unchallenged by those who had authority over him. But perhaps the most terrifying irony of all was that the attitudes which Stafford brought with him from public school were not moderated to accommodate the as yet unraised level of self-confidence of the students. The attitudes which Stafford brought were, indeed, apparently amplified. For most public schoolboys are probably subject to comparatively less intense competitive pressure and allowed a more relaxed academic pace in relation to amount of self-confidence. Nothing, therefore, could underline more sharply the Unit's self-concern regardless of the educational needs of its clients. Indeed, third year students were often treated as if they had intellectual buckets into which as much 'education' was forced as they could carry, regardless of clients' attitudes to education, uncertainties about it, thoughts about what it would do for them in the future and all the various other considerations necessary for the devising of a sound and viable educational system.

3. A school At the end of the second year, the Management Committee decided to take on the direct responsibility of teaching its students in classes on the premises. This development was described as an 'intermediate school'. The currently fashionable term 'intermediate' in the parlance of rehabilitators, as in the phrase 'intermediate treatment', is, unfortunately, yet another beguiling catch-all word, which so frequently disguises with the image of a stopping place on a straight road what so often is a cul-de-sac. It was, indeed, hard to perceive this new venture as other than a retreat from, rather than a preparation for, such features as the large lecture halls and individual self-direction of the university environment, which, with the advent of Stafford, was seen more singlemindedly than ever before as the proper destiny for every student accepted for the Unit. Ron wrote to NACRO: 'It is worth noting that an important aspect ... as we plan to operate it will be that of control. Because I now have the time, I shall be able to lay down regular work patterns for the students, hold regular discussions with teachers, organise periodic tests, mock exams, and end of term reports' (emphasis mine). Ron and Stafford were themselves to do much of the teaching. It was also planned that they would have a weekly hour's 'tutorial' with each individual student to discuss his progress. At classes, 'attendance would be compulsory for all students not on courses elsewhere. The curriculum would include certain "core subjects" ... to be followed by all students'.

In discussing different contemporary ideologies of education, Corrigan (1979, p.144) refers to:

> ... the body of opinion that sees ... most people, and especially children, cannot cope

> with a wide range of choices and as such they really need strong intellectual and moral direction ... What is needed is a return to discipline in schools, and this must be enforced with as much force and as many sanctions as necessary. Attendance must be ensured, with systematic prosecutions for truancy. Once this has been enforced, then the school must set about the coherent and direct transfer of moral values to the pupils.

In organisation and outlook, the Unit's school approximated to this body of opinion. As Stafford put it, 'The argument would be that they need external adult pressure applied because they haven't got it in themselves ... We are not dealing with wholly mature people. It's wrong to leave them to their own devices'.

In Regier's account of the development of detoxification units, the third stage of 'policy rationalisation' does not appear to have significantly emerged until all the attempted models in the second stage of 'policy critique' had manifestly failed. Not so with the Unit. Although it was now recruiting a more treatable clientele, it was also devising new policy critique type models for treating it. One of the models prepared for third year students was similar to what Regier calls a 'suprarational model'. This is attended by the catchphrase, 'We can only intervene when we have control' (Regier 1979, p.91). One of the ways in which this notion is put into action is in timetabling almost every hour of the client's day for 'treatment' in the faith that not only is the treatment benign but one cannot have too much of it:

> Head Nurse: The TV went on here at 7.30 AM. The man who turned it on is not dealing with his drinking. I recommend no TV after lunch, and no TV after midnight. We have to eliminate things which keep the men from dealing with their illness. That's one of the reasons we haven't been getting results (ibid., p.73).

In a similar way, any third year student engaged in an activity other than studying was suspected of not dealing with his recidivism.

Moreover, yet a further policy critique model was coming strongly to the fore at this point of the Unit's history; what Regier calls a 'medical-moral hybrid' model. Clients were perceived as not only too feeble to know what was good for them; they were also perceived, even though they had served their sentences, as morally discreditable. The picture of the client thus came to conform to what Douglas Curtis had referred to as 'existing prejudices'. In this way, any policy regnant in the Unit could remain more or less intact because 'program failures were blamed on service recipients' (ibid., p.153).

E. REVIEW AND ASSESSMENT OF THE UNIT'S SECOND YEAR

1. Absence of community As far as most of the Unit's second year students are concerned, there is little reason to suppose that the Unit was a new element in their lives which would break a well established pattern of burglary, robbery and violence followed by imprisonment, followed by similar offences, and so on in that syndrome which has come to be called 'the revolving door' (e.g. Fitzgerald and Sim 1979, p.134). Indeed, there are reasons to believe that the Unit precipitated earlier recidivism than would otherwise have been the case.

Most of the second year students came to the Unit with a very low opinion of themselves. Paper qualifications were their only claim to status. They lacked self-confidence quickly to increase these qualifications in the outside world. They were anxious not to betray their self-doubt to one another. They were embarrassed about how transparent they might be to other students regarding their history so far of failure both in crime and in gaining status in prison society. They did not form a mutually supportive community; indeed, as in other years, there is little sense in which they even constituted a 'community'. Levey (1976), a sociology undergraduate who made a short study of the Unit in a period when I was mainly engaged in documentary research, noted that 'although there were communal kitchens communal cooking took place only infrequently. Everyone kept his own food/utensils etc. in his own room and cooked meals for himself which were usually eaten in his own room' (ibid., p.65). She, like others twice before, attempted to organise voluntary house meetings, but they were soon discontinued because few clients attended. She perceived that '"informal" interactions were the exception rather than the norm. The common ground they shared as students didn't seem to facilitate interaction' (ibid., p.69).

That common residence seemed not to contain any rehabilitive or other benign element was not denied by staff. Why not, then, sell the hostel, allow the students to obtain their own accommodation in Cambridge, as, indeed, a number of students had already succeeded in doing, and hire an office or day/evening centre to conduct business with clients there? The answer lies partly in the wider national bureaucratic structure. [2] The Department of Education and other statutory grant awarding bodies had no interest in financing clients' education with the consideration in mind that they had committed crimes. The Home Office, on the other hand, was geared to provide a 'bedding grant' to hostels for offenders and ex-offenders. By means of a complex financial formula which taxed the wits of NACRO's accountant this grant was used not only for defraying the costs of the project's administration but also for paying teachers and for providing maintenance grants not available from other sources for the Unit's students. The Unit in the third year, therefore, did not become a boarding school. It became what might be described as a 'bedding school'.

2. Organisational passage from volunteer to detainee In sharp contrast to the lack of social solidarity between students, there was a remarkable amount of moral obligation felt by clients to staff. Overcommitment is evidenced, for example, by the many letters of remorse, referred to earlier, which Ron received from his former clients after their reimprisonment. Each letter tends to follow a most uniform pattern. It states how sorry the writer feels for letting staff down. It expresses sensitive appreciation for whatever favours staff did for the writer at a time when staff had other problems to cope with. The letter ends with hopeful wishes that the Unit might still succeed if it receive in future more meritorious students than the writer. Such letters re-enacted gestures of situational adjustment that clients had expressed in the Unit out of their desire for approval from staff and for a mitigation of a mental conflict which nevertheless led students to escape to the familiar environment of prison.

In Chapter 2, we discussed the judicial status passage whereby some of the Unit's students came as 'volunteers' but, because of subsequent court cases, became 'detainees'. In this chapter, a main theme has been an organisational transition from one status to the other. After the students arrived at the Unit, many took upon themselves strong moral commitments to the programme which the Unit had set for them. However, when they, sometimes in a very short time, decided to withdraw commitment, the Unit imposed sanctions upon them. Thus, students who came as volunteers became hooked into detainee status. Many clients seem to have felt that, if they tried as hard as they could, their anxiety and stress in no way decreased, whereas, if they stopped trying, they were punitively made to feel anxiety and stress. They could not win either way. They were not set a suitable level of educational effort consistent with the performance which they felt themselves capable of; a level which could have been progressively raised as self-assurance lifted. Such juxtaposition of expectation and response was merely one form of educational opportunity of which students were deprived. Staff, in the educational sphere, instead of 'encouraging independence [as] the best way of achieving successful resettlement' (Crow 1979, p.3), set the students standards external to their felt abilities and then concerned itself with overdue library books and other matters which students could look after themselves. Before long, staff had to deal with court cases. A pattern was set. Many offences of second year students were escapes from the fire of academic competition to the daily frying pan of routine reincarceration.

The reactions of staff, moreover, were no less patterned. Of all the institutional domains of society the educational system is perhaps the one which receives least critical appraisal from its participants. Again and again in my research, I was impressed by the extent to which structural contradictions in the Unit scarcely deviated from similar contradictions in the world outside, where, for example, high school falls short of successfully preparing its students for new patterns of life which they must encounter when they leave, whether in employment (or unemployment) or even university. The Unit's staff, similarly, seemed unaware of any discrepancy between schooling and education in any other sense of the term. In consequence, when formal education was manifestly not transforming ex-offenders into well adjusted citizens the axioms on which the system of formal education is based went unquestioned by staff members who had so long participated in it. The fault, therefore, was considered to be the lack of conformity of the Unit to the prevailing system of education. The transformation of the Unit into a school was, therefore, the logical consequence of a determined attempt to correct a supposed fault the existence of which came so readily to minds of committed pedagogues. Nothing could speak louder of the extent to which the organisers of the Unit had themselves become detained in the educational ideology upon which the Unit had become increasingly based.

3. Control versus change; the short term versus the long term Apart from whatever other functions schools perform, they are decidedly people controlling organisations, in which the mental and moral abilities and activities of a large age group of the population are invigilated and supervised by state agencies. There is evidence that the people controlling functions of schools have people changing effects (though not necessarily the intended ones) during their scholars' formative or teenage years (e.g., Morrison and McIntyre 1971; Willis 1977). The extent to which such a sequence can take place among fully grown burglars and armed robbers, or even thieves and shoplifters, is rather more questionable. Moreover, as far as students at the Unit are concerned, most had been in people controlling organisations, such as prisons, so often already without noticeable people changing effects of the kind which the Unit would have considered desirable.

The possibility that controlling people might not change them, as shown by what happens as soon as people are freed from control, may be compared with the way the second year of the Unit was assessed by its members. That year came to be referred to in various pejorative ways. Indeed, in that respect, NACRO, the Management Committee - and even clients of the years which followed - were at one, even though they may not have been in complete agreement that the amount of increased control which developed was the answer to the possibility of a recurrence of the second year's problems. Yet objectively, in one of the terms of reference of the Unit, the second year was very successful! Two of its clients, Leo and Gene, later became university graduates, as against none from the third and fourth years. The only year comparable with the second for such pride of place would be the first year, from which two clients, Adam and George, also went on to graduate in higher education, though Adam lived elsewhere in Cambridge and refused to live in the Unit. This 'success' of the Unit's second year calls for explanation.

The 'bright young guys' recruited for the Unit's second year had been bright in prison. This was no guarantee that without proper preparation they would continue to be 'bright' at the Tech or anywhere else. What they needed was not more control, for they had had many years of that already. What they needed was learning how to 'relate to the Tech', if that was where they were to be placed, or, alternatively, plenty of time, such as they had enjoyed in prison, to fulfil their academic programme. But the distinctive feature of the two clients of the second year, as well as of Adam of the first year, is that they had studied <u>privately</u> in prison, without any of the low status of schooling in the prison education system. Such autonomous brightness, it seems, had been an excellent preparation for university!

Once the premises of the established educational system, therefore, are put on one side, such as the principle of control which became so prominent in the Unit's second year, it becomes possible to perceive the educational outcomes of the clients of the Unit who became university graduates in an alternative and clearer framework. Such clients may, for argument's sake, have daydreamed in the lectures which they attended after they left prison, as, indeed, so many quite ordinary students do. When it came to private study, however, on which tertiary education is largely based, they were able to perform as effectively as in prison, where their education had consisted entirely of private study.

The theme here, becomes, therefore, that of continuity and discontinuity. A person can succeed in one educational environment if one of the styles of learning in it is continuous with a style in which he has previously been successful. There is, however, an additional possibility. A person may perform well in an educational environment if he is adequately prepared, informally or formally, for the discontinuity of its style of learning with that to which he has previously been accustomed. Neither of these principles, however, were ever embraced by the Unit, which instead was lured back to the familiar educational charms of pedagogic control. In assessing a candidate's educational capability the members of the Unit's committees scarcely looked further than paper qualifications. Having taken the client on, the Unit exerted intense effort to achieve 'results' by trying this way and that, within the limitations of its own understanding of education, quickly to add to his paper qualifications. <u>Moreover</u>, what happened to the client later - indeed, whether he had, in fact, <u>changed</u> in personal academic prowess or attitude to the law - was of comparatively little concern.

The argument might be put forward that the Unit was unique and that, having no prototype, it could hardly be expected to concern itself with long term, unintended consequences. Possibly this point might be granted. I hope, however, that the last two chapters have begun to give indications that it might be a good idea in the future for a rehabilitative project of any description to be as concerned with thinking about long term rehabilitative and other effects as about dramatic occurrences, whether promising or disappointing, in the immediate term. This recommendation will be strengthened in the next chapter, whose story, in certain respects, is the converse of that of this chapter. For we shall see two students achieve noteworthy GCE results and go on to higher education, where the most noteworthy features of their undergraduate careers are an inability to cope with their new educational environment and a speedy return to crime and punishment.

NOTES

[1] The specialist will note that I have not, strictly speaking, 'applied' Cloward and Ohlin's theoretical system, but used parts of it for my analysis. It may, therefore, be useful, briefly to criticise, from the point of view of empirical research, those aspects of their system which have received much attention. Cloward and Ohlin identify retreatism not with behaviour leading to prison but with drug-taking. They themselves insist, however, that 'the anticipated official response [including imprisonment, presumably] to deviant actions is an important part of the definition of delinquency' (1960, p.6). Although the only evidence cited about drug-takers seems to suggest that they tend to be loners (ibid., pp.185-6), these authors identify the practice with subcultures. Moreover, they identify drugs with forbidden ones, thus excluding alcohol. The latter, however, is more accessible than criminalised drugs, being located in the nearest pub or liquor store. It is also a 'supercultural' phenomenon, as any advertisement for Skol or Scotch in Seattle, Southampton or Soweto proclaims. Silent on alcohol, Cloward and Ohlin neglect the fact that indulgence in it often results in delinquent acts. This negligence is unfortunate in relation to their basic premise that 'delinquent acts are distinguished from deviant acts by the very fact that they result, or are likely to result, in the initiation of official proceedings by agents of criminal justice [including imprisonment, presumably]' (ibid., p.4).

[2] Part of the answer may also be a strange preoccupation with the sensitivities of landladies. At intervals, I asked Ron why the hostel could not be dispensed with

and I received the response repeatedly that clients might cause trouble for landladies. Whether this answer was a cover for the other reason for maintaining a hostel or merely an anxiety I cannot say. It is hard to see how clients could be 'resettled' if they did not try to obtain accommodation, which, in any case, they would have to do at some point. Moreover, there was, in fact, a spillover in Cambridge of students who, at one point or another, were able, mainly on their own initiative, to leave the Unit to take private accommodation, for example, George, Leo, Ava, Bert, Stan, Ken, Ellis and Harry. Remarkably, these clients did not get themselves evicted or in any other way become involved in any noticeable disharmony with their landlords or landladies, though I have no data on such details as whether all these individuals paid their rent on time. It is possible, paradoxically, that the Unit prepared students for harmonious relationships with landladies because of a yearning to avoid tensions which they had recently found inescapable in the Unit. In any case, the resilience of Cambridge landladies in dealing with 'students' should not be underestimated!

7 The Unit's Third Academic Year, 1976–7: the Policy Rationalisation Stage

At the end of the first term of the third year, Ron summed up the new approach in the following way:

> The instruction is given by part-time voluntary and paid teachers, by certain of the students and by the project's education officers. The Unit has organised its own classes, because the only way of getting the majority of its students through their courses seems to be to tie in education as closely as possible with the total life of the Unit. It is education based on small classes, organised by an education officer who is accessible most of the time. As a system it is flexible to take on students released from prison after the academic year has begun. It prepares students to sit examinations in the summer with the aim of bringing them "into phase" with the general education pattern each July, so that as many as possible will be able to move on to Higher or Further education elsewhere in September.

This presentation of the new system, however, concealed a number of difficulties in operating it. Moreover, its management became increasingly overcommitted to its success (see Appendix B), feeling, as Stafford put it, that 'otherwise there'll be no hope of future funding'. This overcommitment did not result in great success.

A. DIFFICULTIES IN RUNNING A MINI-SCHOOL

To meet the new plans students often found themselves obliged to take subjects in the 'core curriculum' in which they did not have the slightest interest either intrinsically or for any intended career. They acquiesced to subjects they were instructed to take, even when such subjects were highly unpopular, such as logic, one of the disciplines in the 'core curriculum'. Outside the hearing of staff, they complained. It was only in the fifth year that Ron first remarked on the great distance there could be between verbal acquiescence and expression of genuine preferences. In the third year, however, an acquiescent student soon found himself hooked. As Stafford put it: 'Once you've put your hand to the plough you must continue to the end'.

By the middle of the year, however, negative or lethargic responses to such a policy made it apparent that it was not viable, and some scholars were allowed to drop certain subjects. As Stafford put it: 'There's a little shedding of subjects to get them to what they can really manage ... one must take a realistic view, say, four months before the exam, see that one is riding for a fall and give up one [A level] in a sensible way in order to concentrate on the other two'. Thus, even the 'shedding' of subjects was presented in terms of optimising the students' results, rather than in terms of allowing them to proceed with their studies at a more comfortable rate.

Not much later in the year, the 'realism' about which Stafford spoke took a different turn. Stafford said that 'now that we have given out money for exams there's a financial reason for not allowing subjects to be given up'.

These vacillations caused confusion. It must be stressed how small numbers were. There were only nine students most of whose residence fell into the third year. There were also two 'second year students', Ava and Ilse, who attended classes for a short time (and very irregularly) in the third year; and two 'fourth year' students, Jim and Brian, who came during the third year. Thus, there could never have been more than thirteen students in the school at any time. Most classes were much smaller than this. Any students who dropped a subject, therefore, represented a significant proportion of the total and demoralised or discomfited those who remained in the class.

Indeed, even students attending other classes could be offended. For example, when Cyril's determined absenteeism from certain classes was grudgingly accepted by the staff, Ellis and Fred became angry and said he ought to be expelled. Their resentment when a less pliant student got his own way reflected their own educational anxieties and dissatisfactions, and possibly a certain envy.

Most students in the third year had been selected on the basis of their level of 'risk', rather than according to similarity of educational level or ability. As a result, some of the classes, such as English or mathematics, did not represent any fundamental departure from the individual tutoring of previous years, save that several students of mixed ability were in the same room at the same time, receiving the necessarily divided attention of the teacher.

Not only did selection criteria clash with educational needs but also management relationships with students distorted teaching relationships with them. For example, two students in the A level sociology class were also taking A level history with Stafford, who accepted no excuses and responded to 'idleness' with threats. As a result, history homework was always given priority, at the expense of sociology and other subjects.

As the school could not provide some of the subjects which students considered that they needed, such as art or physics, recourse had additionally to be taken to the Tech or private teachers, as in previous years. Soon, the Unit found itself involved with at least fifteen teachers. Thus, the increase in staff was largely vitiated by the burden of administering both a school and the usual educational arrangements. This burden led to some gross anomalies. For example, the Unit was unable to give the time and effort to find a suitable biology teacher for Ian, who was aiming to be a nurse.

Students <u>also</u> were burdened by a heavy academic programme, and its accompanying anxieties. The third year students, like previous cohorts, found themselves in a recidivising environment. Ron, indeed, remarked about one student:

> Ellis has allowed his knapsack to get overfilled with all the work we and Stafford and the Tech have given him. And he's taken the work he's been given conscientiously. I would say that the reason Ellis has just got himself into trouble again is that he has felt the educational stress too acutely. He's tried very hard to meet the expectations that he thinks his teachers have.

If such an insight had been fully appreciated much earlier then staff might have become much more relaxed in their expectations regarding students' educational performance. By the third year, however, the Unit had committed itself to a school and to producing qualified scholars whom, it considered, it had failed to produce in previous years. It could hardly maintain such commitment, however, without, as a rehabilitation hostel, anomalously being prepared to increase the risk of reoffending of clients whom it had selected mainly on account of their estimated low or medium risk of reoffending. It seemed as if, after the supposed poor second year academic results had been attributed to a high crime rate, good academic results now had by all means to be achieved regardless of the effect of such effort on the crime rate! The anomaly is underlined when we look at the actual results produced by the school.

B. THE PERFORMANCE OF THE SCHOOL

Although third year clients had passed more GCE subjects before coming to the Unit than clients of previous years, and although their residence in the Unit was occasionally interrupted by court cases but not by reimprisonment, and despite whatever advantages there may have been in small classes the academic results achieved by students in the third year were unimpressive. Four of the nine students, Arthur, Harry, Cyril and Ian passed no examinations at all, while Fred and Des passed one O level only. Geoff, who did his studies at the Tech only, and Ellis each passed one A level.

The best results were obtained by Ken, with two O levels and two A levels, although he had obtained a certificate of a vocational, but never of an academic, kind previously. Ellis, who had previously passed another A level in prison, and Ken went on to higher education. Ellis's polytechnic career was quickly terminated by reimprisonment, as was Ken's university career, after he had been on the run for several months for multiple crimes. At the time of writing (27/7/82) he is still in prison for the sentence imposed on him at the subsequent court case. The magnitude of his offences after leaving the Unit seems to be proportional to his academic success as a client of the Unit. Indeed, in his case study, I shall argue that Ken's difficulties at university, and his use of crime as a way of quitting it, may be closely connected with the negative effect of schooling on adjustment to university life.

C. TUTORIALS AND THERAPY

The reinstatement of counselling sessions, referred to as 'tutorials', in which students could individually discuss problems with a member of staff on a regular basis brought an intimacy into the staff/student relationship which had been missing since the first year. The ex-prisoner had been a cypher in a multitude; becoming the centre of undivided attention each week from a senior person a step or two away from the penal and probation services was often a desirable experience. This was the positive side of tutorials in the third year.

Tutorials, however, contained not only intimacy but also resentment and hostility. They emphasised an assumption about the effective performance of the Unit which was in no way gratifying to the students. The assumption was that education could provide a basis on which an educator could initiate scrutiny into, pass value judgments on, and give gratuitous advice about, the student's personal life.

From the Unit's earliest days, this assumption had been been resisted by students, even to the extent of hostility to the educational programme on which unasked for direction of one's personal life was based. Thus, Ron said of Dulcie:

> She probably equated teachers with social workers and probation officers - a class of person trying to give her help she didn't particularly want ...

> She had pride ... She didn't want to feel ... that she needed shaping by the project.

The theory was held by management that by associating education with an exploration of a student's personality his criminality could be dealt with. It is interesting to note, by contrast, that the Oslo Education Project, which works with young drug offenders, holds the opposite theory: that teaching and anything resembling psychological therapy should be kept as far apart as possible (Frøysa 1976, p.1):

> Almost any offer of educational instruction is taken as a vote of confidence in his strength of will and abilities, whereas an offer of therapeutic help is declined by the client since it tends to focus on a pathological condition.

It may be interesting to point out, therefore, that the assumption of a psychotherapeutic role rather than one of responding to requests for assistance of a practical kind may have become part of tradition in British people product organisations, in spite of its undesirability in the eyes of their clients:

> Much careers information, however well or badly implemented, is conceived as pastoral or quasi-psychotherapeutic ... and this tends to be at the expense of hard information on the realities of the working world (and unemployment world) ... It may ... be because the personal guardian role is more appealing to teachers in terms of professional status than mere transmission of information and technical skills (such as how to sign on as unemployed) ... When we asked how schools should prepare young people for working life it was work experience which came first in every case - and the more work experience the school provided the more popular it was (Sawdon et al. 1979, pp.64-6).

> A study of social work clients in Southampton (Social Work Today, 15 November 1973) showed that whereas most social workers thought clients expected most of all to be able to discuss personal problems and to receive advice, sympathy and information, less than 10% of the consumers said they expected help of this kind ... most expected practical help ... (Dronfield 1980, p.41).

The practical help which most students at the Unit wanted was permission to carry a lighter academic load, with less emphasis on a core curriculum, subjects which they did not find interesting, and impressive examination results. To obtain this practical help, however, required many sessions of wearing down the threats and disapproval of counsellors, as well as such gestures as manufacturing plausible excuses for absence from class or lateness.[1]

Staff's continued lack of recognition, however, of this

kind of need for practical help resulted in an amplification of the tendency of staff to discover personal weaknesses. For example, Fred suggested to Ron that Cyril was losing self-confidence in his unsuccessful competition with the only two other students in a certain class, and thus beginning to drop out of it. Routine managerial consultation in running a mini-school impelled Ron to pass on the suggestion to Stafford. The latter, however, dismissed the matter, indicating that Fred was a patronising busybody. Weakness of personality was, therefore, now attributed to Fred. What could not be entertained was the possibility that there might be a grain of truth in Fred's concern: that students (including, perhaps, Fred himself) might be suffering loss of self-esteem because of academic pressure.

Throughout the third year, much time was given over to finding a personal weakness behind every failure in academic performance; behind every resistance to the hypertrophied value placed by our culture on academic success, examinations, deadlines for essays, and so on.

Another form of practical help to which little attention was given was simply the acquisition of study skills, which could have been given as and when required and which was not necessarily most efficiently provided by a mini-school. This point was distressingly evinced in February 1979, when I had lunch with a young man who had just been interviewed in connection with his application to join the Unit. He seemed concerned about the theme of personal problems. I was perplexed, but we proceeded to conversation on other topics. Only after about half an hour did I grasp what he meant by personal problems. He found difficulty in getting started in writing an essay, especially under pressure of time; in writing down his ideas in the right sequence; etc. Moreover, he considered that these problems were entirely personal to himself and completely lacking in the established members of the competitive academic system which he had applied to enter! None of these 'personal' problems, however, had been discussed with his interviewers.

Lack of early discussion with the applicant about such educational problems by the Unit's education officers had, however, produced a personal problem of an unambiguous kind. The previous night, because of anxiety, he had been unable to sleep. Insomnia is often habit forming.

When people are regarded as having personality weaknesses by those who have authority over them there is always a danger that their basic rights, such as freedom of movement or association, may be threatened, to however minor an extent. One hostility between students and staff in the third year was expressed when Ken and Ava decided to move out together and take a flat elsewhere in Cambridge. Ron described the cause of the resentment:

> At first, he wanted to talk about a comment I had made the previous evening when he and the probation officer and Stafford had had a talk in the office and I had said I didn't think it was a good idea for him and Ava to go and cohabit because they weren't in a position to commit themselves to each other in marriage - both their futures were very open at the moment, and if they were to move out, which I thought would be better for them, it would be better for them to live independently and less claustrophobically, giving each other more options. Otherwise, it might be very difficult for each of them to pull out of the relationship later on. So he wanted to talk the remark over. Then he said, 'We found somewhere we rather like. Is the offer of help with rent still open?'. I said that it was still open but I want to know more about it ... If you ... criticise him he just says nothing at all. He won't treat it as an argument. He'll wait till you've stopped and then gather himself and carry on as if you've said nothing. He's able to argue in sociology classes only because he's not personally involved.

Ava and Ken moved out, and between them and Ron there was considerable bad feeling, which, however, slowly improved.

An important point in this conflict is that when staff intervened in students' personal lives then differences in attitudes appeared which reduced the understanding and 'affective bonds' which Lofland (1969, pp.271-3) considers essential for 'escalation to normal identity'. Concern for keeping options open, for independence and social space, and for the commitment implications of cohabitation seemed to be preoccupations quite alien to those of Ava and Ken.

D. TUTORIALS AND STUDENT RELATIONSHIPS

Tutorials were part of the process of what Ron referred to as, 'endeavouring to contain and control all sorts of disruptive, unpleasant, violent, devious, immature and criminal behaviour, quite apart from the normal problems of keeping students at work'. Such a function could hardly avoid expanding distrust between students - just about as soon as X discovered that a staff member possessed knowledge of a piece of the jigsaw of his life obtained during a tutorial, or even in casual conversation, with W, Y or Z.

A typical example occurred after Fred requested a loan from Stafford, saying that, after many years, he felt that he needed to visit his family. In fact, when the visit was supposed to take place, Fred prepared a meal for Ellis. Ellis subsequently mentioned to Stafford that he had enjoyed a very good meal with Fred. Stafford thus found out that Fred had been lying. Ellis felt acutely embarrassed and directed his anger at Fred, complaining that Fred had not informed him that he had misled Stafford. Had he done so he would have known not to mention the meal to staff. As the result of a series of events based on such triangles of distrust, the fairly close relationship which had developed between Ellis and Fred in Wormwood Scrubs prison fell apart.

In tutorials, Ron and Stafford sometimes mentioned to a student a fact about him which the latter assumed another student had revealed. After the tutorial, the student would rampage through the house to find out who had told on him. Ken and Geoff were the two main witch-hunters. What had actually happened, according to staff, was that the discrediting fact had inadvertently been disclosed in an earlier tutorial by the student himself, who subsequently forgot that he had done so, or it had been deduced from other facts which the student had disclosed.

What we find here is a paranoic atmosphere similar to that of previous years. Hostile avoidance developed, which eliminated any cohesion between students, whom Ellis depicted as 'just a number of suction pads stuck to a wall'. Stafford's perception of social relationships between students, however, was one of romantic contrast, for he surmised that 'some of them will be in touch with each other the rest of their lives, which is a bonus which I don't think they could have expected'. In fact, with the exception of Ken and Ava, students completely ceased to be in touch with each other as soon as they packed their bags at the end of the year.

E. AFTER THE THIRD YEAR

My assignment was to study the performance of the Unit during its three experimental years. In fact, I continued to follow events in subsequent years to see whether any significantly new patterns might develop. Since few did, I present here a mainly chronological account of the Unit's post-experimental years.

In February 1977, the Home Office agreed to provide for the life of the Unit to be prolonged to the end of the academic year 1977-8. Stafford was given a further leave of absence by his school. In addition, two more full time teachers were obtained under the Job Creation Programme of the Manpower Services Commission. This meant that the number of 'outside' teachers could be reduced and that the new full time teachers could take on part of the tutorial work. The students selected for the fourth year were 'lower risk' than those in the third year.

The doubling of staff further tangled the web of tensions. Much time was taken up with staff meetings sorting out recriminations when, for example, a student was rebuked by Ron or Stafford because of information coming from a junior teacher and the student made counter-accusations against the teacher. The guardians now had to watch over not only their wards but also over their ward's guardians, as shown by 'the CALA phase'.

In the fourth year, the school was moved from the Unit to rooms some distance away belonging to the Cambridge Arts and Leisure Centre on the theory that clients would increase their effort if they were obliged to go to school instead of just rolling out of bed into it. This change was later reversed, and the school returned to the Unit. Ron regarded teaching performance as unsatisfactory, and because it was not under his close supervision. The move to CALA had been actuated by the desire to get the students out of the Unit, the reverse change by the felt need to bring the junior teachers closer to management.

In February 1978, the Home Office agreed to continue with the Unit till the end of the academic year 1978-9 and to pay the salaries of the junior full time teachers. Stafford returned to his own school and was replaced by a prison education officer in the summer of 1978.

At the time, the funding of the Unit may have seemed rather like Rhodesian sanctions, being extended routinely by the authorities from year to year. Ron may have felt that the Unit was under less threat of being ended, for he went in for a less strict selection of students for the fifth year, 1978-9, thus giving himself the opportunity to work with more 'hard core' offenders. The high risk students produced a high rate of reimprisonment.

In November 1978, however, the Home Office agreed to provide for the continuation of the Unit till the end of the academic year 1979-80 but stated that it could provide for the hostel side only and not for teachers' salaries. In April 1979, Ron announced that he was resigning in July to take up a new administrative position. The other full time staff members also moved on at the end of the academic year. Plans were initiated for converting the Unit into an ordinary probation hostel. Consequently, the Unit's sixth year, 1979-80, was a transitional one, catering both for students left over from the previous year and also for probationers from the Cambridge area, in equal numbers. The new staff consisted of a project leader, who had no teaching duties, being responsible for the general running of the hostel, and an education officer for the student remnant.

F. REVIEW AND ASSESSMENT OF THE UNIT'S FINAL YEARS

The dubious theory on which the Unit was run, and its value laden and unscientific notions of personality, are indicated in a report by Ron (during a month of sick leave occasioned by, among other things, the severe exhaustion of running a mini-school). In the report, he gives scores to each of the third year students for (a) personality development, (b) extent of abiding by the law and (c) 'overall educational experience'. He then adds these scores for an overall rating on 'progress in intermediate education'. Plus grades are received by Ellis (+2) and Ken (+3), whose recidivising tendencies were evident throughout their stay in the Unit. By contrast, Arthur, who has been completely law abiding since he came to the Unit, but showed no interest in the school while he was there, is the only third year student to receive a minus, as the result of 'worse' personality development (not responding to the Unit's programme?) and 'valueless' educational experience. According to the Unit's own assessment, therefore, by the third year, if not before, rehabilitation, i.e. the Unit's aim, and the Unit's educational methods and/or developing a personality of which staff approved were operating at cross purposes.

Unlike, apparently, the detoxification units studied by Regier, the Unit lacked faith that even the more treatable clientele which it recruited in the third year would respond to treatment. Consequently, the Unit repeatedly turned to the type of educational experience which the majority of the population undergo for guidance. Hence the school, and hence the temporary exercise of locating the school away from the Unit to force pupils to go to school. One almost wonders why the Unit did not locate its management at the school which had been located away from the Unit! For what was never questioned was that the reference point, the overall educational system in the country as a whole, might be faulty.

Since doubts were entertained about the treatability of even the supposedly more treatable clientele selected for the third and fourth years, the Unit was forced before long to go back to the policy critique stage, attempting yet further models of policy change which go with that stage. One of the main models attempted from the third year was the tutorial counselling sessions, a development which, in her study, Regier labels as a 'transactional model' that 'presents the cause of system problems ... as a personnel problem which involves lack of self-awareness, lack of understanding among actors, and deficient communication skills' (Regier 1979, p.74). I do not, however, consider that students were deficient in communication skills (except, perhaps, in a narrow academic sense). What was lacking was the allowability of certain ideas which they wished to communicate, such as that they did not regard as a suitable method of acquiring knowledge a 'core curriculum' backed by sanctions.

Another feature of the transactional model was the assumption that 'personality inadequacies were impeding goal realisation' (Regier 1979, p.153). Interestingly, since staff had embraced the dogmas of the transactional model, students sometimes responded by adopting the same absurd rehabilitation discourse in order to back out of the Unit's educational programme. Thus, after Fred had reported to Ron about Cyril's dropping out of a course, Ron, convinced that, as he told Stafford, 'behind this front, I think we've got a very timid little chap' went to see the latter concerning his missing classes. Cyril, however, pointed out that, unlike any of the other students [including Fred, who was on a deferred sentence], he had not been in trouble for more than two years [which was true at the time], and was, therefore, quite capable of managing his own affairs. Ron was thus bereft of a case for Cyril either attending school or having his personality weaknesses exposed, since such devices were intended to rehabilitate clients, and Cyril had supposedly rehabilitated before he came to the Unit!

A characteristic of policy implementors who have tried every kind of model for understanding the difficulties in achieving their goals, except questioning their own assumptions about the institution which they are using to implement the policy, is that they eventually become deconverted from total idealism to total cynicism. As Regier (ibid., p.155) puts it:

> ... the participants ... were not comfortable with what they perceived as inauthentic resolutions. Their journey was an unsettling one; after the long search, they experienced no palpable rewards, no sense of emergence or clearing up, no victory. Furthermore, in the process, caretaker was set against client, client against client, and caretaker against caretaker. The implementation process, which had commenced with considerable idealism, slowly paled into a shadow of the original vision. Hence we may conclude that the implementation experience not only inspires idealism, but may breed deep cynicism, as well.

I consider, however, such a development unfortunate because there may be as much, if not more, usefully to learn from a project which went wrong as from a project which achieved its goals.

G. SOME GENERAL RECOMMENDATIONS

It may be useful at this juncture to list some principles which seem to emerge from our account of the history of the Unit which the reader may wish to keep in mind as he peruses the case studies to follow:

1. If alternatives in the treatment of arrested offenders are between short sentences, on the one hand, and long sentences subject to parole, on the other hand, then the former are, in most cases, preferable. By and large, Parole Board decisions seem to be based on dubious guidelines, such as prisoners' sentiments and behaviour in custody. Prison welfare officers and probations officers recently holding Cropwood Fellowships at the Institute of Criminology in Cambridge with whom I have discussed the subject aver that a prisoner's conduct in custody is normally a poor predictor of his conduct outside. Moreover, prisoners who are released on parole and also subject to conditions of licence may thereby be subject to feelings of stress, which may get them into trouble again.

2. The greatest encouragement and opportunity should be extended to ex-offenders to improve their education, if, like so many other citizens who dropped out of school many years previously, they wish to do so, and particularly as so many make a success of so doing. I do not consider, however, that it is desirable or beneficial to subject ex-offenders to the discipline of schooling. The main needs of ex-offenders who wish to return to education, as of so many other other citizens who wish to do likewise, are for study skills, learning how to learn for oneself, and learning how to make the best use of whatever resources are available, for example, lectures, libraries, local experts and, one hopes before long, borrowable video tapes. The personnel catering for such needs are not necessarily former schoolteachers, but, for example, people who have expertise in educational psychology and technology.

3. Like researchers from the Home Office (e.g. Sinclair 1971; Sinclair and Snow 1971), I find that a hostel, other than for providing a discharged prisoner, unless sick, with a base from which he can find other accommodation, has no rehabilitative advantages. Hostels supported by the Home Office are generally used as a device for providing alternatives to prison, that is to say, forms of punishment and supervision. To pretend that such hostels have major functions other than instruments of control is unfair to their staff, who find themselves constrained to devise superficially plausible policies and programmes to justify the continued existence of the institutions of which they are in charge.

4. Education, as some kind of blanket concept, is not a panacea for social problems and, certainly, in itself, possesses no rehabilitative virtues. To pretend otherwise is to subject people implementing an educational programme for the rehabilitation of ex-offenders to move, step by step, in the direction of applying educational methods which operate in the country as a whole and in which they have themselves been socialised. Such methods, even if they were ideal for the country as a whole, may not be beneficial to offenders as a whole, or even to ordinary citizens of a similar age group.

5. That education 'in itself' does not have rehabilitative properties does not mean that, for example, commitment to an educational programme, or any other commitment for that matter, may not have a 'normalising' effect. This is an hypothesis to which we may now return, subjecting it to case-study data.

NOTE

[1] Staff members, of course, had a different perception of the course of their interaction with their tutees. As Ron, in the third year, complained, 'Students in the project go through two stages. At first, they are in love with the idea of education. But then they realise the realities and hardships of the educational programme before them, and then they distance themselves from staff, and it becomes difficult to talk to them'.

8 Case Studies of Students who did not Rehabilitate

Discussion of Errol, for example, in Chapter 5, indicates how important it is, in evaluating the performance of a rehabilitation project, to gather data on clients for at least three years after their clientships ended. An earlier cutting off point would have spuriously indicated that Errol had rehabilitated to a remarkable extent instead of being in the process of having his relationship with the woman who was 'holding him together' worn down by the stresses of the educational programme which he had been processed into and which ultimately led him to criminal acts of a most disturbing kind.

The three year rule which is adhered to in this study is soundly based on previous researches. For example, the Fricot Ranch study (Jesness 1965) portrays an educational rehabilitation programme with features in common with those of the Unit. At first that programme seemed to show success, which, however, later wore off. For 'the overall difference between the experimental and control groups tended to decrease the longer the follow-up was continued, and by the end of three years it was no longer significant' (Hood and Sparks 1970, p.202). I am not aware of follow-up work which has been continued beyond the point where formerly discrepant reconviction rates reach equilibrium. With the Fricot Ranch enquiry, for the experimental group to have reached parity with the controls, there must have been an acceleration of reconvictions among the former towards the end of the three year period. There appears to be no reason that such acceleration should not have continued after this period, making the reconviction rate of the experimental group higher than that of the control group.

That the three year rule is rarely followed in evaluation studies is regrettable particularly when we consider one of the main reasons:

> Because most researchers produce frequent permanent products (articles, chapters, books) in order to receive reinforcement in the form of raises, tenure, social acknowledgment by peers, editorships, and job offers, they are likely to avoid any delay in terminating a particular research effort, especially if the delay is as long as the one or

two years often required to collect adequate follow-up data (Emery and Marholin 1977, cited in Farrington 1979, p.364).

The present study, however, is also not without a methodological flaw. I was asked by NACRO not to use a control group, but only to compare individual clients with each other. Nevertheless, the comparisons which follow have an important part to play in sociology at the present time, for, as Taylor (1976, p.16) complains, the type of writing which has been conventional in the field of deviance 'can lead away from a consideration of individual delinquents and the treatment and punishment they routinely receive'.

I would like to stress again, however, that I am primarily concerned, which many studies are not, with rehabilitation rather than with not being reconvicted, since the latter variable is frequently quite unrepresentative of actual conduct or misconduct. I have, therefore, included Leo in this chapter, even though, unlike all the other individuals with whom it deals, who were repeatedly reconvicted for offences of which they were guilty, he frequently reoffended without being convicted. His status as an unofficial offender is also important as far as Becker's hypothesis is concerned.

The chapter after this one, however, is more problematic, for I cannot claim that each of the individuals discussed there never reoffended in the three years and more after he or she left the Unit, though I would claim to have had a relationship of trust and rapport with them. I shall, however, as with Adam, indicate where there is room for uncertainty about the individual's relationship with the law - as, indeed, I consider there is likely to be to some extent with most citizens. What is more important, however, is that I am confident that whatever offences the clients in the next chapter may have committed are quite minor in comparison with their offences before coming to the Unit - Adam, again, would serve as a good example of such change in behaviour.

In each group of 'not rehabilitated' and 'rehabilitated' I shall present the case studies in the order in which the clients concerned arrived in Cambridge and made use of the Unit's services.

To prepare our case studies for tabular comparison which will assist us to explain rehabilitation or reoffending I shall use the following symbolic notation:

1 Staging post
2 Resort
3 Colony

X Overcommitment
Y Undercommitment

PP People processing
PCh People changing

PS People serving
PCo People controlling

I shall use arrows to indicate change and directional transformation from one category to another. When neither X nor Y are attached to 1, 2 or 3 then the corresponding client may be considered to have been neither overcommitted nor undercommitted.

I hope that such symbols will simplify matters rather than complicate them. Thus, the coding of the first case study, 1X↑;PP, is a shorthand way of indicating that (1) Ben saw the Unit as a 'bridge' (from a dreary round of dead-end jobs, crime and punishment to a variety of high ambitions); that (X) he tried to cross the bridge in a desperate manner (in the absence of proper educational guidance); that (↑) such overcommitment tended to increase as his efforts to cope became more and more obsessive and compulsive; and that (PP) the main office which the Unit performed for him was that of advocacy and patronage.

A. BEN: 1X↑;PP

Ben left school at the age of fifteen. He joined the army but was discharged fourteen months later as medically unfit. He moved through various unskilled jobs, and served nine terms of Borstal and imprisonment before coming to the Unit. Of his many convictions none was for violence, and only one, burglary, would normally be classified as of a serious nature. During the sentence before he came to the Unit, he had the opportunity to attend prison classes, and he claimed to have passed two O levels. When he heard about the Unit he wrote saying that he had discovered what education had to offer. He listed ten subjects, which ranged from Norwegian to building construction, that he wished to take at O level, and also proposed studying for two A levels. He was accepted at the Unit at the age of twenty-eight, and was its first resident. Ron said that 'Ben arrived with a deeply ingrained sense of failure, a severe lack of confidence which made his attempts to relate to the opposite sex, fellow students and teachers stilted and formal'.

We have seen how, in the conflict for popularity among the clients, Conrad lost and how, because the latter's expulsion from the Unit was felt as a blow against the clients as a whole, Ben did not win. Ben then assumed an air of superiority and disdain towards his peers, giving the impression that he was intellectually absorbing a vast amount of reading, while at the same time adopting towards the staff an increasingly ingratiating manner. He deemed the class discussions at the Tech puerile, and frequently contradicted his classmates on the basis of their limited knowledge of life, He contrasted their bookish learning with his wide experience.

Before long, however, Ben repeatedly absented himself from the Tech, retreating into the labour of transferring but a few items on his reading list into voluminous and almost verbatim notes. He was, therefore, trying too hard in the educational programme because of an exaggerated perception of its demands. He concentrated hard on one aspect of the programme, reading, and thus neglected other aspects, such as lectures, or even other essential reading which he left himself no time for. He concentrated hard on the mechanical, note taking, aspects of the programme, and consequently left himself no time for careful thought and reflection. Feeling the pinch of working so hard with little money for the relief of leisure he took a job as a clerk in a university department, but he was soon fired for deception. The case did not come out into the open.

When mock examinations came along Ben did not take them, apparently afraid to put his knowledge to the test. He also handed in his entry form for the June examinations late, but was nevertheless allowed to sit them. Although he completely failed, he was able, on the basis of a strong recommendation from Ron, to obtain a place at an adult residential college to study a liberal arts course.

Ben maintained his attachment to the Unit long after he left it. In February 1976, Ollie burgled silverware, which Horace buried under the floorboards of his room in the Unit. Ben at the time was on a weekend visit to the Unit. Ever faithful to its aims he revealed to Ron where the silver was. Ron took the loot to the police, who did not enquire about its travels.

Ben stayed at the college for two terms. Ron considered that the syllabus there was very similar to what he had studied in Cambridge. He visited the Unit during the Easter vacation. He said that he was including the visit as part of his work as a researcher for British Rail on the pattern of potential use of the railways by students. (It seems that British Rail had sent a circular to the college saying that it might be prepared to offer its students discount railcards, depending on how many used rail transport. The student representative council, of which Ben was a member, was asked to send British Rail a figure.)

Ben did not return to college at the end of the vacation. He remained in Cambridge, staying at Horace's girlfriend's flat and doing odd jobs. His endless loyalty to the Unit, however, was duly rewarded. In July 1976, Ron wrote to two other NACRO schemes which had vacancies for project workers a laudatory testimonial which approvingly referred to Ben's value in people control:

> Ben has identified himself closely with the project and, I think, has a real understanding of the ways

> in which residential projects influence and support their residents. Perhaps more than any other student we have had he has attempted to see the work of the project from the point of view of the management. He has on occasion shown a considerable sense of loyalty which has helped greatly in handling difficult situations.

Soon afterwards, however, Ron went on vacation, and his place was occupied by a locum who normally worked for a Manchester charity. By the time the locum returned to Manchester Ben had accepted the offer of a well paid research position for the charity.

Ben suffered renewed stress. He was asked to find out the attitude of various institutions to handicapped people, but he did not know how to go about the enquiry. He was sent once a week to attend a class at Salford University. He found the course, however, too difficult and dropped out. Fortunately, there was another research assistant, who was able to cover up for Ben's deficiencies.

Ben's job came to an end when he was arrested in May 1977 for having, at intervals, passed three forged cheques of the charity. Ben knew that the forgeries were likely to be discovered eventually. According to Ron, he committed the offences 'as a means of bringing to an end a situation he couldn't endure any longer'.

Ben returned to Cambridge because he had nowhere else to go, and because he needed a testimonial from Ron for the court case, which, in fact, resulted in a suspended sentence. As it was the summer vacation, he was provided with a room in the Unit. However, as the result of the change of policy with respect to clients contacting staff after hours Ben felt that he was being shunned. He obtained a poorly paid job as a cleaner, but he did not clean himself or his clothes. He was not able to find a girlfriend. The barmaid of The Nearby Inn, however, gave him alternative lodgings in her house. She tried to comfort the depression into which he had sunk as the result of his many defeats. He imagined she had a romantic interest in him, but no romance was forthcoming. One night, extremely drunk, he stole the car of the barmaid's former husband, who was living in the same house. As a result, he was reimprisoned. The barmaid said that she had now 'washed her hands of him' and expressed her contempt by referring to 'that autistic, mentally retarded girl' whom he had associated with. (This was Ilse, a client who was troubled by a stutter, and would sleep with anybody for the sake of attention.)

When Ben came out again, in the Unit's fifth year, he entered the Unit's office and sat on the radiator. Normally loquacious he was now taciturn. Ron was very busy and spoke to him cursorily, quipping that he looked good on prison life, thereby signalling, as Ron later reaffirmed, that he had no time for Ben. After twenty minutes, Ben left the Unit. He then went to visit Horace's girlfriend, and, while her back was turned, stole £200. Soon afterwards, he was back in prison, at the age of thirty-three.

The ultimate rejection of Ben by Ron was an unhappy ending to a relationship in which each side expected much. From the beginning, what Ben expected, even though he may not have precisely articulated it, is indicated by Ron's statement that Ben 'found working in a classroom situation well-nigh impossible. Yet he clung desperately to his studies - as if to a lifeline'. Ben, however, did not receive appropriate educational support and guidance to loosen his clinging. Ron reflected about Ben that 'the job he got in Manchester gave his fantasies and pretence a new lease of life. He felt he could be on the same level as professional people whom he'd known as teachers etc. I think he is an example of someone for whom education can provide a dream world, insulated from real decisions'. These cogitations, however, are only part of the story. No doubt education can provide dreamy insularity. The Unit itself, however, was also insulated from real decisions. If, for example, Ben had received instructions and advice to prevent him from carrying out the manifestly ritualistic study methods which were associated with his fantasies then, as psychological research indicates (e.g., Beech and Liddell 1974, p.147), Ben would have gained a measure of psychological stability and self-assurance. Processing people with fantastic testimonials is no substitute for such educational guidance, least of all in an educational project.

B. LEO: 1↑;PP,PS

Leo grew up in a lower working class neighbourhood where upward social mobility was virtually unknown. In his early youth, like his peers, he occasionally got into delinquent adventures, and, again like his peers, he 'grew out of' delinquency as he became older. With adolescence, however, he was no longer a delinquent, but he had become a deviant, with erotic drives directed only towards his own sex.

According to the laws of England, a man commits a crime if he sleeps with a girl before she is sixteen or with a boy before he is twenty-one. Boys sleeping together who are both under twenty-one, however, are rarely prosecuted; prosecutions of homosexuals are usually directed against older males. Many years after the Wolfenden Report, which led to radical changes in laws regarding sexual behaviour and enshrined the principle of the rights of consenting adults, Leo suddenly found himself sentenced to four years imprisonment for homosexual offences. He would have been unlikely to have met such retribution if he had examined the birth certificates of his partners or associated only with fellow homosexuals who in appearance were decidedly older than twenty-one. (In 1978, a Bill to lower the age of homosexual consent was rejected by the House of Lords.) [1]

Leo served thirty-two months, and came to the Unit at the age of thirty-eight. When I asked him when he had first become interested in furthering his education he replied that he always had been, in the sense that he had always preferred non-fiction to fiction. He did not know why he had left school as early as possible except that everyone else had and that he did not like school. He did not find it easy, in fact, to talk about any events before prison, which appears to have had a mentally disturbing effect in this regard. As Leo put it, prison had created a 'wall' in his mind and he could not remember much behind the wall. Almost every past experience seemed mentally inseparable from the time referent, 'prior to imprisonment'.

Leo spent all his spare time in prison in private study, because 'there was nothing else to do'. A prison education officer encouraged him to take examinations, an idea which had not occurred to him before. He consented reluctantly for he considered that the prison education service would dishonestly claim the credit for his performance. He passed five O levels and one A level, with a top grade in almost every subject. At the time of his release, he had completed most of the work for a second A level and for several more O levels. He was recommended to NACRO because he had almost all the requirements for university entry.

Leo came to Cambridge with some diffidence, because he was mainly interested in obtaining a job. Indeed, improving his chances of employment was his main motive for taking examinations. APEX, the advisory service for ex-offenders seeking employment, however, had been completely unable to find an employer willing to employ him in spite of his good examination results. Ron telephoned several places of higher education before obtaining an offer for Leo for the following year. (The prison education service had also already applied to twelve.) Leo said that had he tried on his own he would have said 'to hell with it' after the third try. Leo considered that positive decisions about admitting people to a university had to be made unanimously by about five academics and that the university which accepted him must have had five 'liberal' decision makers at the time. Cambridge University, with its high proportion of teachers with single sex boarding school backgrounds, evinced no interest whatsoever in his application.

Leo came to live in the Unit because he was homeless. His previous accommodation had been rented, and repossessed when he went to prison. He was disturbed, however, by the noise of record players late at night and by filthy kitchen utensils all over the place. He found other accommodation after nine weeks. But he maintained contact with the Unit, working as a mathematics and physics tutor for it, though he was considered by Ron as having a supercilious attitude to his students. Moreover, even three years after going on to university, he was still coming every month to audit the Unit's accounts, a job which he considered would never have been offered to a 'real' criminal.

Since leaving prison, Leo was able to avoid rearrest by means of various stratagems. For example, he changed his address repeatedly shortly after starting university so as to minimise the chance of the police knowing where he lived. He also took pains to make sure that the different people he went to bed with did not know each other. In this way, any further charge which the police might have wished to bring against him would have 'involved one man's word against another'. But he did not exclude the possibility of being arrested at any time. [2] This estimation was in agreement with the prison psychiatrist's assessment before Leo was released. It did not agree with Ron's retrospective estimation of Leo as having a low risk of reoffending.

Before his final undergraduate degree examinations, Leo was pessimistic and fatalistic about the future. In spite of much abuse which he had received from queer bashers and others at university he had enjoyed his studies there. He would have liked to have gone on to do postgraduate studies, but the mines which are laid at every staging post in the educational system were present in this case too. He was told that he had outstanding ability in compiler design and numerical analysis but only 'adequate' skill in computational physics, systems modelling and linear programming. He considered, therefore, that, on aggregate, he was not likely to obtain a 'good degree' which would enable him to pursue research, even though the latter often requires exceptional ability in only one or two specialised fields.

Leo obtained a third class honours degree. He considered that he would have obtained a better result if he had not been going through the emotional turmoil of a broken love affair at the time of his examinations. When I last saw Leo, shortly afterwards, he was searching for a job but unsuccessfully. He had little doubt that discrimination was continuing to operate against him as a homosexual ex-prisoner.

Leo's case casts doubt on the notion that 'it is far from impossible that in the not-too-distant future a large proportion of the adult population would be unemployable simply because they would not be endowed with the innate capacities necessary to acquire the highly developed mental skills which may be called for by a more complex technology' (Mishan 1969, p.228; emphasis his). While Leo was in prison his last employment as a Salford bus conductor was automated, and he would have been likely to have become unemployed even if he had not been a homosexual and even in spite of his apparently innate mental capacities.

Since there is unlikely to be any correlation between sexual preference for younger people of one's own sex and academic ability, Leo's return to formal education was biographically fortuitous. He received a grant, as it were, from Her Majesty's prison service, in the form of low quality but rather expensive (£112 a week, according to 1979 Home Office estimates) bed and board for thirty-two months. Many other people of all ages, both upholders and breakers of the law, would no doubt return to education if they were properly funded and if traditional schoolish principles were removed (Geddes 1979, p.350).

Leo's case must surely also demand a reformulation of Becker's hypothesis. A programme whose goal is academic qualifications may lead one to check deviant impulses, but it may also lead to careful attempts to reduce the risk of sanctions for <u>not</u> checking deviant impulses. The point may seem obvious, but I do not think that the obvious should be neglected in propounding any hypothesis. Moreover, a proper understanding of rehabilitation seems very limited unless we consider the alternative strategy of reducing the risk of being arrested. Indeed, we may even regard rehabilitation as one way of reducing such a risk to a minimum (save that a person may be wrongfully arrested and punished). This way of looking at things is, of course, the opposite of the viewpoint of many evaluative studies in which, implicitly or otherwise, absence of reconviction is treated as evidence of rehabilitation. Furthermore, the approach adopted here may be considered a potentially fruitful one theoretically. For it leads to the important question regarding, on the one hand, the circumstances in which a committed person will check any deviant impulses which would otherwise adversely affect his line of action, as against, on the other hand, the circumstances in which he will <u>not</u> check his deviant impulses but, instead, check that none of his indulgence of them will lead to adverse effects. After further case studies have been considered, a line of conjecture will be hazarded which may help to answer such a question.

C. <u>JACK: 1X→Y, 3; PCh</u>

Jack claims that, however his feelings may later have changed, he began his prison career with a sense of pride and triumph. Of his status as a 'villain' and a man who could easily do time if necessary he regarded a Glasgow law court as a most effective broadcaster, with an informal social network outside prison also spreading the news. At Peterhead Prison, where he was sent, moreover, he had opportunities to become acquainted with men with high reputations for violence; to gleam in their reflected glory; and even, on occasion, to compete with them.

Jack explained that students in prison classrooms tend to be recruits from two [presumably among other] categories. The first are inmates who have no status whatsoever in any other area of prison life. Such men are commonly labelled 'softies'. The other category contains men whose position in the inmate hierarchy is so high that 'you can rest on your laurels' and attend classes, since nobody can make the label 'softie' stick. Indeed, Jack claimed that one can even advance one's status further by showing that one not only had repute as a fighter but that one also had a brain. Jack attended a class at Peterhead Prison with this strategy in mind, and because the teacher was an attractive woman. Other 'villains' followed suit. They were required to recite poetry and plays. At first, they responded negatively, but eventually she brought them round to an appreciation of English literature. [3] As a result, Jack obtained a Scottish Higher Certificate (roughly equivalent to an English A level) in the subject, and thus became an attractive candidate for the Unit upon his release.

Jack came to the Unit in its second year at the age of twenty-eight. My observation of the way in which any other client with whom he came into contact seemed to defer to him lends credibility to his statement (1/11/78) that '*Wayne once said that I had done all the things that they wanted to do; and Ollie once commented in front of Ron that he thought I was "number one"*'. It was noticeable during this period, however, that Jack's violence seemed to be based on reputation only. Once, for example, he was in a queue for hot dogs with a few other clients. A member of another group of youths aggressively jumped in front of him. He restrained himself from responding to the insult and, instead, he pulled at another student who was beginning to display violence on his behalf. The other student immediately fell back. It seemed as if Jack was using his authority based on reputation to enforce a decision not to start a fight, while, simultaneously, avoiding what, in his late twenties, he may have been fearing: putting his reputation to the test. The only time he actually used violence during this period was when he kicked out of the Unit a drunk outsider who had intruded into the bedroom of one of the girls. Moreover, as we shall presently note, when, three years later, he was forced into fights, his stature was declining from what it may have been in the past.

Another letter from Jack (10/9/78), which it is useful to quote at length, discusses his first few days at the Unit and, in particular, his short encounter with the Tech, an institution so distant from his experience and status. The letter shows, among other things, how a weirdly structured edifice of overcommitment can quickly crumble into undercommitment:

> *You asked for a list of experiences concerning the "tech". My dealings there were so brief as to be confined to one lecture, which I remember was a very passive and unexciting experience ... I certainly didn't develop any attachment to the place - I didn't give myself a chance to. But I somehow doubt that I ever would have.*
>
> *I remember the event well. I had fifteen minutes to make it to the "tech" from the Social Security. Despite all the holdups and time spent asking directions I somehow made it to the classroom ... There were perhaps twenty others milling around when I arrived. One look at them and my heart sank: they were exactly as I had feared - twenty little, bright, shining and gleaming academic faces, most of them peering at me through nine-carat gold National Health replicas and looking like they had stepped off the end of an assembly belt that very morning. You know the type - they all look like they've been caught up in a car wash, or hit with a tin of Johnson's Wax on the way out the gate. Everytime I see one I imagine their middle-class world as an archipelago of domestic production units fastidiously turning out spotless examples of middle-class "superiority".*
>
> *I drew some questioning glances and self-consciously stood there in direct contrast to them and two months late into the bargain. The lecturer arrived and suddenly I found myself alone as they all piled in behind him. I steeled myself and followed, enrolment card (which I had been told to give him) in hand, looking for an opportunity to present it and introduce myself. His eyes swept over me and fixated on someone else as I hesitated in the background obviously waiting to gain his attention. The class was beginning to settle down, so I chose a seat at the rear, hoping that no-one had become accustomed to sitting there, and by this time in half a mind to reply to any objections with a few well-chosen expletives.*
>
> *After the lecture I saw my chance to introduce myself. His eyes swept over me and fixated on someone else. He didn't seem at all interested and kept interrupting my attempts to discover which books I needed by involving himself in unimportant conversations with some of those remaining. I got the impression I wasn't getting through to him and was on the verge of making one of those sarcastic remarks like "Am I talking too fast for you?" when he suddenly gave me the information I needed. I then stayed long enough to reach the door - all in all, my first experience*

wasn't exactly encouraging, nor (looking back) stimulating enough to make me want to return. Probably he felt every bit as awkward as I did and wasn't sure how to react to me.

I think the most off-putting thing was of not being a bona fide part of that world. I always felt different enough to feel like an actual interloper - an imposter. I hadn't been brought up or confirmed in the main stream and would always be an "outsider".

I used to hate meeting other students [from the Tech], *as I looked and felt so obviously different from them. In fact I was so obviously different from them that communications became a bit of a problem. Not only were we from different backgrounds but in most cases I'd be a good ten years older than them, so it seemed there was no way I could fit in. I had entertained the idea that I would have liked to attend college 5 days a week. But many things got in the way of this - Social Security for a start ... it was another means of stigmatically differentiating nacro students from normal students - at least that's what it felt like having to rely on the Social Security and queue up every week with the rest of the status-robbed unemployed to receive State handouts. In effect we were neither one nor the other; neither available for work nor proper students* [Jack was one of the second year's 'bright young guys' for whom the Unit was not able to obtain a student grant].

The above account indicates different ways in which overcommitment can manifest itself. Ben, we may recall, devoted himself to some components of the programme to the neglect of other components. He spent so much time taking longwinded notes on all the books about Napoleon mentioned by the lecturer that he had little time for reading about other nineteenth century despots, or for attending lectures, or even for pondering the arguments which he was taking notes on. By contrast, Jack tried too hard by filling his programme with more components than are normally required. No sooner did he arrive at the Tech than he added components which to the less committed would be superfluous, such as choosing where to sit, working out an account to explain late arrival, etc. [4] Ben put too large a weight on the scales - Jack put too many weights on the scales.

Jack, so much older than the other students at the Tech, seems to have been social psychologically in a similar, though converse, situation to that of a mentally retarded child who must, with dread, behave in accordance with his chronological, rather than mental, age:

> They must lead lives something like the heroes in stories of impersonation, who, pretending to be someone else, must continually remember to walk,

> talk, whistle, sing, scratch, move a certain way - always - with detection, capture and death [?] the penalty for forgetting (Holt 1964, p.64).

Jack's predicament may also be compared with Schutz's (1944, pp.502-7) portrayal of the 'stranger', who:

> becomes essentially the man who has to place in question nearly everything that seems to be unquestionable to members of the approached group. To him the cultural pattern of the approached group does not have the authority of a tested system of recipes ... he has to make sure that the solution suggested by the new scheme will also produce the desired effect for him in his special position of an outsider or newcomer who has not brought within his grasp the whole system of the cultural pattern but is rather puzzled by its inconsistency, incoherence, and lack of clarity ... Hence the stranger's ... distrust in every matter which seems to be so simple and uncomplicated to those who rely on the efficiency of unquestioned recipes.

Interestingly, however, though Jack made a fast and futile attempt situationally to adjust to the Tech, he did not make any attempt to find refuge by situationally adjusting to the Unit's staff, its students or the neighbours. He differed, therefore, from Ben, who continually boasted to all these people connected with the Unit of how much he was accomplishing academically (even without the Tech) and of how much he supported the 'idea' of the Unit. In consequence, Jack was subjected to rebuke for lack of effort - another social process about which Schutz has something insightful to say (ibid., p.507):

> Very frequently the reproach of doubtful loyalty originates in the astonishment of the members of the in-group that the stranger does not accept the total of its cultural pattern as the natural and appropriate way of life and the best of all possible solutions of any problem ... But these people do not understand that the stranger in the state of transition does not consider the pattern as a protecting shelter at all but as a labyrinth in which he has lost all sense of his bearings.

Again, however, 'strangers' can react in different ways. In the case of Ben, the attitude of heroically trying too hard resulted in protracted retreat into glorious fantasy; in the case of Jack, it resulted in lightning retreat from what he saw as a nightmarish fantasy.

It did not take long, in a state of inordinate stress, before Jack and Wayne got together - 'off the cuff', as the chairman of the Steering Committee expressed it - in a defiant gesture. They broke into an electrical equipment shop. They lacked access to a garage, and the stolen car in which they took away their stolen goods was quickly sniffed out. Paraphrasing the conceptualisations of Cloward and Ohlin we may say that Jack and Wayne failed to achieve a 'success goal' because of lack of any legitimate means to an illegitimate end.

From custody, after the court case which followed, Jack wrote:

> *I will be going to Nottingham, but prison being like a second home to me, I will feel settled immediately I enter the place* (17/3/76).

This homely feeling reminds one of another observation by Holt (1964, p.67), this time of one of his school students who:

> was deliberately turning back from the world of success, which was strange to him, and which, though it offered new and sweet rewards, might also contain hidden dangers, in favour of the world of failure in which, even if he was not very happy, he was at least at home.

Jack was released in May 1977, but was soon imprisoned again for burglary. The prison in which I visited him is officially claimed to be progressive. Inmates are visited by relatives and friends in a large hall with many small tables, and there is a rocking horse in the corner for the kiddies. Jack had recently been 'thrown out' of another prison and he was about to be thrown out of this one because of a fracas with other inmates a few days previously. A prison officer gave emphasis to this incident by telling me that I would have to be positioned especially near to him and his colleagues, and at a distance from the prisoner. The situation emphasised my wonder about Jack's current status in the violence hierarchy, but it was impossible for me to judge how it might be changing until his next release.

Before that event, Jack wrote to say that he would still like to improve his education, particularly as he hoped that from it he would derive greater political and social awareness, in which he felt himself to be lacking and which he hoped would make some sense of, and yet somehow take him beyond, the Glasgow gang life which had dominated his world outside prison. Jack considered, however, that he had probably 'burnt his bridges' with NACRO. I consulted Ron, who on previous occasions had been loth to reacquire the Unit's failures; Wayne, for example, had been rejected completely when he made a second application during the the Unit's fourth year. It was now, however, the beginning of the Unit's fifth year, when Ron was heroically prepared to accept 'hard core' offenders. Ron accordingly responded, 'Third time lucky'. I conveyed this magical formula back to Jack, who thus reappeared at the Unit during its fifth year.

A few days later, Jack came to see me and unexpectedly

asked me if I had kept letters which he had written so that he could show them to members of staff. Some of the letters discuss psychological and sociological literature and, indeed, testify to Jack's analytical and critical skills. In fact, each member of staff read the material and averred that she or he was very impressed with Jack's manifest educational ability. This expression of confidence in him, however, did not lead on to consideration of the ways in which Jack could, step by step, further the intellectual interests, reading and thinking in which he had already invested much of himself. Instead, he received a gesture which contradicted the earlier message of belief in his ability. He was asked to take an 'aptitude test', which aims 'to incorporate as many different biases and principles as is consistent with a reasonably short test ... under conditions of speed' (Heim 1970, pp.1-4). It gives marks for 'right answers' and takes no account of any ability to reflect, question, doubt, assimilate reading of one's interest or any other educational capability which can be immediately built upon. As Jack went through this procedure he shivered uncontrollably. A member of staff said that, if he was feeling cold, she could fetch him his jacket. He thanked her. He told me afterwards that he had not felt cold. He had been overcome by nervousness, but he had not wanted to say so. I was disheartened by such information, for, as Holt (ibid., p.60) points out, 'the scared fighter may be the best fighter, but the scared learner is always a poor learner' (see also Levitt 1968, pp.173 and 182).

Jack was then required to add himself to the class in English literature. As he already had a pre-university qualification in this subject, it was patent that this requirement was actuated by the idea of raising the morale of the English literature class rather than that of Jack, as well as impressing on him the great favour which the Unit was doing him by accepting him back.

The Unit lowered Jack's self-esteem in a further way. Instead of possessing the unchallenged aura of a man not to be trifled with, as in the second year, he was now forced into fights by several of the fifth year students. He lost each fight indisputably and won none. These encounters reduced the Unit for him to little more than a colony of his recent prison experience. Unwilling to adjust to the requirements of the staff, he had, indeed, to make the most of the Unit as a colony. Such an opportunity presented itself one night in February 1979, when Joan got drunk again, and this time broke windows in different rooms in the Unit. In the morning, Jack 'owned up' to the damage, and Ron removed his studentship. Jack thus took the rap for another inmate and left with some glory, clinging to an heroic ideal of prison culture, as well as repeating the pattern of being thrown out of punishing institutions - although, this time, not to be thrown into another one.

Soon afterwards, Jack moved into the flat of a girlfriend who was studying accountancy. Here, for endless months, he hibernated and aestivated, sleeping long hours, cadging money from the girl for cigarettes and drink, but otherwise doing nothing in particular - except, perhaps, reflecting. During this period, he admitted to me that he had passed his peak in fighting ability. Discounting his heroic moments in the past, he expressed his sense of failure to me in terms very similar to those of McVicar (1979, p.197): 'As a criminal I have been a lamentable failure. Whatever money I have gained by crime, I could have earned as a labourer in half the time I spent in prison'.

When I last spoke to Jack, in August 1981, he was still vegetating. With regard to crime, he was stealing only very occasionally. Prison had lost its attraction. Indeed, he had been out of prison for more than two years, by far the longest time in thirteen years. His only recent convictions had been for assaulting his girlfriend and for criminal damage arising out of domestic disputes, for which he had not been reimprisoned. It is possible that an awareness that his days as a high status man of violence were over had rehabilitated him to some extent. He could have learnt the same lesson in prison, but because he was sober and, therefore, a more alert fighter in prison it might have taken longer to learn the dismal truth. If, therefore, we were to assess his outcome, not from the period after his first studentship in the second year - in the experimental period of the Unit - but from his second studentship in the fifth year, then there would be a case for reallocating Jack to the next chapter rather than this one.

D. KEN: 1X↑;PP, PCo

Ken came to the Unit at the age of twenty-six, a few weeks before the end of the second year. His education in prison had been entirely vocational. It had enabled him to obtain a £70/week welding job, which he considered soul-destroying. One of Ken's first remarks in our first conversation soon after his arrival in the Unit was that he felt he would need someone to keep reminding him what the goals of the Unit were. He seemed to be expressing a desire to be shown the way and kept in check continuously. This was a trait which infuses the whole of his case history. When I asked him if he had any friends he said yes: a solicitor, two psychologists and a probation officer. He said that the basis of these friendships was that he could relate to these people on an intellectual plane.

In the same conversation, Ken told me that he had been a thief because, in his observations, everybody exploited everybody else, and he had conformed to the pattern. He added, however, that nowadays he could think for himself and find his own satisfactions.

But, in fact, Ken may have achieved very little liberation from his conformist tendency, as can be seen, for example, in the following episode:

> Ken said that he had had enough to drink, and that it was time to walk home for lunch. I said that that was OK, but I asked him to wait while I went to the toilet. I came back a couple of minutes later, and found Ken standing with another pint in his hand. I said that I had thought he had said that he had had enough to drink. Ken replied that he had had enough to drink but everyone else in the pub was drinking, and while I had been away he had been on his own, so he had bought himself another drink.

Ken seemed to have stronger intentions of getting down to study and keeping out of crime than I had observed in most other clients. He found himself, however, in a Unit where little study was being done and where various offences were being committed. Ken told me that all his life he had felt the need to 'belong'. His earnest study intentions, however, conflicted with the activities of other clients and, therefore, with his desire for a feeling of belonging. He soon, therefore, started to reoffend, explaining to me that, if he was caught, he was quite prepared to return to prison, where he had enjoyed some measure of status, identity and belonging. It seemed evident, however, that he was also motivated by the desire to obtain prestige even if he were not caught. On the criminal exploit for which he was convicted soon after coming to the Unit, for instance, he took along another student merely to admire his skill. On this occasion, however, he was, in fact, immediately arrested.

Ken was not reimprisoned for the conviction and he thus continued his studentship into the third year. By then, however, having failed to win pre-eminence among the other clients he had developed two attitudes that were similar to those which were earlier observed in the situational adjustment of Ben: an over-identification with the staff of the Unit and an air of superiority towards his fellow clients. The following interaction demonstrates this situational adjustment. It also shows different ways in which nervous tension in the students could manifest itself. One protagonist seems to find relief in bullying ridicule, the other responds with defensive seriousness:

> After morning classes, Ken and I went to the pub. We passed Des on the way, and I invited him to join us. After giving me his opinions on other topics, Ken turned to the subject of drugs. He said that he didn't think Ron was able to learn anything from the Unit. For example, he was allowing

> Lee (a drug taker who had lived in a bedsitter for a short time) to return to the Unit even though there were drug problems in the Unit. Des, whom Ken had completely ignored till this point, then said, 'Who's got a drug problem?'. Ken replied, 'Harry, Geoff and you'. Des insisted that he did not have a drug problem, unlike Geoff and Lee, who shot up heroin. He took only cannabis, but that was not something he could get addicted to. Besides, he had kept his promise to Ron not to bring it into the Unit. Ken then insisted that that proved that Des had a drug problem - otherwise why didn't he give it up? Des said that in Jamaica [where he grew up] everybody smoked it even though it was illegal. When he came home from a hard day's work he liked to put on the telly and smoke. In any case, it was not as harmful as nicotine. Ken said that what he had just said proved he had a drug problem. He (Ken) had smoked it millions of times, but because it was illegal he had easily been able to give it up. He would bet Des 10p that he couldn't give it up, and, if he couldn't, that would show that it wasn't worth 10p. At this Des got very excited and said that he could give it up if he wanted to. There had been times when he had had the opportunity to smoke but had resisted it. For example, at Borstal, kids who went away for the weekend had brought it back but he had not taken it because the screws were all around him. Ken smiled superciliously. He said that what Des had just said proved his point. By smoking pot Des was putting himself 'on offer' [making himself liable to be picked up by the police].
>
> We left the pub, and Ken departed from us. Des was very upset. He said that he didn't like people being sorry for him: if people got the idea that he had a 'drug problem' they would get sorry for him. In trying to mollify Des, I 'labelled' Ken. I said that Des shouldn't worry about Ken. Ken was OK, but he liked having arguments. Didn't he know that about Ken? Des said that when he came to the Unit he had preferred to keep to himself, so he didn't know Ken well.

Ken was an extremely diligent student at the school set up by the Unit in the third year. Particularly after he had moved out of the Unit because of the noise of other students, and in the circumstances described in Chapter 7, he always came early to the Unit's classes, waiting for the arrival of the teacher and the other students. He seemed pleased to fit in with Ron's 'idea of starting a school to provide an increased amount of teaching in a more <u>controlled</u> setting than we have had hitherto' (emphasis mine). Moreover, he depended very heavily on individual contact with Ron, Stafford and other teachers in the Unit, often meeting, or having long telephone calls with, them after class in the evenings or at weekends to discuss his homework.

One of the subjects which Ken studied at the school he also took lectures in at the Tech. Possibly because of the more personal educational help which he could fall back on at the Unit he responded to feelings of threat at the Tech with fight rather than flight, in contrast to Jack and others. Ken said that he could never resist the temptation to show off his knowledge and make fools of the other students at the Tech. The urge was particularly strong because of 'my working class accent'. Moreover, he became very friendly with the teacher at the Tech, a young postgraduate close to him in age. It seems, however, that he was unable to reproduce this supportive pattern of social interaction when he went to university and found himself again in a social void.

Reaction-formation The concept of overcommitment as one of the most prominent attitudes of the students closely resembles what Albert Cohen, using psychoanalytical theory, calls reaction-formation:

> If a new moral order is evolved which offers a more satisfactory solution to one's life problems, the old order continues to press for recognition, but if the recognition is granted, the applecart is upset. The symptom of this obscurely felt, ever-present threat is clinically known as "anxiety", and the literature of psychiatry is rich with devices for combatting this anxiety, this threat to a hard-won victory. One such device is reaction-formation. Its hallmark is an "exaggerated", "disproportionate", "abnormal", intensity of response, "inappropriate" to the stimulus which seems to elicit it. The unintelligibility of the response, the "over-reaction", becomes intelligible when we see that it has the function of reassuring the actor against an inner threat to his defenses (1955, pp.132-3; emphasis his).

A notion similar to reaction-formation was sometimes used by the Unit's staff. Ron, for example, wrote to Daryl's solicitor that 'his efforts failed because he tried too hard, set himself impossible standards and pretended to himself that his break with the past was complete'.

Where then does the difference between reaction-formation and overcommitment lie?

Reaction-formation, as presented by Cohen, puts its stress on 'the old order', the past. Overcommitment by no means denies the individual his life history, but it puts equal emphasis, like the concept of commitment, on the actor's concerns about his present and anticipated future. The conceptual difference is slight, but important:

> Having spent several days in the torpor of the

> summer of 1976 reading Kant line by line for a philosophy teacher, Ken came to visit me at university. While sitting on the lawn we were approached by a postgraduate student and invited to a party to be held that evening. At the party everyone sat in a circle. Introduced to a student doing research in ecology I asked her about her topic. While she was explaining, Ken was concentrating with rapt attention, which, I think, all interpreted as evidence of some kind of expertise, only to discover that he had been listening in order to demonstrate his superior mind. 'Why do you call it all "organic"? ', he asked. 'Don't you mean "biological"? "Organic" isn't scientific, it's dialectical'. [5]

Later, I discovered that Ken understood 'dialectical' as the adjectival form of 'dialect' and as pertaining, therefore, to an inferior form of language. In his determination to reach the goal set for him, Ken was taking his philosophy lessons extremely seriously, clutching at every word as if it had a single meaning relating to eternal truth.

While the concepts of reaction-formation and overcommitment overlap, therefore, the former tends to seek for the source of the behavioural problem in the past, whereas the latter is equally interested in the anxieties of the intended future, which in Ken's case was becoming an undergraduate.

The connection between overcommitment and concern about the future was evident in many of the Unit's clients. In the case of Brian, one of the students in the Unit's fourth year, for example, overcommitment expressed itself in a preoccupation about obtaining elocution lessons. He was not so much repressing 'the old order' as responding to the university and professional career goals to which he was being directed. The situation is reminiscent of Jackson and Marsden's (1962) discussions of the ways in which working class grammar school pupils begin to become more middle class than the middle class as they are made ready for middle class careers.

<u>Authority figures and upward mobility</u> If a programme is to be used as a means towards an upwardly mobile career then an especially treacherous kind of overcommitment is one which is closely linked with situational adjustment to particular sponsors or authority figures. Upward social mobility necessitates providers of opportunities for success to be readily replaced in such a role as each stage is completed. Those who, accordingly, are recipients of chances for advancement must be:

> able to continue relating themselves to figures of authority, never too close for disattachment when necessary - never too far away when continuity and closeness are necessary for attachment ... The

> mobile man must be able to depart: that is, he must maintain a substantial emotional distance from people, and not become deeply involved with them or committed to them (Warner and Abbegglen 1955, pp.80-81).

Soon after Ken heard about his excellent examination results, he and I went for a country walk. It was a cool and soothing day in late summer, the kind of day when an undergraduate might feel particularly cheerful and relaxed, optimistically daydreaming of personal independence, of further academic or other acknowledgments and of fresh challenges - as well as of mischievous but tolerated escapades.

But it was not a walk which elevated one's spirits.

I was not in the company of a privileged youth looking forward to new surroundings offering new promises which he might confidently expect to be fulfilled. I was in the company of a very different personage altogether, who, if he was looking forward, was also looking backwards; whose silence, so discomfitting to sponsors who had so often chastened him for his own good, was now broken by a newly added anxiety about what he was about to lose. The main agony was whether he would be able to obtain where he was going all the personal attention which he had received from education officers and teachers in Cambridge. I found myself powerless disingenuously to reassure him. For I soon found myself considering further anxieties which he himself had perhaps not yet contemplated, but which it was my professional task to contemplate and my moral obligation to pass on to those who had been appointed to help him and others like him facing similar puzzling futures.

1. Firstly, there was the anxiety which Ken himself had articulated. The teachers at the mini-school had been highly accessible. The structure of the mini-school had ensured that. The teacher at the Tech had been highly accessible. Coincidence of age grade had somehow brought that about, along with a feeling of responsibility which had begun to grow at the Tech for the constituency of potential learners wider than the one it usually served which the clients from the Unit had fleetingly and skewedly represented.

What Ken did not need to spell out was that he had become habituated to these mentors in Cambridge, who, indeed, had given him no guarantee that where he was going he would find substitutes for themselves, to whom he would be able situationally to adjust as easily as before. The first anxiety to be considered, therefore, was the accessibility of new authority figures. Few of Ken's fellow undergraduates were likely heavily to feel such tremors. If they had felt the need or right to personal attention they had long since come to terms with, for example, relating to different form-teachers each year. They may also, passed through so many academic hands over the years, have acquired 'disattachment'.

2. Ken had been an apt pupil of how to be a 'good' GCE pupil. At no time had he been given preparatory lessons in how to be a 'good' undergraduate; lessons which middle class students learn informally. The Unit had never taught him, for example, that attendance at lectures is to some extent at the mature discretion of the student, to be used if the lecturer can provide him with a new, different or unpublished perspective, for a refreshing break from the printed word, or to keep in touch with how other students are tackling their studies. Just as hostels for ex-prisoners once taught their inmates to play the role of members of the warden's family (Turner 1961; Miller 1964; Griffiths 1970; Peryer et al. n.d.) so the Unit had taught its clients to be good schoolboys. As Stafford put it:

> At university, lectures exist and an undergraduate either turns up or not, and that's his choice; in a school, classes exist and every boy who doesn't turn up is likely to be in trouble, and has to explain his absence. The first pattern says, 'We lay on classes - it's up to the student to decide if he'll turn up and pick the flowers growing in the garden'. I think we run much more closely to a school now - we impose the embarrassment of apology to the teacher for absence. My own approach - perhaps not unnaturally - is more school-like than Ron's.

3. It has come to be questioned whether a high school regime necessarily efficiently prepares even conventional students to be university students (Lunzer and Gardner 1979; New Society 1979). Even conventional undergraduates, overadjusted to school-like methods of study, sometimes feel stress in their transition to university. Lacking complete self-reliance they sometimes become, in fact, dependent, and seek the guidance of parents, chaplains or psychotherapists. Other undergraduates, whom delinquency has separated from parents and alienated from counsellors, may return to delinquent 'solutions' to their stress.

4. Ken had had little time to develop resistance to the competitive pressures which prevail throughout the formal educational system. Indeed, in the rivalrous atmosphere of the Unit, such pressures may have been reinforced. It seemed unlikely that the coping mechanism of disdain for fellow clients which Ken had developed in the Unit would be of any benefit to him at university.

I could, therefore, hardly claim clairvoyant powers when, in the summer of 1977, I reported that I considered that Ken had been prepared by recent educational experience for being an educational dropout and that, regardless of his earlier classification, he was very much 'at risk'.

His predicament, however, was not fully conveyed to his university tutor, and it was rather late in the day when she 'tried to reassure him and keep him in touch with reality'.

For no sooner had Ken arrived at university than he found it impossible to feel comfortable sitting in a lecture hall. He felt that students sitting near him would in some way be able to find out about his short experience of formal education. He was not only a 'stranger'; he also lacked a biography. Help with his educational problems was never more than superficial, and it was not long before he was in trouble with the law again. Most of the academic year he awaited his case. At the end of the academic year, he abandoned his studies and disappeared for some time. When Ron discovered his whereabouts he encouraged Ken to renew his determination and find some way of starting his degree course again, either at the same university or elsewhere. Ken obediently returned to the town where his university was. While awaiting trial Ken wrote to Ron:

> *I do want you to know that in my own twisted little way you managed to make me, and still have me obligated to you ... to such an extent that it probably transcends rationality and logic ... perhaps by placing offenders into the stresses of education it's possible that you speed up the process whereby they reoffend ...*

The judge placed Ken on a Community Service Order. This measure seems to have little rehabilitative effect on most offenders (Pease et al. 1977a; 1977b; Young 1978; Thorvaldson 1978, pp.319-20). In the course of serving it, Ken's rate of recidivism accelerated. From prison he writes that he receives no replies to any of his letters to NACRO, no reassurance that, though it may never have any future dealings with him, it has not rejected him. In constantly brooding on the subject, he seems to consider that to people who once found some worth and something redeemable in him he has become an object of repulsion, so that he writes (26/6/82) of Ron's silence: '*Perhaps I did trouble his conscience then again it may just have been a form of self-preservation that he didn't want any adverse affects contact with me and the contents of my letters might have ...*'.

It may be noted that the coding of Ken's case study is similar to that of Ben's, except that Ken came under the Unit's daily schooling system, whose control he accepted and, indeed, depended on. Ken's drive to conform recalls one of Cloward and Ohlin's (1960) basic arguments that conformism is not inconsistent with a highly competitive society and that pressurized efforts to conform frequently cause mental strain, which in turn may lead to both failure and deviance. About where the latter will lead Ken in the future one cannot be optimistic.

E. <u>IAN: 1Y↔X,2,3;PP,PCo</u>

Ian was the eldest child in a large family. He was put into care at the age of six, and was then moved through six children's homes. From these he passed on to approved schools, Borstals and prisons.

Ian spent the short intervals between these institutions back with his family. Ian's father had been a petty criminal most of his life, a violent man given to drink, sometimes living in the house, sometimes elsewhere. Ian tended to follow his father's example in getting involved from time to time in insecure business deals connected with old cars, such as stripping off parts for sale. Some of Ian's offences were connected with stealing from cars. The only other work which Ian stated on his application form as having done before coming to the Unit was a badly paid job in heavy engineering.

Ian's mother, when she was not sick, which often she was, worked for mentally handicapped children and, through her, Ian became fascinated with this work. In prison, he obtained certificates for passing first aid and home nursing courses. When Ron visited him in prison and asked him why he wanted to become a nurse he said he wanted to help people who could not help themselves.

Ian's application form, therefore, referred to rudimentary qualifications in skills directly connected with the career which he would have liked to enter. The form also referred to musical abilities. When, however, it came to academic attainments, on which the outside world places so much status, the story was rather different. The prison education officer reported that 'Ian has attended remedial English classes and he has made satisfactory if ... slow progress'. (Ian, however, told me that he had learnt all his 'remedial English' from a friend in prison.) The officer added, 'I would consider his chances of passing his RSA exam [in English] as rather remote. I am of the opinion that Ian has limited academic potential'. The prison welfare officer commented, 'Ian is over-stretching himself and is not realistic in aiming for Further Education ... He would need a lot of support in concentrating his mind on the task at hand, when he is open to the influences of the outside world. He is said to be happier when under the close control offered by prison ... He responds to care and concern'.

Control, care, concern, the Management Committee's classification of Ian as low risk, and the Unit's supreme faith in schooling as a method of dealing with offenders' 'immature' behaviour were among the main factors which led to the decision to invite Ian to take up a studentship in the Unit. He arrived towards the end of the second year with considerable undercommitment. He:

> expected it to last about two weeks ... 'cos I thought: come to a place like this where there's people who 'ave either took O levels themselves and who's 'ad a good educational background, and therefore with someone like me who's really illiterate, I'll be wasting my time, but I came down 'ere to see what I could do. When Ron came to the prison I was still reluctant to come 'cos I didn't know much.

Ian was nevertheless assigned to the incipient school to study five O levels, a goal which demanded a fantastic acceleration of the educational progress which Ian had recently made. To set Ian such an unreachable goal may seem contrary to all reason, unless we remind ourselves that educationalists tend to equate intelligence, which Ian manifestly possessed, with academic potential. Moreover, educationalists tend to be people of authority, an attribute which Ian had never possessed. He was, therefore, in no position to balk at the academic goals which were set for him, given the authoritative equation between intelligence and academic potential, without 'admitting' that he was a person of rather low intelligence.

Low intelligence, however, was not the only notion he could not admit to without being false to himself. Whenever his mother was particularly sick he went back to Manchester, his home town, to visit her. He could hardly forsake such visits in favour of trigonometry lessons without denying that home nursing was one of the central interests of his life.

Such 'truancies', however, were bound to be reflected in his performance in the school. Necessarily, therefore, after some months, members of staff came to realise that unless they lightened Ian's academic load, as by this time they had been cajoled into doing by clients with stronger academic backgrounds than Ian's, he might not come back from his next visit to Manchester. Such an eventuality had to be avoided at all costs, for a definite pattern, which, indeed, was never to change, had already become manifest. All Ian's reconvictions since he had joined the Unit were the result of offences committed in Manchester; in Cambridge, Ian had never reoffended.

Even after Ian's subject load had been lightened, however, the downward trend in his academic performance continued. Loneliness based on feelings of inferiority in relation to the others soon led increasingly to drinking, and drinking to impoverishment. Impoverishment necessitated finding odd jobs, and jobs in turn took time away from study. Thus, a report on Ian's English declared his attendance and punctuality as fair at the end of the first term, and as not good at the end of the second; his examination prospects as 'poor to average' at the end of the first term, and as nil at the end of the second.

At the end of the second term, Ron solemnly informed me that he was 'beginning to wonder whether Ian seriously believed in education'. Ron was not entirely wrong. For I do not think that Ian seriously believed in Ron's conception of education.

The nearest Ian ever had to a friend among the Unit's clients was a man as 'uneducated' and as unpretentious as Ian who stayed at the Unit for a few days and then bid it farewell. In the short period in which Kerry sojourned in the Unit he interacted with Ian in a most informative way, accurately and sensitively expressing Ian's unease. One afternoon, Ian was trying to puzzle out and react to the mixture of mind analysis and advice which he had been just subjected to in a tutorial. Kerry summed up the whole situation better than I could have done (or should have done if I could have done). The time might come, said Kerry, when one needed a rest from a subject; one should then be able to go to a teacher and tell him how one felt, with no personal offence meant; but what was more likely to happen was that one would take too much study - like smoking so much that one's mouth would begin to taste stale - but would be afraid to let the teacher know; and then, all of a sudden and without prior announcement, one would cease taking classes in the subject. Ian indicated that Kerry had hit the nail on the head.

Yet it was actually a very long time before Ian made his final departure, a fact all the more remarkable in relation to an expectation which passed through Ron's own mind at an early stage:

> At the beginning, I feared that he would one day look in the mirror and say to himself, 'Gosh, you are no good', and give it up. I am still waiting on tenterhooks with him, fearing that one day you might come in and find out that he had gone, and decided he couldn't do any more.

Even at the beginning of the Unit's fourth year, however, Ian was still toying with the idea of trying a further year. In the end, though, he went back to Manchester, to disagreeable home conditions, to second hand car jobs, to further criminal convictions, and to prison.

The question still remains, however, why for so long Ian did not take the definite step which Ron had feared. For the Unit's programme, and Ian's ways of coping with it, confronted him with manifold hardships. I once asked him, for example, if he had a girlfriend, and he replied, 'Yer can't afford it, can yer? On £20.70 a week!' [Social Security money].

In order to catalogue the sad attractions of the Unit for Ian I shall use the typology of meanings which the Unit had for its students.

Staging post Ian was lured into the Unit because of its promise to help him to realise his ambition. During Ian's prison sentence before he came to the Unit, Ron wrote to him that 'educational requirements vary considerably. Some hospitals will accept applicants for State Enrolled Nurses Training without any 'O' levels ...'. This was an unduly optimistic forecast, though Ron did go on to indicate that, when there was competition for training opportunities, O level passes were an advantage. The letter was a foretaste of further authoritative declarations from Ron, after Ian was released, which at times made him feel assured, even buoyant:

> I was going to go into night school when I finished [prison], and work during the day. 'E introduced me to this business, which is much easier 'cos I don't 'ave to work and I can spend more time on it, and get a job at night-time, which is better than studying at night after work, 'cos if you've done a good day's graft you are tired and ready for sleep. 'Ere you can work and get a cleaner's job or something at night-time. I'm 'oping to do me O levels, I 'ope to get grade B, that's me aim. I 'ave two English teachers.

Six weeks after this statement, however, concrete facts began to lodge in Ian's mind, where false hopes had dwelt before:

> The only thing that 'as changed is that I came 'ere to do two O levels, and now I've been informed that they require more ... to get into nursing. They do like to see someone with at least one A level.

But so long as the Unit continued to offer Ian any hope at all that there would be a flight to his ambition it kept him waiting irritably in the transit lounge. Thus, although Ian would sometimes say things like, 'Even today I've considered just packing up and going', nevertheless, as Ron put it, 'Even Ian wants to be a nurse, knows it's going to be a hard slog, but the thought of being a nurse is what sustains him.'

What sustains most people, however, is not only their goals but also the means of achieving them. When the means which society lays down cannot easily be related to one's familiar experience then one's slog is likely to take the form of overcommitted fantasy. Hence, according to Ron, Ian would sometimes 'work twenty-four hours a day, and then emerge with a vast, rambling essay, or a huge mass of maths exercises, which are all terribly wrong'.

Merton (1940, p.562) pointed out that our bureaucracy suffers from what he called 'trained incapacity'. But, through those who serve as its agents, it also suffers other citizens to go through the same training, not least in education itself. Thus Ron commented on Ian:

> He is not able to do much for himself. He is not able to deal with problems, in the sense of translating verbal statements into algebraic symbols. He is trying to tackle the basic mathematical processes. He's made a great stride with vulgar fractions and could answer a question in O levels - after a certain amount of prompting (emphasis mine).

But I find it very difficult to see what algebra has to do with the work of a State Enrolled Nurse. As Leach (1977, p.32) points out:

> Those who teach elementary mathematics, in any of its guises, like to imagine that their task is to develop in their pupils a love of highly abstract transformations, which must not on any account be contaminated with the problems of real life.

A very similar criticism can be made of O level English Language, which seems to continue to be based on such notions as that there is only one 'standard' form of English useful for communicating or thinking in and that deviations from it constitute some form of 'slang'.

Ian could read and write and use a simple calculator. He knew some of the basic principles of nursing. He could communicate his ideas and feelings more directly than most of my informants. According to Ron, he was 'in personal terms a generous, warmhearted, courageous young man, second to none - a very nice kid'. He seemed to have qualities which go beyond those considered vital for entering training as a State Enrolled Nurse (Korving and Davidson 1975, pp.41-7). But the powers that be affix incapacitating regulations at the staging posts which they set up. As Leach (ibid., p.4) again points out:

> It is the graduates of Oxford and Cambridge, with their bookish background and assumptions, who tend to run the country. It is the children of the graduates of Oxford and Cambridge who collect the top university degrees, because the system is set up in such a way that the knowledge and skill that is highly valued is just the sort of knowledge and skill which these people are most likely to have.

The writ of such élitism runs far and wide, regulating a gamut of occupational staging posts. But though the elite applies to so many citizens restriction of passage to socially valuable work it does not prevent them from sojourning at staging posts and watching others embark. It is to Ian's sojourning that we must now turn our attention.

Resort As we noted above, Ian went through periods

of unstable, fantastic overcommitment. But eventually he returned to an attitude of undercommitment. People who become undercommitted to the official programme of their organisation, however, do not automatically drop out. For such people may be highly committed to unofficial features which they perceive in the organisation.

Ian told of unpleasant experiences in prison and in the hands of the police. But home, a staging post back to prison, could be even more uncomfortable. Between the Devil and the deep blue sea of the 'community' and prison the Unit came down from heaven and offered respite:

> I think the change is 'cos of not living at 'ome. In our 'ouse there's always tension, fighting, arguing seven days a week. With being away from there, and 'aving a place of me own and being able to sit down where it's nice and quiet and peaceful it's like being in paradise after being brought up in a mad'ouse. It's given me a chance to unwind, relax ...

Indeed, when Ian first came to the Unit, one of his chief anxieties was that the contrast between the new surroundings and home might not be strong and wide enough. When asked by Ron to 'describe the room in which you slept last night' he wrote:

> *the walls are very thin and you can hear all the other people's noses* [noises] *as if you was in the same room; is like home sweet home* ...

Whenever Ian returned from home visits he was swept in by an angry, distraught mood, which became a recognised stereotype among other students. One evening, when I was about to go out of the Unit, two students jokingly told me in lowered voices to watch out - Ian had just come back from Manchester.

Moreover, even though the Unit might not have <u>completely</u> calmed Ian and made him feel serene, it gave him a second form of security (which, however, encouraged him to make further excursions back to Manchester):

> At one time, me and me father could never see eye to eye, but now we can sit down and talk, but then if I stay in Manchester more than three or four days we still clash. We still 'ave our different viewpoints, and in a lot of ways it 'asn't changed much. This change is mainly 'cos me father doesn't see me as much as 'e used to, and secondly 'e knows that if 'e throws me out of the 'ouse I've got a roof over me 'ead. At one time, 'e would tell me to get out and I'd 'ave nowhere.

Such 'resettlement' by NACRO (of which it was probably not aware) should not, however, be exaggerated, for there may have been another cause of more harmonious relationships which Ian considered were developing in the home. A man's life cycle within the traditional condition of the working class in England must also be taken into account: under the influences of old age, hard labour and sickness Ian's father had 'slowed down':

> 'E starts when 'e's 'ad a lot to drink. But 'e's slowed down a lot. 'E's old and very ill. And 'e spends most of 'is time in bed. Goes to work, comes 'ome, 'as 'is teas and goes straight to bed. Up five or six in the morning and off to work.

During most of the period in which the Unit knew Ian, he went through several cycles. He swung into the Unit from the area of his criminal activity, whither he swung back again, then back to the Unit, and so on. He did this four, five and perhaps more times, until he was seen in Cambridge no more, even though its rehabilitation unit may have remained in his memory for a long time as a resort from his normal, dulling and annoying routine. He once wrote from Manchester about the Unit providing him with 'a fulfilling life of joy and understanding'. Wishful thinking had its place, in Manchester. So did other facts, in Cambridge. There he was surrounded by anxious competitors putting on airs. He was confronted with ever inflating entry requirements to his chosen profession. He was never provided with a competent biology teacher. Finally, he was forced to recognise that he 'could come to the stage where I could say, "Fair enough, it's not my cuppa' tea" and go'.

Colony Silberman (1969, p.90) refers to after-care clients who:

> could be described as the uncared-for children of deprived families belonging to an underprivileged class. Usually from large or disrupted families or reared in institutions, they lacked sufficient attention and care during the most formative years of their lives ... they often found themselves in large and under-staffed institutions where it was difficult to take account of the individual needs of each resident.

That the effects of residential institutions on people of formative years are distinctive has, indeed, long been recognised (e.g., HMSO 1895, vol.2, p.9).

Ian revealed several ways in which the Unit served as a colonial extension of the experiences or fantasies of the institutionalised childhood to which he could never return:

MG: Don't you socialise with people in the house?

Ian: I talk to them only when they talk to me. I've been used to being on me own, being in children's 'omes. I'm used to quietness, and I'm used to being on me own, and that's something that can never be broken. No matter 'ow 'ard they try they can never break what's been embedded in one.

In one of Britain's children's homes, whose 50,000 inmates 'are more and more exhibiting signs of delinquency and maladjustment' (Phillips 1977, p.493), a sixteen year old, long term resident said, 'There are disadvantages: you have to tell people when you are going out and it gets a bit embarrassing ... But you get everything done for you here' (ibid.).

The management of the Unit not only provided Ian with an environment in which he could keep to his own small room without the feeling of being lost in a crowd of other emotionally deprived and neglected minors. It also sorted out his problems, including administrative ones, as when the Department of Health and Social Security 'conned' him (see Chapter 10). It also coaxed him into avoiding complications outside the residence, into keeping to the rules of the residence, and even into being mothered:

Ron: ... for the first time in his life he was living somewhere where he was cared for in such a way as allowed him to feel a certain dignity, a certain kind of relationship with the people looking after him that he had not had much of before ... we gave him the feeling that ... if he got into muddles ... we could sort out the muddles for him ... he goes up to Manchester and gets very unsettled and upset ... he gets pulled apart by his mother and father's behaviour and the way they live. When he gets back here he has increased debts to us, his rent has not been paid while away, and with the car he has acquired he seemed to be going to pieces ... Now he's back with a dog and a charge of siphoning petrol ... I had a long talk with him one afternoon and everything was 'fucking this' and 'fucking that' - really putting on a brazen front. Eventually he calmed down and became more sensible, and we've reached an agreement now that instead of his wild ideas he's got to recognise that he's not a businessman. He comes back and says that he's got all these cars to repair and spray in Cambridge. I had to persuade him that ... he'll only get conned by people, and that his destiny doesn't lie in that direction ...

MG: Why do people con him?

Ron: You look at him - scruffy little bloke, obviously semi-literate at best, working himself to a frazzle to get jobs done ... He's just a kicking boy really. He'll say, 'OK, I'll do the job - £18'. They come to pay him and say, 'Look, I've only got £2 in my pocket, I'll pay the rest on Friday', and then never turn up ... So I said, 'You put yourself in ridiculous positions like this - what will people think of you when they see you come back with a car you can't

> afford and criminal charges against you, and a dog you oughtn't to have here?' ... So I told him his self-respect and dignity would come by having his affairs in order, with savings and no debts ... He agreed ... We shook hands on it ... he sold the car [for £5] and got rid of the dog. Mary is going to have him round to the house now and again for lunch ... and we'll jolly him along with extra special treatment to make him feel he belongs somewhere.

But Ian was as sensible as any other citizen and knew that he couldn't live in a colony of his institutionalised past forever. He decided that the Unit did not suit his kind of life style, that he felt 'boxed in' and that he 'wanted out'. He returned to his family in Manchester. Soon afterwards, he was prosecuted for burglaries but not reimprisoned. When I went to visit him a little later he was in hospital. A car he had been working on illegally had fallen on him, making him the victim of an industrial accident in the 'hidden economy'. I last received a letter from him (17/9/79) from a remand centre, saying he was expecting four years imprisonment if he was found guilty, but consoling himself with the notion that such a sentence would give him plenty of time to build up his English. According to Thorpe (1978, p.69), 'those who have little to lose by delinquent activity while attending school suddenly find themselves with a great deal to gain by staying out of trouble as the rewards of adult life become more apparent'. For Ian, the opposite would seem to be the case. The dubious rewards of adult life were both apparent and familiar once he had left the Unit's school.

F. ELLIS: 1X↑; PP, PCo

The coding of Ellis's case study is the same as that of Ken's. I briefly include it because of the considerable difference in social class background between the two: Ellis came from a more or less middle class background, Ken came from a very low working class background. However, unlike the other middle class client we have alluded to, George, whose biography seems to have been conventional in every way, except for a period spent in Borstal for using cannabis, Ellis had a very disturbed background. Moreover, from the point of view of a study of the effects of the Unit, both Ken and Ellis, from the time they entered that experimental institution, faced a very disturbing 'foreground'.

Ellis was the eldest child of business people. Parents and children mixed with middle class friends. Ellis's early life, however, was far from comfortable. In particular, his mother often subjected him to humiliating punishments and frequently reminded him that he had never been wanted and that he had been the cause of her unhappy marriage. He was seventeen when she ejected him from the home. He went to London and moved from job to job. By the time he came to the Unit at the age of twenty-two he had had several prison sentences.

When Ellis came to the Unit his father became filled with expectations. Since the time his boy left home his business fortunes had sunk, his marriage had finally ended and he had taken a job as a lowly paid steward of a Labour club. He considered that if Ellis could obtain a degree he would be able to speak of him with pride to his close relatives and, in particular, to his sister, who was a magistrate and a county councillor. Ellis himself was no stranger to this strategy. He said that every time he had been in prison he had felt apart from other inmates, for, while they were planning the crimes they would commit after release, he was thinking about plans for becoming a respected member of society by passing A levels.

Arrived at the Unit, Ellis expressed much anxiety about whether he would succeed. Possibly he was feeling the conflicts described by Green (1946, p.41) as afflicting the middle class young 'neurotic', in whom:

> ... the god monsters will be appeased only by a combination of submission in his role of child-in-family and assertiveness in his play-group, school-pupil and other roles enacted outside the home. An integration of these conflicting roles is impossible. His conception of himself becomes one of abject failure. Any striving is painful for it violates the initial submissive adjustment. But he feels equally guilty for not making the effort to achieve.

Ellis's father's expectations, however, were not the only source of anxiety. For a feature of the Unit was that even students who were already abnormally anxious were confirmed in that state of mind by the impression that staff felt particularly uneasy about them. Thus, Ellis moved into the Unit on 21 September 1976. Though Ellis is almost invariably of a cheerful disposition it was quickly evident that he was impatient to start studying hard. Meanwhile, Fred, whom Ellis knew from prison, was applying to come to the Unit. In a letter to Fred of 29 September 1976, Stafford wrote: 'Ellis has settled down very happily here, and we are beginning to get some work out of him!' (exclamation mark his). In an atmosphere where workaholics could be so flippantly cast as workshy it seems surprising that it took as long as six weeks for Ellis, loaded with task of passing three A levels in a few months, to get away from Cambridge, revisit London, quench his thirst for respite with alcohol in a dance-hall and repeat his habit of stealing a handbag. The irony of the situation was compounded when Stafford made the remark that he regarded it as 'tiresome' to have to go to London to testify to Ellis's good character at his trial since the latter was 'obviously a reformed character'. The article of faith that the more education one accepted the more one's rehabilitation could not have been more poignantly expressed.

The first few weeks of Ellis's life in the Unit may be regarded as a period of peak anxiety. A second peak occurred after his A level examinations. Worry about the results was his main conversational topic. In fact, they did turn out worse than one might have expected. For example, he had passed an A level in Law in prison the previous year. After coming to the Unit, he studied it again in order to improve his grade. Instead, he failed. Soon after hearing the news he went to London and stole a handbag in circumstances virtually identical to that of the earlier offence. He was, however, given a two year suspended sentence. He was thus enabled to proceed to a polytechnic which had accepted him to study for a degree on the basis of the A level subject he had passed at the Unit and the A level in Law which he had passed in prison. I last heard from Ellis in a letter from prison of 2 October 1979. I do not know the reason for this sentence for it was not officially recorded and Ellis wrote that he would let me know the details after his release. He wrote that he considered that his ties with NACRO had been broken, and he ended his letter, 'See you soon'. Such a reunion has not yet taken place, but I hope that one day it might.

G. GEOFF: 1X → Y,3;PS,PP

Geoff, the oldest of six children, had a severe upbringing. His strictly Catholic parents impressed on him that wicked thoughts were as sinful as wicked deeds; a notion which seems to have remained with him throughout his short life. During his schooldays, Geoff considered that his father, a factory worker and former policeman, resented him for his outstanding ability in mathematics and writing essays and despised him as a cissy for being less interested in sport than in books. After five O level passes Geoff left school at the earliest opportunity; his father did not want him to succeed in a career and expected him to help to support the rest of the family. According to West and Farrington (1973, p.59), 'high achieving boys whose mothers maintain low job aspirations for them are rendered especially vulnerable to delinquency'. It is possible that, for older boys than the ones about whom these researchers write, fathers may exert a similar influence (see, e.g., Curtis 1973a, p.8).

Geoff found unskilled labour unbearably boring, and, like other young unskilled workers (e.g., Yeger 1970), he found compensatory stimulation in heroin. 'At that time' [about 1960], according to Geoff, 'there were no addicts about then. If I'd seen addicts and the problems they have I don't think I would ever have taken it'.

Geoff became addicted to the drug, and his involvement with it led to criminal convictions. Geoff said that he studied hard in prison (mainly on his own) because he wanted to show that he was not a fool: 'Everybody else in jails are fools, otherwise they wouldn't be there'. Although not a fool, Geoff nevertheless indicated that he may have been fooled on two occasions by the police, who wanted to put him behind bars. Geoff said that his first imprisonment resulted from wrongful conviction for stealing heroin, which, in fact, had been planted on him by the police. There was no significant evidence against him. He heard two members of the jury say that he looked guilty because he was shivering, whereas he was thin and feeling the cold. Geoff also said that the prison sentence which he served before coming to the Unit was also unjust. He was accused of stealing the heroin with which he was found, whereas he had, in fact, bought it from another user.

When Geoff came out of prison in October 1976, the Unit provided him with accommodation right away so that he could immediately enrol at the Tech to study mathematics and physics at A level. Geoff took no subjects at the Unit's school. He regarded lectures at the Tech merely as an adjunct to private study, much in the same way as he had regarded classes in prison.

<u>Indecision</u> Geoff's transition to the Tech would have been a smooth one, except that he found himself plunged into a morass of indecisiveness:

> When I came out I wasn't sure what to do. I thought the best thing was to keep off drugs entirely, but I didn't know if I was able to. On previous occasions I've come out I've gone back on, most times straight back on; also to help me put off decisions, to keep myself in limbo. I really didn't know what to do.
>
> You really can't make your mind up, but I didn't want drugs to get a grip on me, 'cos they have got a grip on me now and again. It's easy to say, 'I'll never use heroin again', but that's easier said than done. If you promise to yourself that you won't do it again and you do then it's worse for you than if you never had promised yourself. You feel let down and you go on to your next fix. If you say to yourself you <u>might</u> use it now and again but realise it's a bad thing but can happen then you'll probably have just one fix and then leave it.
>
> Another thing is that it is easy to kid yourself that things have gone wrong before because you haven't managed your addiction properly, but it will be

> different next time, blaming yourself. In fact, I've met people who have used heroin for years and are stable, and you wonder, 'Why can't I be the same?'.

Geoff's indecision also seems to have been prolonged by unintended contact with other drug users:

> I met two people in Cambridge who I had known from years ago when I used to take drugs quite heavily. I began to neglect my work and would probably have gone off the rails, I think.
>
> I only used one fix. It was the social milieu that was the problem. But I was using a lot of Collis Browne - and two preludin tablets. I was also fixing now and again and getting into a bit of a state. I was mainly taking Collis Browne, a medicine sold over the counter, which contains morphine. It was upsetting me emotionally because I didn't intend to use it. I would start the day deciding not to take it and I would end up with a couple of bottles. I was in a dilemma, whether to take it now and again or to give it up completely.

It may be recalled that Walster (1964, pp.112-3) speculates that 'social support' decreases indecision. In Geoff's case, on the other hand, he was receiving social support <u>for</u> drugtaking from the former acquaintances whom he came across as well as <u>against</u> drugtaking from the staff of the Unit.

<u>Patronising a patient</u> One evening, when Stafford was in the Unit unusually late, he discovered Geoff in 'a bit of a state'. As a result:

> I've got a prescription [for methadone] from the doctor now. He registered me. Ron and Stafford helped me to see this doctor, and made it easier than to have approached him myself. I'm glad I was living here at the time 'cos it seems to have worked out alright when it might not have otherwise. They said at the clinic that they usually take people into hospital for twelve days but that they wouldn't do so in my case.

I asked Geoff why he would not have got himself registered (as a person allowed to be prescribed controlled drugs) if he hadn't been at the Unit. He revealed the difficulties which he considered there might have been without middle class patronage:

> I might have got myself registered if I had been living on my own, but the clinic would probably not have put me on methadone. They usually say they will help you only if you've got a habit. I didn't have a habit, though I was developing one. Besides, if you've got a habit you don't want methadone, you want the real thing. Also they may have offered to

> take me into hospital. Again this would have been pointless, since I didn't have the habit at the time.

The term 'junk' has come to be applied to both heroin _and_ methadone. So I asked Geoff about the differences between the two, the relative advantages and disadvantages.

Geoff said that 'you can manage on methadone, whereas with heroin you just can't function'. Moreover, 'methadone lasts a lot longer, whereas heroin lasts only about two hours. You want it all the time'. Another point is that 'when you are on methadone then heroin gives you no pleasure - it's "overtaken" by methadone'. It is hard to know whether this effect is an advantage or a disadvantage, particularly as Geoff, a man with long experience of drugtaking, asserted that he had known many people who had been able to come off heroin on their own, but none who had come off methadone successfully on their own. Also, long term use of methadone has various side effects, of which one of the most common is pneumonia. Furthermore, Geoff considered the withdrawal symptoms of methadone to be worse than those of heroin.

It seems, in retrospect, unfortunate that Geoff was put on a methadone regime at about the same time as its main protagonists (Dole, Nyaswander and Warner 1968) recanted their earlier claims about its supposed virtues (Dole and Nyaswander 1976). Evidence was also being presented about the same time about methadone's addictiveness and about its ability merely to arrest, but not to eliminate, the heroin craving for which it is prescribed (e.g., Raubolt and Bratter 1976, pp.326-7). The side effects of methadone have long been known (e.g., Osol and Farrar 1955, p.836). Recent years have merely brought greater knowledge of the mechanisms by which its deleterious effects operate (e.g., Wade ed. 1977, pp.967-8; Pharmaceutical Codex 1979, p.546).

Decisiveness The provision of methadone enabled Geoff to _manage without_ heroin. It did not guarantee him against a preference for heroin. Moreover, the Unit's files contained an unusually large number of reference forms from prison education officers testifying to Geoff's absorption in the arts of pure and applied mathematics, radio and television repairing and cognate subjects. Such intellectual enrichment in prison, however, does not in itself provide a guarantee of an ability to overcome problems in the outside world, nor that release from prison will have an ultimate outcome any different from that of previous entries back into the outside world:

> The last time, I came out into a different world. Prison then was so much a different world, it was so far from reality, it was just like it never existed except in my imagination. But prison had been a reality, so that time I was into drugs immediately I came out. I didn't work or discipline

myself or anything. I was reacting to my new freedom.

This statement may seem convoluted. It nevertheless expresses the discontinuity in 'reality' which Geoff tended to experience when he came out of prison. Moreover, it appears to have been by means of mentally juggling with the notions of discontinuity and continuity, freedom and discipline, compulsion and choice that Geoff was able to resolve the indecisiveness which gnawed at his efforts to address himself to the educational programme set before him - an indecisiveness which continued after his being put on the medication of methadone.

The cognitive processes whereby Geoff was able eventually to succeed in overcoming his stressful indecision were striking. He identified the Unit not as an alternative to prison, nor as a form of after-care but as an extension of prison. He indicated, in other words, that the Unit was a colony of his routine prison experience. He expressed the argument in action - by, for example, studying in his room seven days a week and only emerging to go to lectures at the Tech and quickly return - as well as in conversation with me that any difference between his life in the Unit and his recent experience in prison was fallacious:

> I've been living much the same as I am now ... the two years since [before] I came here. I haven't changed my life since I came out of prison. All my spare time in prison I was studying anyway.
>
> The only difference is that what I'm doing is more out of choice, though what I was doing in prison was out of choice anyway. They can't take much away from you in prison. All they can do is keep you locked up. But it's what I intended in prison, and it's what I hoped for.

Moreover, once Geoff succeeded in reducing cognitive dissonance in order to get down to his studies he had no difficulty, it seems, in being dismissive to anyone else who was still taking heroin:

> I'm still seeing one of my friends. He's still on it, but there's no question of his influencing me; the other has lost touch with reality.

Temporary relapse After Geoff's A level results he stayed on at the Tech, beginning an HND programme in September 1977. Before leaving the Unit for private accommodation, he told me that he intended to 'let up' and give himself more time for social life. During the first year, however, he was able to put this intention into practice only to a slight extent. He explained that he did not know how he measured up to other students. His examiners, however, provided a measure, for he came out top of the first year HND students. Moreover, early in that year, Geoff had his dosage decreased from fifty millilitres per day of methadone linctus to thirty.

The HND programme is a sandwich course, with practical experience in industry during the summer vacations. Usually, placements are arranged by the Tech, but Geoff, being an individualist, arranged his own, in the summer of 1978. He expected that, as a trainee, he would be moved around from one operation to another. In fact, he was given a very tedious task in product testing, and, when he complained of boredom, management refused to transfer him to another activity. He was thus in a similar position to 'Janet', discussed by Sawdon et al. (1979, p.171) in their section on the misuse of young people in industry, who 'thought she was a trainee ... part of the Work Experience Programme. There was no education or training programme and she spent six months filling shelves (which she learned in a week)'.

Janet, we are told, ended up unemployed. Geoff, back in the unstimulating world of work of his late teens, coped by having his prescription increased to seventy millilitres. Temporarily abstaining opiate takers, as Lindesmith (1968, p.51) points out, have a low boredom threshold. The increased dosage, however, made Geoff's job only marginally more bearable. He went to see the clinic consultant again, who, however, had by this time gone on an extended holiday, while his colleague was unsympathetic to increasing Geoff's dosage further. Geoff, therefore, obtained extra amounts of methadone unofficially. But he returned to the prescribed seventy millilitres in readiness for the second year of his HND studies.

From in-patient to outsider Were our case study of Geoff to end here, two years after he left the Unit, we would have had to regard him as one of the Unit's star successes, as we would have had to regard Ken or Ellis if we had ended their case studies with their entry to university or polytechnic. Unfortunately, however, not long before the end of the second academic year of the HND programme, things took a sharp turn for the worse. Geoff obtained a job for the summer of 1979 for the second practical experience part of the club sandwich. For the interval of two weeks before starting the job he went into hospital, having been assured and reassured by the doctors at the clinic that he would be able to withdraw from methadone within that period of time. But this was not the case. He found the withdrawal symptoms unbearable. Moreover, at the end of the fortnight, there were no signs of a cure, and Geoff was in no fit state to take up the arranged job without returning to methadone. The ten to fourteen day upper limit which was operating at the detoxification centre in Cambridge is doubtless connected with the 'cash crisis in drug treatment centres because of the Government spending cuts' (The Guardian 13/8/80). No such upper limit operates in the teaching in an education centre not far away. The

Director of the Institute of Criminology in Cambridge, Professor Donald West, told me that in his psychiatric experience, physical withdrawal symptoms can last much longer than two weeks, while psychological effects, such as 'flashbacks' of pleasurable moods of the drug, can last longer still.

After Geoff came out of hospital, he had what he called a 'nervous breakdown'. He considered that he had let himself down by not being able to have himself 'cured' in two weeks. He found it depressing to think of the rest of his life as an addict. He was, however, able to hold down and keep his job assignment, though only by unofficially obtaining cocaine.

According to Burroughs (1977 [1953], p.xvi), 'junk is not, like alcohol or weed, a means to increased enjoyment of life. Junk is not just a kick. It is a way of life'. But for Geoff it was becoming a way of death. He talked of past junkie acquaintances who had died quite suddenly, and considered that he was likely to be facing the same fate. For well over a year, he had been complaining of pains in the area of his lungs, and after his 1979 job assignment he was hospitalised with pneumonia.

After this hospitalisation, Geoff was too weak to hunt for accommodation and he moved into a squat. He had only six more months of study to complete the academic part of his qualifications. However, identifying himself now as a confirmed junkie, he found it hard to concentrate. This weakened state of mind in turn led to feelings of guilt for he considered that unless he could improve his concentration to cope with his studies he would not be contributing to society. In this mental turmoil he dropped out of the Tech:

> I never thought I would be on permanently. I was assured I could come off. When I couldn't manage it, it destroyed confidence in myself 'cos I couldn't do what I expected to do. It would be so much harder the next time, and I knew I wasn't getting any younger. I knew it wouldn't be easy ever to come off. If I'd known what I know now I wouldn't have attempted it except when I had enough time, 'cos it takes two <u>months</u>. It made me feel I was a junkie, so I now had something else, guilt, to carry around with me. I didn't feel it right to go back to college, I didn't think I was good enough to mix with people who were not junkies.

After his withdrawal from the Tech, Geoff obtained his first reconvictions since coming to Cambridge, but they were more closely connected with police, rather than with Geoff's, behaviour. Each year, as the summer tourist season arrives, skid rowers and other vagrants become less visible. Having been hounded out of his squat by the police Geoff set up a tent on one of the less frequented commons. He found himself repeatedly stopped, searched and harrassed by the police. One night, Geoff visited me and, but a few minutes after he left, a man knocked on the door and, on being admitted, burst into the house, loudly announcing, to the distress of the children present, that he was from the CID. The policeman held up a book and asked me if it were mine and if I had lent it to Geoff. When I said yes the man stormed out. The book was a Directory published by NACRO which included information on treatment centres for withdrawing from drugs.

One evening, in July 1980, Geoff went up a small passage to urinate. He found himself at the back of a radio and TV shop, where pieces of polystyrene, in which the shop's wares were delivered, were lying about. Geoff rummaged among this material, in the hope of finding a piece of suitable size to use as a ground sheet. Not finding a piece large enough he walked back to the street, at which point he was arrested. He was kept at the police station over the weekend, and when I visited him there he told me, in the presence of the invigilating jailer, that he had been informed that if he pleaded not guilty he would be remanded in custody for two weeks while the prosecution prepared its case, during which time he would be blackmailed into admitting to further offences which the police had not yet cleared, by being deprived of his medication.

At the court on Monday, Geoff's barrister was told that Geoff had the choice of pleading guilty to a charge of trespassing, which would result in a short sentence, or of pleading not guilty of attempted burglary. Geoff, whose deprivation of methadone had already begun, said that he wished to plead not guilty. The barrister said there would be no hope of bail unless Geoff had an address. I left the two in the cell and telephoned the Unit, but it would not give him a room without a meeting of the Management Committee. I then telephoned the Cyrenians, a charitable organisation which provides temporary hostel accommodation for the homeless. I was told that they did not usually accept a resident without an interview. However, the young man at the end of the line said that he would think the matter over and I could 'phone back in ten minutes time. I did so, the Cyrenian worker gave Geoff a place, and in court five minutes later Geoff was granted bail to appear again in two weeks time.

Just before his reappearance Geoff was given the same choice as before. He chose to plead not guilty. The counsel looked askance. The notion entered my mind to say to him that I knew that in law drunkenness was not usually a sound basis for arguing lack of intent, but what was the position on other drugs which affected the mind? The legal adviser did not stop to give me a reply. He addressed the court with the argument that not only had Geoff had no intent, he had not even had 'an intent to have an intent'. Geoff was acquitted by the two magistrates (a criminologist and a university administrator).

The social construction of dying I take it as axiomatic in the field of social work that a client does not accept help without embarrassment when the helper is no wiser in the ways of the world than himself. Embarrassment is particularly likely when the help comes spontaneously, as in this case, rather than from long experience of the client's problems. But whatever the reason, Geoff seemed to be seeking me out less often than before the court case. Meanwhile, I considered, as I wrote in an earlier draft of this book, written in this period, that Geoff had little hope of physical survival unless he received proper medical attention, which, indeed, he was more than willing to obtain.

I therefore contacted various individuals and agencies but, alas, with very little useful response. A full account would go into many pages. Here, however, it may be important to set down a few of the cultural premisses of general practitioners whom I approached which structured their belief system regarding methadone addiction.

Firstly, we may recall Mills's (1959) concept of 'the sociological imagination', according to which a task of the sociologist - and the citizen - is to find the social problems behind 'private troubles'. The GPs I approached expressed a mode of thought remarkably similar to that of Mills, though in a form he would probably have regarded as grotesque. If Geoff was not able to get better in fourteen days, I was informed, then his trouble was an incurable disease which, however, was 'social' rather than 'medical' and, therefore, beyond the province of medical science. I found it curious to come across the notion of a social disease, once applied to VD, reappearing in the 1980s.

Secondly, I was confronted with what anthropologists, in particular, call 'secondary explanation', a second order premiss which functions to preserve a first order premiss to which one is even more attached. If Geoff did not respond to treatment then some inappropriate factor must have been operating, of which the most likely would be Geoff's having taken more than the 'correct' dosage. With the aid of this secondary explanation the premiss that the treatment was completely adequate remained intact. It may be noted, however, that attachment to such a premiss seemed to exclude proper consideration of the tendency, discussed in the medical literature, for the effectiveness of methadone at any given dosage to decrease over time.

Thirdly, I was faced with the principle which Becker calls 'the hierarchy of credibility', whereby the amount of credence given to a person's actual or putative statements depends on his social status. One way in which this principle was applied was in the allegation by GPs that Geoff could not have given the consultants at the clinic the whole story. Here GPs seemed to view senior colleagues as passive receivers of information rather than as professional persons who enter into dialogue with their clients.

Fourthly, there was the notion of what one might call an 'ecology of curability'. Like the police, though in a different manner, some GPs urged that Geoff should get out of town. Only in a large city would he find physicians who might be prepared to hospitalise him for an appropriate period, rather than in Cambridge, where there are few places for hospital patients. It would seem that there are varying zones of incurability.

Fifthly, GPs not only presented themselves as advisers in human traffic control; they were also deeply involved in what might be called 'the neutralisation of politics'. One GP, for example, near retirement age, regretted the good old days when there were large asylums (his term) which were 'thrown open to all'. Thus, a social problem is seen as the result of bad (presumably 'administrative') policies, the decline of the asylum, rather than of bad politics, such as public spending cuts. In any case, it is arguable whether asylums have declined. I assisted Geoff to keep out of an asylum, prison, the number of whose inmates has increased steeply practically every year in the last decade.

Geoff's final asylum was a wooden shed in a Cambridge cemetery. The shed burnt to the ground not long after his final court case, and his body was identified by forensic experts. A council official spoke of 'no problems with tramps in the cemetery, although in the summer people probably did bed down there occasionally'.

I trust that our detailed, though short, case study of Geoff has not diverted us from some of our main themes, with which it may be useful to renew contacts at this juncture.

We are reminded of how circumscribed any study of an organisation and its work tends to be if in analysis they are dissected from the wider social structure. Light cannot be expected to operate in a house whose wiring has been disconnected from the national grid. Thus, we have seen how the medical services of the state provide methadone for the treatment of an opiate addict or proto-addict but do not provide adequate treatment for withdrawing from the medication. Such a state of affairs, deriving from the political economy, cannot be explained in terms of medical norms, which have little coherence and themselves call for explanation in macrosociological terms. Still less can gross anomalies in the medical services be the responsibility of a small, inexperienced rehabilitative outfit such as the Unit, for what limited powers it had, such as processing people, enabling Geoff, for example, to obtain methadone more quickly, and more officially, than would otherwise have been the case, were as likely to worsen the plight of the client as to ameliorate it. The greatest service which the Unit rendered Geoff was probably supplying him with accommodation when he came out of prison.

Geoff's case also sharply reminds us of the principle that a minimum of 'a three year reconviction [or reoffending?] rate for "old boys" might be considered the most appropriate measure of a regime's performance' (Sinclair 1971, p.73). Money is wasted on evaluation studies which compromise with this principle. Our case study of Geoff also, incidentally, emphasises the distinction between evaluation and the allocation of blame. It is not the task of a sociologist to be a Commission of Enquiry. His/her work is to elucidate 'how the system works', if, indeed, that is what it does. There is far too much guilt in crime, justice, education and rehabilitation already. Moreover, if any blame has to be dispensed then I am as much entitled to it as anybody for my interference in Geoff's problems in his final months. My plea of mitigation is that, in such intervention, something was intended to be learnt which could be applied to ameliorating the welfare of fellow citizens, including, I hoped, Geoff himself.

Geoff emphasises for us again, and in a particularly sharp way, the deleterious effects of overcommitment to education for the rehabilitation of offenders. He, perhaps more than any other student we have studied, seemed to have devised a foolproof shock absorber to those deleterious effects by treating the Unit as a colony of his prison routine, thus cushioning himself against the strain of discontinuity between education in the prison environment and education in the environment of the outside world. Defence mechanisms, it seems, almost invariably break at an individual's weak points when he is subjected to such strains as highly competitive education. Such breakage raises policy issues which, I consider, are probably not restricted to ex-offenders. If, as policy makers still sometimes claim, punishment does not need to be retributive, embittering those who are caught in the dragnet of the criminal justice system, does learning necessarily have to be so intense and competitive, crushing the best endeavours of those who are dedicated to perform well in the educational system?

NOTES

[1] 'As Malcolm was the first person with whom I had the full experience of the physical act of sex,

some people might consider that he seduced me, since he was thirty-two and I was sixteen. But to my mind a statement like that would be ridiculous: the fact that he was the first was purely coincidental. It could be said too I suppose that in the same way I seduced Peter since he was fourteen and I was eighteen. Yet I knew him for over six months before the subject of sex even arose, and by then we were so much in love with each other that what took place was no more than a logical progression of what already existed ... that's why I've stayed in London since I came out of prison. If I were to go back there, I couldn't very well help running into him before long and then we'd be back where we started. He's seventeen and I'm still under twenty-one, so the change in the law about homosexual behaviour wouldn't cover us' (Parker 1969, p.113).

[2] Niederhoffer (1969, p.130) studied 186 policemen and asked them to rank sixteen categories of people with whom they had to deal from those they disliked the most to those they liked the most. Juvenile gangs and drug addicts were among the categories included. Homosexuals came out as the second most disliked group, after 'cop-fighters' (cited in Plummer 1975, p.109).

[3] 'Joyce Laing, the art therapist, was coming in from time to time and though we were very wary of the therapy bit we liked her coming as she was a pretty good looking bird. So we had to compromise and pretend to have an interest in art in order to keep her coming back. One day she brought in a 7 lb bag of clay for us to mess around with and the five of us sat there humouring her and having a good laugh till such time as she had to leave ... The day was hot and we sat in the prison yard and I sat messing with the material doing a portrait of one of the guys. I liked it and that was what mattered ... and knew that I had stumbled onto something inside myself. It was tremendously exciting to discover this latent talent, especially in art as this had been poofy stuff to me in the past' (Boyle 1977, p.250).

[4] 'In October 1973, I was allowed out to attend college on a sociology course ... When I arrived in the classroom ... I began almost to sweat with fear and embarrassment. I did not know whether to sit down or stand up. I felt at one point that my panic would take over and that I would just flee from the room and go back to prison' (Probyn 1977, pp.219-20).

[5] A friend who was with me most of the day reminds me that 'perhaps it would be worthwhile recording the frequent visits to the WC brought on by his extreme anxiety throughout the visit'.

9 Case Studies of Students who Rehabilitated

A. <u>ADAM: 1;PP,PS</u>

Adam grew up in Liverpool at a time when Mays (1954, p.81) reckons that three-quarters of all juveniles in the city were delinquent, and in a part of the city which produced three-quarters of all official juvenile delinquents in Liverpool (ibid., p.82). He was of English birth and descent, but most of his neighbours were black, and when fights took place between blacks and whites he sided with the former.

During the period of Adam's upbringing, school 'didn't mean anything' to him. Looking back, he said that middle class kids went to middle class schools, working class kids to working class schools and ghetto kids to ghetto schools. The eleven plus meant that if you passed you went to a 'posh' school, otherwise you stayed with your 'comrades'. [1] (Similarly, Mays (ibid., p.74) refers to 'the aversion many young men expressed to standing for promotion during their military service. To take a stripe is to become "different," to lose one's pals and be cut off from "going with the boys"'.)

Adam learnt his first lessons in crime from the window cleaner. In his early teens, Adam robbed with other whites, but avoided them at other times lest, if they were caught, he might be arrested; thus conforming to the common pattern whereby criminals minimise their contacts with accomplices (e.g., Maurer 1949, p.298). The money which Adam derived from crime he used mainly for clothes, so that, unlike many other youths, he could, for instance, walk in shoes without holes. He thus acquired high status, but he found the 'hierarchical competition' with which it was associated annoying. He went out with prostitutes older than himself. This increased his status further, but, in compensation, he felt on a level of equality with these women, rather than in a position of dominance, which would have been the case if he had been older.

School offered little of educational interest. Adam

recalls science lessons as typified by endlessly repeated experiments to produce salt by boiling saltwater. Teachers often attacked pupils with sticks, and, unburdened by the middle class conception of punishment as the withdrawal of approval or the inculcation of guilt (Green 1946), he retaliated. At one point he was sent to Detention Centre for three months, but when he returned to the ghetto school he made it clear that he was doing so on his own terms. The teachers were apparently not loth to meet them. Instead of lessons he was assigned other school tasks. One of the most profitable to himself and his kin was delivering school milk to the classrooms, an excellent opportunity for fiddling.

When Adam reached fifteen there seemed to be only two alternatives: factory or crime. Factory was completely ruled out: 'Factories don't attract me now, and they didn't attract me then, and there was just no way I was going to be factory fodder'. Adam's attitude to factory work was remarkably similar to that of the jack-roller:

> I didn't know how to do anything but steal. Manual labor was my only choice, and I thought I was above that, and, besides, it was monotonous and poor pay ... I was no fool, to be kidded by the circumstances of life into manual labor and a life of slavery to fill the pockets of grafters and snobbish people (Shaw 1930, pp.160-1).

The us/them relationship which had prevailed in school continued on the street between Adam's friends and the 'filth' (police). The latter normally arrived in groups of six and picked on one boy. One day that boy was Adam. He fought them for more than ten minutes before being taken away. The event turned him into a hero, a 'superfuck'. The street would be saying for a long time afterwards, 'He fought six of the filth on his own for ten minutes before they took him away'.

Incarceration meant that the us/them relationship became an even more prominent part of Adam's existence. 'They' used both the stick and the carrot, and he disregarded both. If he had agreed to such arrangements as remission for good behaviour he would have given in to 'them', an unworthy bargain.

Adam's imprisonment prior to coming to Cambridge was for a variety of charges, the most serious of which was conspiracy to rob. He was shoved about by prison officers and threatened with deterrents, but he lashed out every time against his tormentors. As a result, he spent his custody in Dartmoor Prison in almost permanent solitary confinement, which was repeatedly renewed by the Board of Visitors. This regime meant spending twenty-three hours a day in a damp, verminous cell measuring seven feet by twelve, with only a concrete block for furniture. Horrible as life was, psychiatrists found no evidence of mental disorder.

Having spent nearly twenty months in solitary confinement, with the exception of eighteen days, Adam smuggled out a letter to The Sunday Times. The story was taken up by other newspapers, some of which showed pictures of his exercise yard, which looked precisely like a lion's cage, with iron bars curved and spiked at the top.

When questioned about the cockroaches and other features of the cell about which Adam complained, the Home Office stated, 'In fairness to all concerned ... Dartmoor weather can be hot and muggy, and on these occasions the atmosphere will be as damp as anywhere else in the Dartmoor area. It is heated efficiently and inspections disclose none of the nuisances suggested'. More than a decade after Adam was sent to Dartmoor a young prisoner committed suicide there. Investigative journalism then revealed that he had been petitioning the Home Office about damp and cold conditions (The Guardian 15/12/78, p.2).

Apparently as the result of the publicity Adam received he was released from solitary confinement two months later and transferred to Hull Prison. As he arrived there he was photographed by the press, with prison officers submissively carrying his belongings.

In Hull, Adam played a prominent part in sit-ins, strikes and demonstrations, with searchlights and a large number of officers continuously glaring at his cell. Adam reckons that in this prison, which makes more use of solitary confinement than any other British prison (Hymphrey and May 1977, p.8), he was costing the prison system an additional £1000 a day.

Throughout most of Adam's imprisonment the pattern of polarised violence continued. Several times he was truncheoned to unconsciousness. He sometimes thought that eventually they might kill him. He did not want to die, but he was strengthened by the thought that, if he did, they would have defeated his body but not his mind. [2] When they chained him to the wall and kicked his testicles he spoke to them in what Adam called a language which they understood: 'Look, what you are doing is only making me hate you more, and the more I hate you the less I'm going to love you, and the more scared you are going to be, and the more black eyes you are going to take home at some later time'.

As time went on, however, Adam came to perceive that the warders were only part of a wider social system. It was that system that he would have to be ready to fight. He started by preparing to take on the governor. Not long after such preparation the assistant governor was imprudent or vain enough to call at his cell without the preliminary precaution of having Adam physically restrained and searched

- a procedure, however, which would have involved further violent resistance and possible loss of consciousness. In this interview with the assistant governor, the weapon of hate, constructed from a toothbrush and a razor blade, was produced at the right moment and put to use.

In prison, Adam became a man of thought as well as of action. [3] When they gave him The Daily Express and other right wing newspapers he read closely between the lines. He applied the same scrutiny to the 'library' cupboard. A book which affected him most particularly glorified the terrible story of British colonialism in India. He came to realise that the social system of which he was part was itself part of a wider, global system, and in the latter he identified with oppressed black people. When he came out of prison he would participate in the liberation struggle in Africa. This 'conversion' is similar to one expressed by a prisoner in San Quentin:

> All these years, man, I have been stealing and coming to this joint. I never stopped to think why I was doing it. I thought that all I wanted was money and stuff. Ya know, man, now I can see why I thought the way I did. I been fucked all my life and never realized it. The white man has been telling me that I should want his stuff. But he didn't give me no way to get it. Now I ain't going for his shit anymore. I'm a black man. I'm going to get out of here and see what I can do for my people. I'm going to do what I can to get those white motherfuckers off my people's back (Irwin 1970, p.81).

In a letter of 21 May 1974, Adam wrote to Ron:

> *I may appear reluctant to discuss my long-term plans, this is not because they lack precision, on the contrary much thought has gone into my future and it is now quite definite ... I'm acutely aware that to give total involvement, to make a real active contribution to my cause I'm going to require much more knowledge ... Which brings me to my interest, in one word - Africa, or more precise colonised and oppressed Africa, ie Guinea-Bissau, Angola, South Africa and primarily Mozambique and Rhodesia.*

By the time Ron went to give Adam a preliminary interview the prison had practically capitulated to him. The governor had conveyed to him that for the remainder of his sentence he could do what he wanted provided he did not give his officers any trouble. Adam told the governor that he wanted to do physical training, and asked for a heavy object to carry on his back. Each day around the exercise yard he endlessly ran, the product of stolen school milk and an iron will, until his custodians grew tired or hungry. [4] When prison officers conducted him to the room set aside for the interview with Ron, the latter found them virtually bowing and scraping and Adam treating them with contumely.

Within days of his release Adam made more political contacts in Cambridge than Ron said that <u>he</u> had made in all the years he had lived there and been a member of one of the main British political parties. The inertia and introversion which Adam saw in the students coming to live in the Unit he had no difficulty in explaining. Each had at some point or at many forfeited his spirit to the social system in order to enjoy the carrot or avoid the stick; the social system might need to cosset such products for a long time to come.

Adam negotiated terms with the Unit with the same spirit of independence as he had with the prison from which he had just departed. As a grown man he was not interested in syllabuses, curricula and examinations designed for schoolboys and schoolgirls. He informed Ron of the areas of knowledge he wished to study, and Ron accordingly obtained for him university lecturers from the University of Cambridge and the London School of Economics with whom he could study such subjects of his choice. One newspaper reporter wrote:

> Ernest Miles, fellow and tutor of Princely College, talks of a "thirst for knowledge" shown by his particular charge, Adam (28), in the special liberal studies course arranged for him. With no formal educational contact for the last 14 years, Adam is particularly interested in post-colonial Africa. "His first essay was quite slender, but the second one filled 45 pages. We are now past Nkrumah, and are having a go at China. He has an enormous thirst for knowledge under the general rubric of revolution, a need to identify with a minority other than his own [Miles thought Adam was of Irish extraction]. He is a student who will read anything I suggest - it was merely a question of throwing him the tool-kit and leaving him to get on with it".

Adam considered that since his release he was offered sham deals many times. Ron asked him if he would like to live in the Unit. But Adam saw its cellular living arrangements as just another prison. Prison had given him strength of purpose but he did not need it anymore. (Of our total population of forty-five Adam thus became the first of three clients who was never a resident in the Unit.) Ron and Doug invited him to the official opening: his background and determination would impress the newsmen. Adam turned the invitation down. [5] The admissions tutor of one of the University of Cambridge colleges offered him a place for the following year on condition that he did not visit the guerrilla camps in Mozambique, thus putting the college in danger of bad publicity. Adam told the tutor that he could keep the place - he would be visiting the guerrilla camps. The tutor, accustomed to candidates abasing themselves for a place, reconsidered the matter and offered Adam a place unconditionally.

Adam accepted, thus, like many 'mature' students, bypassing normal entry requirements, and later graduated with an upper second class honours degree. This outcome was totally at variance with earlier prophecies about Adam's future attainments by Ron. In a letter of 17 September 1974, for example, requesting the Cambridgeshire Education Authority for a grant for Adam, Ron wrote, 'It is unlikely that in a conventional sense Adam will gain any academic qualifications'. The assessment was perhaps partly affected by the fact that Adam completely failed the inane Heim 'aptitude' test. Of the twenty-one students of the first three years who took it only three scored fewer marks.

As an undergraduate, Adam met a medical student at a women's rights advice centre where they were both doing voluntary work. They settled down and married. She is the daughter of a wealthy Tory and former Cambridge mayor. In his intimacy with a woman of high status, Adam thus reproduced the kind of relationship which he had had with prostitutes in Liverpool, and, indeed, I have not seen a home run on more egalitarian lines.

When I asked Adam if the Unit had been useful to him he replied that he had his goals and the means which he used were secondary. There were always means of gaining education if one was forceful enough - Robert Mugabe gained it, and degrees to go with it, in Rhodesian detention camps. Adam said that he was studying history because he needed to understand the forces behind the contemporary world in which he wished so actively to participate. He contrasted his situation with that of other undergraduates who studied the subject because their school teachers had told them that that was what they should do and who suffered from parental pressure. He said that he did well in examinations because knowledge was more important than obtaining a degree, whereas so many of the other candidates suffered from nerves. He used the analogy of tennis: when you play to win your muscles tighten up; when you feel relaxed and detached you gradually improve your performance.

Throughout Adam's undergraduate days in Cambridge, Ron regarded him with increasing hostility, a great misfortune considering how much Ron might have learnt about education and rehabilitation from Adam. Once, after a fierce argument about Africa (and only a few days after Ron had included Adam as one of the Unit's successes in a report to the Home Office), Ron sententiously described him to me as congenitally subhuman. This judgement needs to be explored further, especially in terms of differences in orientation to education and rehabilitation between Ron and Adam, for it was strikingly in contrast to a judgement of Ernest Miles, who, when he wrote a testimonial for Adam for a University of Cambridge place, expressed reservations about his excessive humanity:

> He has made a lot of social contacts already in Cambridge and has been exceptionally sensitive

> and supportive in dealing with some of their difficulties. He seems to be the kind of man whom others seek out for objective advice. In a college situation it might be as well to warn him early on about being exploited too often by others in this fashion.

Ron's hostility to Adam appeared to derive from the feeling of being threatened which middle class people experience when individuals from the lower strata become too uppity for their comfort and refuse their patronage. More specifically, Adam's educational programme was largely under his command, being part of his greater programme in life. As we have seen, by contrast, the residents of the Unit became from year to year increasingly under the command of <u>its</u> educational programme.

We are confronted once again with the distinction between commitment and situational adjustment. It is interesting to note, therefore, that my records show that whenever staff members used the word 'commitment' they tended to equate it with situational adjustment, taking traditional pupil roles and organisational expectations as their reference points. Ron, for example, viewing Adam after nearly three years at the University of Cambridge, saw him as uncommitted to education! He referred to the fact that Adam started university terms as late as possible and ended them as early as possible because of his other activities. He considered that Adam would not return from a leave of absence which he had just taken for the purpose of active service in Africa. Ron thus contrasted Adam with Ken: 'Adam never placed himself in the hands of his teachers. He tried to use them cleverly. Ken sat at people's feet, he committed himself'. Ron was unable to foresee that just about as soon as Ken budged from the Unit's specialised educational environment to which he had overadjusted he would feel confused about the right way to place himself in people's hands or sit at their feet or perform any other kind of body ritual and that his overcommitment would eventually result in severe maladjustment. Ron was unable to see that Ken was, as it were, undercommitted to himself, being led by others to a future disaster, whereas Adam, on the other hand, had no lack of self-confidence, using the university, and its expertise in such subjects as neo-colonialism, revolution and the dominant trends in human history, as any clever - and self-confident - citizen might use the resources of a public library.

Ron's comparison between Adam and Ken was confused but, nevertheless, exceedingly apt. In a letter from prison of 12 April 1981, Ken wrote, '*I think you are wrong to adopt Philip Bean's definition of rehabilitation. The fact is that I'm "leading a more law abiding life" now*'. In no way has Ken's academically induced preoccupation with semantics diminished. The more significant point, however, is what

Ken's statement seems to reveal about his conception of rehabilitation. For Ken, it seems to be a matter of being under institutional control, rather than having the freedom to choose commitments in life which happen to be lawful. Indeed, I would not be at all surprised to learn that Ken, in sharp contrast to Adam, rarely if ever breaks the law in prison. But who will ensure that he will be kept under control when he is discharged from prison? Moreover, if he is again placed under control after he is discharged what will happen when he is again released from such control?

But Adam also provides a striking contrast to so many of the Unit's other clients, in terms of autonomy, lack of anxiety and self-esteem. Moreover, one can hardly avoid seeing the connection between these attributes and the stance which he maintained in prison. As we discussed earlier, courts and prisons had exerted on most of the students a conception of themselves as very discreditable individuals whom society could not tolerate. Adam had refused to accept this definition of the situation and had taken no part in the desperate, individualistic status competition, either in violence or in formal education, going on between other prisoners. He had directed all his violence against his imprisoners and had despised prison intellectuals as people who readily associated with the authorities, who tended to be chosen for demeaning 'privileges' such as setting the table with knives and forks, and who could not be relied on when it came to collective assault against the prison system. He had not competed, he had opposed, and his refusal to submit, regardless of the amount of corporal punishment he received, had kept his self-respect intact. He had even persuaded other prisoners to do likewise, pointing out to them, for example, that prison officers may subject prisoners to pain but must avoid wounding or disfigurement, as occurs in fights between prisoners, and using this point as an argument for the power which the imprisoned possess in being able to call the bluff of prison officers' threats, thus undermining their morale and legitimacy and maintaining one's own (cf. Biko 1978, pp.152-3).

In the more than seven years since Adam was released from prison no further convictions have been recorded against him, and to the best of my knowledge he has not reoffended in any significant way. At one point, he had a fight with another undergraduate, but I did not question Adam about the matter. I considered that I was in no position to judge the rights and wrongs of the incident and that discussion about what had provoked him would be an intrusion into our conversations about greater provocations which had shaped his life from the time when he was a truant and a hero in a subculture in northern England till becoming an educated comrade with those who have been directly or indirectly oppressed by a superculture in southern Africa.

B. <u>AVA: 1Y,2,3↓;PCo,PCh</u>

Ava explains her extremely short criminal career in terms of 'rebellion'. It is an explanation which appears to her self-evident, requiring no second order explanation. Rebellion is a phase which, in her view, everyone goes through. Questions about how she came to be more rebellious than other adolescents were equally pointless to her: people differ in all kinds of ways. I decided to accept her starting point, her 'rebellion', and probe for no preceeding causes.

Ava conducted her rebellion on both fronts, home and school. At school, her main weapon was supplied by the teachers themselves, the high regard which they had for her intelligence: 'All the teachers used to say, "Gosh, she's really clever, yet she's rejecting it all, we don't know why, you've got the ability to go to university"'. Her parents were similarly obliging in supplying her with ammunition to use against them:

MG: When did you first take any kind of drug?

Ava: When I was about fifteen, nearly sixteen.

MG: What were the circumstances at the time?

Ava: I think somebody knew somebody else. It was grass. It all started with dress at first - dressing hippie 'cos we wanted to rebel against home and school. We went to places where hippies congregate, to pubs and things like that they go to. You don't consciously say you want to rebel, but your parents see a scruffy person in the street and say, 'Gosh, look at the state of that!', and you dress like it and your parents say, 'You're not going out like that, are you?'.

MG: Who dressed like a hippie first, you or your friend?

Ava: We both did really. I would never have done it on me own. It was only 'cos there were two of us trying to enter this kind of group, me and Nicola. So we started smoking grass with them. They were probably people who were quite well known to the police and things, stealing for their drugs.

MG: If you hadn't dressed like they did would you have been able to get in with them?

Ava: I don't think so, 'cos even when we did dress like them it took a long time to be accepted by them 'cos we didn't like to be dirty like they were. Our dresses and things were always nice and clean. We didn't have greasy hair and things like that. Our hair was always nice and clean.

MG: How did you feel, being with them but not completely like them?

Ava: It just seemed a harmless lark at the time. But to any kind of grownups who saw you in the street you were like them, you were one of them.

MG: Did you ever move closer towards them as time went on?

Ava: No, I was always in some sort of contempt of them, even while I was kind of stoned, and getting picked up and things like that.

Ava's rebellion, however, seemed to draw no counter-attack from her parents, still less a truce on new terms. Her parents had drawn contemptuous attention to strange hippies whom they passed on the street. But her parents failed to give her the amount of attention she seemed to be seeking when she put on the guise of the people they disdained. Her parents' refusal to label her, or to be drawn into any kind of strong emotional response, seemed to amplify her deviance and make her psychological battles increasingly determined:

MG: How did you feel when you smoked it and nothing happened?

Ava: It was just done for show ... There was no euphoria, it was just so we could say we had done it. That was more important than the feeling you got from it ... They would never ask ... It was the unspeakable subject. They must have guessed I was taking it but they never actually said anything. Rather weird when you think about it. I remember coming in once when I was on LSD. I was sitting in front of the telly, laughing, tears running down my face. They must have known.

After one of her arrests, Ava was given a court order sending her to a mental hospital. This measure led to at least three psychological consequences. Firstly, her parents had no legal power to have her discharged. As a result she fell into a state of depression centred around the feeling that she had been completely abandoned. [6] Secondly, this incarceration left a worrisome scar on her mind. For years afterwards she felt anxiety that her deviant behaviour might be symptomatic of mental illness. Thirdly, she reacted with remorse:

> I went into Epsom, and Gosh, that was enough to shock anybody ... I thought, 'Oh, I've got to get out of here. I'm not going to take drugs again.'

This last reaction may have been gratifying to the authorities, but it was short term and superficial. Her hospitalisation seems to have been entirely counterproductive. For it did not produce any resolution of Ava's adolescent conflicts, moving her from irresponsible 'harmless larks' to any kind of pride in the acquisition of some acknowledged adult responsibility. Quite the contrary, it made her look back at her remorse as a sign of childishness and a pre-rebellion mentality:

> I only said, 'I'm not going to do that again' in

> Epsom 'cos I was in a loony bin, and it was a childish impulse to not want to do it again.

It was most unlikely that such an outlook would lead to any diminution of her 'rebellion'. Moreover, even if it had, she now felt no sense of invitation to return to one of the mainstream paths of reaching maturity:

> Then, even if I'd wanted to, which I didn't, I was known by people at school and that to be a kind of hippie, dropout and all. So even if I'd wanted to get in with respectable people I couldn't have - I didn't want to at the time anyway.

The result was that Ava was now immersed in 'secondary deviation' (Lemert 1967, ch.3), because drugs now had to be called upon to fight boredom, as well as the tensions of increased parental contact:

> There was no pressure from the hippies. I hated the situation I was in at home, and taking drugs was just the easiest way out. It wasn't so much rebellion then, I just couldn't cope with being bored and things like that.

Not long afterwards, Ava was convicted for possessing drugs stolen from a doctor's surgery. She was sentenced to a Community Service Order, and sent to nurse handicapped children in a special school. In terms of rehabilitation, this measure seems to have been entirely positive. Since its effect is so often the reverse, it requires a little further discussion.

People who have served Community Service Orders with whom I have discussed them tend to regard them as a fraudulent 'con'. They are subjected to the ideology that because of their offence they must make reparations to the community. But frequently they cannot see what they have taken from the 'community'. Also, even, let us say, when they have robbed Peter they can perceive neither logic nor justice in having to pay Paul. Moreover, since the 'service' which they are called upon to perform is often work for which people are paid the 'servant' considers that he himself is being robbed, quite apart from the possibility that, at the behest of the court, they may be robbing others of job opportunities. Moreover, many individuals, such as Ken, who are given a Community Service Order have long criminal records. It seems patent to them and, I would speculate, to many judges, that the order is one of a variety of forms of punishment which the court, at its discretion, may elect to apply. The Service which the offender is then called upon to perform, however, is often of a kind which would ordinarily be praiseworthy. The offender, therefore, feels bitterly that he is being insulted for doing as a punishment what he might otherwise be admired for. Further, if he _is_ praised for the work then he feels that he is being patronised, for he is, in fact, doing it under duress. Moreover, he is denied any form of expression of these feelings of alienation, for, after all, what right does he have to complain? Damiens the regicide (Foucault 1977, pp.3-6), subjected in 1757 to extremely cruel torture, seemed, according to his dying utterances, to have seen more sense in his punishment than many offenders seem to find in Community Service Orders. The latter seem, as the present case study indicates, to have positive aspects for certain offenders. By and large, however, the Order seems to be an example of the way in which Royal Commissions and legislators assume that what makes sense to them must necessarily make sense to offenders of all categories.

But Ava's definition of the situation seems to have been quite different and, indeed, something of a relief in its simplicity. She has never considered herself a criminal or even a hippie. The most salient feature of her Order was that it provided an agreeable opportunity to get away from home, without the implication that she might be insane and with a minimum of any other kind of stigma. Moreover, she seems to have been subjected to very little gratuitous ideology, possibly because the social value of the work which she was doing was patent. In looking after handicapped children she felt a definite sense of adult responsibility, and she looks back at this short interlude in her life with a great deal of self-satisfaction.

With the termination of the order, Ava's probation officer suggested the proposal of applying to the Unit rather than returning home. The idea appealed to Ava for two reasons. Firstly:

> I wanted to continue my education 'cos I left school a year earlier than I should have, and I regretted it.

She could now return to formal education in an area away from home and where she would not be seen as a dropout respectfully knocking on the door to be allowed to drop back in. The Unit thus seemed to her a most propitious staging post.

Secondly, the Unit also presented itself to her as a colony of her 'near group' (Yablonsky 1972, p.306), the hippie deviants back in her home town of Swindon, thus enabling her to maintain her deviant individuality if she so wished:

> I liked being with a bunch of ex-cons. I thought it was quite a ... you know. I've never had any criminal tendencies myself as such like the people in the Unit, and it was something out of the ordinary.

Unfortunately, Ava did not examine the feasibility and mutual compatibility, or otherwise, of these two projected prospectuses. But the drawbacks she had not contemplated soon became evident. The major problem was loneliness:

MG: Did you identify yourself at any time with the other people in the Unit?

Ava: No, I saw them as more or less like the people I had been with ... I kept to myself and only heard other people in the Unit ... I never really got close to anyone at the Unit at all.

Back home, Ava had had a friend to help her to mix with the deviant group, but this was no longer the case. As she pointed out in 1977 (and while living with Ken):

> Nicola moved to London and that was the end. We corresponded once or twice but we were moving in opposite directions. And besides, there was so much opposition. One of the stipulations of the sentence was that we didn't meet or correspond. She was my only friend really over the past couple of years.

Another problem about the Unit was that it did not provide her with a movement back into the mainstream as smooth as she had imagined. At the beginning of the Unit's second year, she was enrolled in the Young Street College of Further Education, but the stigma of living in the Unit resulted in her being just as lonely at the college:

> I didn't want to tell anyone where I lived, and I didn't want to invite anyone back. Well I could have - it wouldn't bother me now, but then it did. It was then that I saw the disadvantages.

Because Ava 'could not relate to college' Ron resorted to the device of providing private teachers for her with whom she was to work under Ron's ultimate supervision. The difficulty here, though, was that Ava appears to have regarded Ron as an authority figure, who could trigger off moods of rebellion again. Moreover, neither he nor her teachers gave her the kind of companionship which she yearned for:

> I was completely on me own. I had been under the impression that someone would be living there, which is what I would have preferred ... I had the vision of someone on my level, perhaps someone who had been in prison and come out, not someone like Ron, an authoritarian person, being there. I envisaged someone more with it [in touch with ordinary people and/or new lifestyles]. His <u>manner</u> and being a lot older, and you thought, 'What does he know about drugs and things like that?'. And you thought, 'Look, public schoolboy'. I mean you could tell by the way he spoke, that's what you can't relate to.

There were other factors militating against educational commitment. For example, few of the second year students were coping educationally or rehabilitatively, and Ava, being impressionable, felt little motivation to be the

Unit's star pupil. She spent some time in the company of Leo, but he did not take long to move out of the Unit. Moreover, he was a homosexual, and the relationship did not go very deep. Whatever intellectual stimulation he gave her was not sufficient to encourage in her commitment to the Unit's educational programme. Thus:

> The decision not to continue my education was a gradual one really. Gradually it phased out until I was left doing one or two things, and then I wasn't doing anything really. It was a complete waste of time at the end. Besides, by that time I'd grown up a lot, and I felt secure enough to do something else, whereas before I hadn't really. I was influenced quite a lot by other people in the Unit. Nobody was seen to be into it, and there wasn't any initiative on my part either.

When Ron became concerned about Ava's lack of involvement in the second educational programme which he had provided for her since she came to the Unit she offered him plausible excuses, one of which was that she was trying to understand Archie, her first boyfriend in the Unit, and solving his problems. Ron did not exert any further pressure, which made her think him astonishingly gullible. The fact of the matter was that the other students were giving him far more trouble than she seemed likely to bring him, and their troubles with the law were making strong demands on his attention. Ava thus remained a resident of the Unit, although undercommitted to its educational programme, by means of the situational adjustment of offering Ron excuses which seemed plausible. Indeed, what little academic work she did was itself a pretext for continuing to live at the Unit:

> ... it became an excuse for somewhere to live, doing the education. I didn't want to move away 'cos it was the only place I knew really.

By the third year, even situational adjustment evaporated. She was allocated to the school and, for tutorials, to Stafford, a public schoolmaster. At the age of more than eighteen, she was not fired with enthusiasm to go back to school. When she and Ken moved out of the Unit he went on attending classes at the school punctually; she dropped out immediately and took a job as a nanny. Interestingly, once Ava had left the Unit, and felt no further danger of being controlled by it, she became close to Ron for the first time, the main occasion for their continuing to meet being babysitting for his children:

> I never really got close to Ron. Now is the closest I've ever got to him ... I feel that I speak to Ron as an equal, but then it was like being a child.

During this period, Ava also considered that she had developed a relationship of equality with her parents:

> When you're young you look at your parents as

figureheads, but when you grow up you realise they are people, and they feel the same things you feel. I feel paternal now towards my parents, 'cos they are going through a bad thing at the moment, on the verge of a split, and I'm the only one she can talk to and she talks to me as a friend really.

When Ken obtained a place at university she moved with him to the town where it was situated, and obtained a well paid job. After Ken was sent to different places under his Community Service Order, she remained in the town for some time on her own. It was a time for further reflection. She reviewed her relationship with Ken and saw his role as that of a companion rather than lover. Ken had been so troubled by anxiety that sex with him had been reduced to a short nightly ritual, similar, as she puts it, to putting out the rubbish each day. It was not long before she fell in love with a wholesale and retail butcher in her home town of Swindon and married him. The only shortcoming she sees in her marriage is insufficient intellectual stimulation. As a result, since her marriage, she often flatteringly invited me to visit them. Before long, however, she obtained another resolution of her need for broadening her mind which is more conventional. She became a part time student at a local college, studying at her own pace, and after a few months took an examination in English Literature just for the fun of it, passed, and thus obtained her first A level. But when she has other things to attend to she drops out and later drops in again. Interestingly, one reaction to this balanced approach to her personal cultural development brings out the extent of Ken's overcommitment to education even after some years of having given up university. For Ken and Ava write to each other, and everytime she takes a break from formal education he pours scorn on her. 'She hasn't changed much', he wrote after one of her breaks from college. He seems to find it impossible to conceive of the process of education as other than one of anxious intensity, and perhaps feels threatened when others take a more relaxed attitude.

We are left with the questions of whether and to what extent the Unit functioned to rehabilitate Ava now that she has long ago given up illegal drugtaking. For some might argue, and persuasively, that Ava would have rehabilitated eventually regardless of her experience in the Unit, as the following generalisation indicates:

> Many parents seek to "live through" or "wait out" their children's adolescence by not noticing what they do, hoping thereby to avoid painful emotion. (There is also a good measure of parental indifference.) Young people, of course, react to this strategy either by further withdrawal ... or by behaving in a way which will "make them pay attention." ... But sad to say, adults, if they are wise, will still have the last laugh; for the way of youth turns out to be deeply influenced

> by what their parents say and do, and by what they are. There is enough of his parents inside a young person, by virtue of early identifications and later positive and negative modeling so that his "independence" will often be, in reality, opposition; his delinquency or deviance, an acting out of parental fantasies; his noblest actions, the practice of what his parents merely preached (Sanford 1968, pp.180-1; emphasis his).

What evidence, therefore, might we adduce to support a hypothesis that the Unit had a rehabilitating effect on Ava?

Firstly, apart from the home for handicapped children, the Unit was, it seems, one of Ava's main resorts, whereby she left home when her relationship with her family and other people was a most disturbed one and returned after events and experience had smoothed it out. Had she remained at home her deviance might have further amplified, becoming immovably heavy:

MG: Had they offered you hard drugs before you were completely accepted by them would you have taken them?

Ava: Yeh! 'Cos I remember we used to really question this guy for ages and ages. He wouldn't, to protect himself if we got picked up, which we were bound to, 'cos we were young. They knew we were doing it for a kind of show ...

MG: Did they ever put pressure on you?

Ava: Oh no.

MG: Did you ever become dirty to please them?

Ava: No, not really. But this went on for a year or two. Things got worse at home, obviously. You just started staying out for days, not hours.

Thus, when I asked Ava, 'What were the main pluses of the Unit if any?', she replied, 'I could have been a lot worse off. It enabled me to leave home and grow up a lot quicker than I would have at home'.

Secondly, the Unit seems to have been an object lesson in the kind of person not to become. Soon after she left the Unit she said:

> I've seen the people in the Unit and what has happened to them and I've come to my own conclusions, whereas, if I'd lived at home it could have gone on for ages and ages.

Looking back at her period of residence in the Unit, soon after she quit it, Ava put her conversion in the idiom of maturation:

> I find the people in the Unit ... very immature ...

> But then they are living there and not really called upon to make decisions, etc. For example, Geoff. I asked him what he was doing, and he told me that he was not interested in anything but studying ... And then seeing Geoff smashed out of his mind in the kitchen and talking a load of rubbish and being silly, and you think, 'Awgh' ...

Ava felt the same reaction whenever she visited home and saw the deviants with whom she had once associated:

> I see them just the same and I think, 'Christ, they haven't passed out of that stage' ... I feel as if they're in a stage I went through as part of growing up. Everyone goes through something like that. I see them as really juvenile.

Since the time Ava left Cambridge she has not taken any drugs, apart from Valium (by prescription) during the trying period of transition from Ken to her husband, and the occasional glass (single) of bourbon whiskey.

It may be recalled that Durkheim (1964, ch.III) formulated the theory that, what we would nowadays call, the negative labelling of the lawbreaking behaviour of some people outrages others into correcting their own lawbreaking tendencies. In accordance with this theory, Ava negatively labelled other deviants, thus correcting her conduct in greater harmony with 'the collective consciousness'. The effect has recently been noted by Meisenhelder (1977, pp.323-4), in his reference to:

> The individual's symbolic use of older inmates as a sign of his own deteriorating situation ... Within inmate cliques, the offender experienced his potential future as acted out by older inmates ... 'My point of view changed ... you don't want to end up like some of these old timers been done all their life. They showed me what would happen if I didn't straighten out'.

(Normally, however, other effects of prison conspire to overwhelm this rehabilitative effect.)

At the beginning of this case study we found a rebellious, dependent, 'mixed-up' girl in middle teens desperately trying to draw attention to herself as no longer a child by refusing to conform and by associating with 'outsiders'. At the end, we found a respectably married, comparatively independent, relatively contented housewife living near her old home in Swindon. In her teens, she was in some danger of getting stuck or damaged at a significant point of her mortal career. The Unit was one of the resorts which lifted her up and put her back on the conveyor belt, with little harm done, at the place she would have reached if she had progressed along the conformist centre of life's journey. Anyone visiting Ava's home today would find nothing deviantly out of place, nothing very different from what one would expect the routines of couples in other houses on the estate to be like. Yet, within moments of meeting her, her conversation conjures with whether, when and how she, I, people we know, people I do not, have changed or have not, as if the society on which her imagination is projected were mostly populated by mortals in pubescence, menopause or the throes of personality transformation. The truth, as is so often the case, lies somewhere between the world view created by early experience and the social situation 'on the ground'. Her years of deviance, clientship and courtship involved a somersault which has left her head a little giddy though her feet stand firmly on the ground of ordinary life.

C. DES: 1X→3,2;PCo,PP

Des came to London at the age of fifteen with his mother from Kingston, Jamaica. His mother was active in a West Indian sect, but Des also learnt his values from his peers:

> In my old circle of friends to be a thief was the thing. You weren't one of the lads if you hadn't any convictions. I remember praying to God to let me go to DC [Detention Centre]. My friends used to say, 'Oh Des, you haven't been to DC, you've never had any experience'. I used to have idols - people who had done bird [prison] and had money to show for it, flash cars, etc.

Williamson (1978) claims that delinquent teenagers do not develop a desire to acquire a reputation for having 'done bird' until they have experienced it. He does not explain how those who have not experienced it remain uninfluenced by those who have. Nor does he provide any case study to support his assertion.

It took some time before Des's prayers were answered. In 1972, he was found guilty of unlawful possession of cannabis and fined. In 1973, he was found guilty of theft and fined. It was not till 1975 that, found guilty of theft, he was detained, in Borstal. Des's wish was thus fulfilled, but ironically. For Des claims that he did not commit the offence for which he was sent to Borstal, and his probation officer concurred, emphasising that his 'last conviction was secured due to identification evidence'. Des was released in 1976 but remained unemployed for several months. His probation officer suggested the Unit, and wrote to Ron saying that she considered that Des had been unable to obtain a job because of racial discrimination. Des thus came to the Unit at the age of twenty-three. He seemed to have a healthy level of commitment to the educational programme:

> Everyone likes to better himself. I've tried working. I've tried stealing and this is something else

> ... I wasn't doing anything. I'd probably end up in prison. So I thought I'd be better off here.

As we shall soon see, however, it was not long before Des became overcommitted. He did so for several reasons, not the least of which was what is often called 'Caribbean matrifocality'. In a letter from Des's probation officer she wrote:

> Mrs - is in the United States of America at present and it seems she intends to prolong her stay, possibly with a view to settling there. It seems, therefore, highly unlikely that Des will become or continue to be mother dependent.

But the probation officer may have exaggerated, as Des indicated in his references to his mother:

> She used to worry 'cos she spent a lot of money on me. So she expected me to be somebody. But then I got these convictions, and I must have caused her a lot of heartache. But the last time I heard from her she broke down in tears 'cos of this Unit and looking at life in a different way.
>
> My mother paid for me to go to one of the best schools in the country. I know that some of the friends I had in school got into the civil service and made something of their lives. They didn't leave the country. But I've been here six years. To go back to Jamaica without anything would be the worst thing. I say to myself, 'I'm suffering now in this Unit. I hope this is the worst possible break in my life, and after it will get better'.
>
> When my mother left Jamaica my grandmother used to look after me. My mother worked and used to buy me clothes, although she was a poor person. I'd like one day to be able to say to her, 'That's your home, mother'. I'll give her some pride. I wouldn't like to feel that I'm wasting my time in the Unit. If at the end of this year I haven't got anything to show for that year [pause], I don't know [pause], I'm beginning to realise that I'm twenty-three and in seven years time I'll be thirty.

Des hoped that he would obtain qualifications to obtain a place in university and a degree which would enable him to earn enough money in America in order to save enough capital to set up a business on his return to Jamaica. He expected that by the time he reached America his mother would be back in Jamaica. The tie between the Caribbean mother and child is often strong and enduring. It is the 'elementary structure' of a social network, a 'line' (Barnes 1972, p.5), the end points of which are held firmly together while the line itself may move across geographical space.

A second reason for Des's overcommitment may be related to the concept of a 'developmental cycle' of the Cambridge school of social anthropology (Goody ed. 1958). The concept has been fruitfully applied to the study of households, not least in the Caribbean area (e.g., Smith 1963). But developmental cycles apply not only to social phenomena, such as kinship, but also to cultural ones, such as honour and shame:

> My goal is to have enough money to support myself and my family, and be respected. I know a few people who are villains in this country and as soon as they get £X they go back to Jamaica, and the life of villainy is left in this country. They go up in society and people don't know, 'cos to be a thief in Jamaica is really degrading.
>
> I don't want anyone to sympathise with me. I've always had this dream ever since I was a small kid that I'm going to be somebody in life. Even in bed last night I thought, 'How will I make money?'.
>
> If you go back with money they respect you. But if you go back after, say, twenty years and you've nothing to show for it then Oh! There are people in this country living in council flats. They would like to go back to Jamaica, but they can't, because of their pride.
>
> I've got a lot of plans. I'll get my BSc. Then I'll go to the States and get a job, work for about five years, saving money, and then go to Jamaica. If you've got capital you can do all kinds of things which Jamaica hasn't got: laundromats, bingo halls, things the public will enjoy. But without qualifications it will take a lot longer, but I've always said to myself I'd rather die than live in poverty ... I've seen enough of it. I want to be respected and don't want anyone to look down on me.

In short, Des seemed to be an example of the principle that 'no man go home unless he rich. Everyone laugh at him'(Lawrie 1960, p.137).

In November 1976, Des failed an O level subject which his mentors had expected him to pass. As the year wore on he increasingly anticipated poor results in the June examinations. But Des coped with such stress in two ways. Firstly, instead of following other clients by turning to drink he surreptitiously (and illegally) smoked cannabis in front of his television to relieve each day's anxieties, thus using the Unit as a colony of one aspect of his usual lifestyle.

Secondly, he came to give less prominence to the significance of the Unit as a staging post, where 'I'm planning fifteen years ahead', and more prominence to its significance as a resort, where 'I don't feel the rat race'. Let us allow Des to elaborate on the rat race from which he was taking a break in Cambridge:

> Where I come from, Brixton, it's very competitive. Everybody is looking to make money and wearing good clothes, and if you look like a tramp people look down on you. So you'll do anything to make money. If you haven't got a suit from Harrods then you're lost. But now, well look at this jacket. I wouldn't be seen dead in it in London. She [girlfriend] came to my room once and she saw it hanging up and said, 'Des, where d'yeh get this?'.
>
> I don't like people feeling sorry for me. At the moment I'm just thinking about it. I've got this TV rental to pay, and they've got a letter about a TV licence upstairs [in the office]. I've got to pay £3 rentals, fare to London that makes £8. I'll be totally broke. That means I can't go nowhere. Normally, friends would come over and say, 'Des, we've got a cab outside, let's go to the West End and enjoy ourselves'. But this time they won't know I'm in London.
>
> If I'm broke I don't tell her I'm broke. Sometimes I lie to her and tell her I'm going to a party - these are parties all the villains go to and she knows they don't bring their personal girlfriends, only girls working for them. But I go straight home - I can't afford to buy Bacardi etc. I don't eat meals so as to [pause] - it's too depressing, let's talk about something else.

Here we find 'the market industrial system' most sharply defined, forever stimulating demands for 'good things within a man's reach but never all within his grasp' (Sahlins 1974, p.4). Here those who have not yet been able to obtain the fortune which they thought the mother country offered them, so that they could return to the country of their mothers with self-respect, either choose crime or become 'trapped in the white man's world by the same greed which once took them from Africa to make him rich and which now keeps them confined to the housing estates and wage labour of the urban plantation' (Dodd 1978, p.599).

From a criminogenic environment Cambridge offered Des respite, as it did for Ian. Des was committed to the Unit and to Cambridge as a resort in various ways:

> I feel relaxed in Cambridge - away from the action so to speak. Everybody here hasn't got any money either, so no-one can look down on you. I don't worry about clothes in Cambridge ... As long as you are clean and not scruffy you can do your own thing ... If this project were situated in London I could never do it.

Moreover, this commitment to Cambridge as a resort made Des more law-abiding:

> In Cambridge everybody is loose with their things.

> You don't have to be a professional pickpocket in Cambridge. But I wouldn't do it.

At the end of the Unit's third year Des passed one O level and narrowly missed passing two others. He did not accept Ron's offer to repeat a year at the Unit. He seemed to have decided to give work another try. For he applied for various jobs, both skilled and unskilled, and eventually obtained one as an accounts clerk. He then applied soon afterwards for a similar job with a British corporation because it was 'a more promising one as far as prospects go' and asked Ron to act as 'a personal referee of recognised standing'.

I was not in touch with Des for four years, partly because the corporation refused to disclose to me whether he was even still one of its employees. His former probation officer felt sure that he had gone back to Jamaica! I therefore tried to locate him residentially, starting off with the address he had before coming to Cambridge, a run down house in Brixton about to be demolished. Enquiries there led to another address, and from that one to another, until after five moves I located him. I feared that I would be regarded as an intruder from the past, whereas I was welcomed as a guest who could visit him and his fiancée with whom he was living anytime. He was, indeed, with the same corporation and had received repeated promotions; something which I had surmised, since the appearance of each dwelling I had called at seemed to represent successive rungs up the social ladder. He was committed to his work and had not reoffended, apart from cannabis, and had certainly not been reconvicted. It seemed that the Unit's processing of Des had compensated for the many insults he had received from British society, not least in Cambridge, where, while walking through town, he had been stopped and searched by the police several times for offensive weapons. It was a satisfactory reunion, though it left me wondering in how many young blacks in modern Britain personal experience had confirmed the view that:

> When you are doing crime ... anything can happen ... If I was still in crime you'd have to be very lucky unless you could lift an Arab's pocket. I wasn't into anything like armed robbery. I've known people living like millionaires, living in hotels with a lot of girlfriends and getting a lot of money from them, and they'd think they are God. Then something happens and they are busted and they go to jail for five years and come out penniless until they start something again.

There may be readers who consider that smoking cannabis is a worse crime than picking pockets. Such readers may wish to reallocate Des to the category of clients who did not rehabilitate.

D. Harry: 1Y,3;PP,PCo,PCh

Harry came to the Unit, at the age of twenty-one, about the same time as Des, and returned to London about the same time. I also followed him up after about the same interval of a little over four years.

Harry's attitude to life was in many ways strikingly in contrast to that of Des. Nothing could be further from his thoughts than planning his life fifteen years ahead. Des responded to my question, 'What changes in your life are you expecting while in Cambridge?' with 'I hope to buy a suit, which will cost £70. How can I get the money? Maybe I can save £5 a week for fourteen weeks'. I would not be surprised if Harry, 'scruffy' in appearance, would have regarded such a reply as absurd.

Harry had been a 'dropout' ever since schooldays, moving from job to job as the mood suited him, and taking various controlled drugs with little concern for the effect they might have on work responsibilities or on the chances of avoiding arrest. Arrest had, in fact, happened on a number of occasions, and had led to conditional discharge, a small fine, probation, a community service order and a suspended sentence. Finally, in the period before coming to the Unit, possession of drugs had led to Harry's being committed to Detention Centre. This was a placement which he hated and from which he could not easily drop out. Other detainees, however, were allowed leave for a short time in connection with their plans after discharge. To be permitted leave to be interviewed in Cambridge was exactly the reason 'if the truth be told' that Harry had applied to the Unit, where he subsequently took up his abode. Moreover, a residential project is one of a number of places to drop into and to drop out of again. Furthermore, the Unit enabled Harry to drop out further than usual by attenuating his links with his sister, his only close relative in Britain, the two having come from Ireland. The interview extract which follows indicates the extent to which the Unit presented itself to Harry as a colonial extension of a lifestyle which he had apparently led for some years:

MG: Why did you choose to come to the Unit?

H: I was working as a gardener for a local council and I was pretty fed up with that, so I thought this takes care of that, so I'd try it. I've nothing to lose. It's voluntary - and if I didn't like it I'd go back to squatting in London. I also wanted to see what Cambridge is like and what this place is like. Living here means that I didn't have to look around for a place to live.

MG: What were the disadvantages of coming to the Unit?

H: Having to commit myself, for a few months anyway, which I wasn't used to in a job or anything before.

MG: What changes have there been in your relationships with your family?

H: My eldest sister lives in London. We get on better now 'cos I'm not there all the time. Where I lived was round the corner from where she lived, and I used to go round there a lot. She used to worry about what I was doing, but now she's at ease.

MG: What are your plans for when you leave the Unit?

H: I'm not really sure. I'd like to just travel somewhere. I might enrol at the Tech but then go away for the summer somewhere, maybe to France or somewhere. If I got into a good scene I might not want to come back. So I'm not sure what my plans would be. My girlfriend went to Italy and France and had a great time. She was there for three months. If I liked the people there I might stay with them.

MG: Have your plans changed since you came to the Unit?

H: No, 'cos I had no plans. so that's a change, from nothing to something, like I might go to the Tech next year.

MG: If in the future you changed your present plans how would you change them?

H: I might meet up with a friend and go somewhere else. I met someone in remand and we were thinking of going to Amsterdam. Anything could happen. If something came along I might like to do it. Everyone else here seems to put great value on getting results in exams as if it was the accepted thing to do. I can't get myself worked up about it as other people, yer know. I'm personally not in a hurry. The Unit is only a passing through place.

MG: If the opportunity to come to the Unit hadn't arisen what else would you have done?

H: I might have gone back to Dublin, but I wouldn't have stayed there long, yer know. I might have got myself nicked again, for cannabis.

MG: What do you think are the interesting topics which the research should look at?

H: Yer could investigate what people see in education generally, and how much they value educational results, whether they're not putting too much value on exam results and might not really want to do other things, though I wouldn't know what, and whether there's not other alternatives for people coming out of jail than education for people to get into.

Stafford summed up Harry's attitude to education thus: 'Harry has a casual approach, idle, disappointing. He's happy'.

Harry's casual approach informed all his activities. For example, at the beginning of the summer of 1977, Ian had a job selling ice cream in the centre of Cambridge. One day, I noticed Harry take over for the afternoon. He said that he was not interested in being paid for the work; it was just another experience to get into.

Harry was arrested several times while in Cambridge, and the offences involved also seemed to have been committed in a casual way. He accepted a friend's invitation to join him when he presented a forged prescription and thus got convicted for forgery himself; he accepted a prohibited drug from a friend, which resulted in arrest for possessing it; he wandered around in private premises while drunk one evening, and found himself arrested for damage to property; he went joyriding on a bicycle belonging to someone else after a May Ball, and was arrested again. In all these cases, the Unit provided the court with good character references.

After Harry left the Unit two problems intrigued me. Firstly, in a letter to the Unit from Harry's sister not long after he left Cambridge and returned to London, she wrote; '*Harry is working in London and seems more responsible and more depressed*' (15/10/77). This report contrasted with Stafford's judgement noted earlier that, in the Unit, Harry was irresponsible and happy.

Secondly, Harry had four convictions while in Cambridge. After leaving the Unit, however, no further convictions were recorded against him. This turn of events seemed out of accord with the generalisation that in, for example, Approved Schools, a 'high level of deviancy in the institution usually leads ... to a high level of deviancy out of the institution' (Sinclair and Clarke 1973, p.289).

I obtained answers to these riddles in 1981. On leaving the Unit, Harry said to himself, 'Gosh, if I keep getting into trouble in a rehabilitation outfit then I'm sure to get into trouble in ordinary life'. Prison was not for Harry a way of demonstrating powers of endurance, nor was it an escape from the problems of the outside world. It was a threat to a hedonistic lifestyle. He had, therefore, decided that if he was going to continue to drift he would have to reduce his delinquency. Harry may be regarded, indeed, rather like the rational man sometimes conjured up by psychologists for heuristic purposes (e.g., Eysenck 1965, p.257) who behaves according to a hedonistic calculus - or so he seems to have become. Thus, Harry had spent every summer since 1977 at music festivals. There food and shelter were provided for people who did not have their own. Drugs such as mandrax and LSD had also been offered unofficially, but Harry had to turn them down.

Another reason for Harry's becoming more responsible and more depressed was that, after leaving the Unit, he was obliged to take jobs again. As in the past, all of them gave him diminishing marginal utility over time, so that he had continued to drop out of one job and later drop into another. His longest job since leaving the Unit, and the one which he liked the most, was working in a halfway house for mentally handicapped people who had been in hospital. He worked there for about a year, but the house was closed down. Many young people strive to obtain a steady job before they marry and settle down (Carter 1975; Glickman 1975), so I asked Harry about that side of his life. Unfortunately, he was in no position to marry as he was already 'married'. A German woman who wished to become a British citizen had offered him £100 if he married her. Once this transaction was completed he had seen no more of her.

E. ARTHUR: 1Y,2;PP,PCo;PCh

Arthur left school after passing eight O levels. A little over a year later, he was brought to court on two burglary charges, which he committed while drunk. He thus came to the Unit, at the age of eighteen, because he:

> was arrested for burglary while working in a restaurant in Littlehampton. I went to see my probation officer [Arthur had been previously convicted of 'Taking and Driving Away'] to see if there was any chance of avoiding penal servitude. She suggested that I get into a study programme. We applied to Chichester and Worthing Techs, but I didn't get accepted. Then she came up with the idea of NACRO ... When you go up before a judge for an offence like burglary or theft, and you're unemployed, you'll get a prison sentence, but if you've been done and whilst waiting for the case you get into education it will stand you in better stead. It was a means to an end which stopped me from getting sent down. It really cons them.

According to Arthur,'it was just too heavy in Littlehampton'. Following committal proceedings in the Magistrates' Court his name was reported in the local press. He was sacked from his job and asked to leave his lodgings. Getting away from Littlehampton for some time was a delinquent's solution.

Arthur came to the Unit on a deferred sentence. He was obligated to reappear in court during his stay at the Unit and give an account of himself as having made educational progress instead of committing crime. He told Ellis, his closest confidant in the Unit, that such arrangements made education seem like punishment. Until his reappearance in court his educational performance was minimal; after his reappearance, accompanied by a testament from the Unit, mere weeks were left before the examinations, and his effort academically was negligible. Corrigan (1979, p.45) says that 'it becomes important to recognise the amount of "passive resistance" ... in the classrooms of the British educational system ... truancy may be seen as an extreme action; "dolling off" [missing individual lessons] as less extreme; "mucking about" as a major activity and "not paying attention" as endemic'. Arthur dolled off and did not pay attention. He did not muck about - the risk of penal servitude would have been too great.

Arthur said that his offences had been exciting and daring. But at the Unit he derived more than an equal amount of stimulation from being in the company of ex-cons and listening to their exciting and exaggerated stories. This sense of notoriety, which Ellis found distasteful, seemed to be Arthur's substitute for crime.

The Unit was useful to Arthur in dealing with threatened imprisonment and in providing a resort from Littlehampton until things became less 'heavy' there. His social world was, however, otherwise unchanged - even reinforced. For even while he was boasting to the ex-cons about his sexual conquests in Cambridge he took pride in the constancy of his steady girlfriend in Littlehampton. Neither she nor her brothers had continued academic education after leaving school, and she could not see why Arthur might wish to. At the end of the year, he returned to Littlehampton and took a steady job. He was the only student of the Unit's third year not to reoffend in any way either in the Unit or afterwards.

Arthur had two main grievances against the Unit. Firstly, any intimation that he planned to take several days off during term time to see his girlfriend was quickly stamped on by Stafford with threats of expulsion. Arthur was both a judicial and an organisational detainee.

Secondly, the Unit's educational programme made little sense to him in terms of his future. Talking about his financial prospects he asked, 'What's the point in taking A levels and degrees and things - by the time I start work I'll be below people who are working now, without A levels etc., just working their way up?'.

It is possible that Des came to a similar conclusion. It is a conclusion which must be seen in the context of an enormous social change which has been taking place in recent years:

> Unemployment, particularly among young people, has soared to unprecedented levels, and has put the question of the transition from school-life to work-life in an altogether different context ... the number of young people (under 20 years) registered unemployed in the Coventry area between 1970 and 1977 increased <u>fivefold</u> in the case of males, and increased <u>ninefold</u> in the case of females (Bazalgette 1978, p.ix; emphases his).

It may be that such increases were not as great in London

and the south, but throughout Britain accelerated increases were on the way. This social trend possibly makes much of the literature on the sociology of youth out of date. In that literature (e.g., Morse 1965, pp.113-14; Downes 1966, p.231) many young people, in the period between leaving school and settling down, go through a dropout phase in which lack of job satisfaction, the main attraction of work for them (Veness 1962, pp.91-3), leads them to shift from job to job regardless of how low paid such stints may be. In one highly instructive study, Carter (1975) found that among school leavers in Sheffield a high percentage went straight into the steel and engineering industries, then dropped out because of 'the vastness, the noise and the dirt' (ibid., pp.94-5) and then returned about five years afterwards as 'intended marriage turn thoughts towards the need for a higher income, with a wedding to be saved for, and furniture to buy' (ibid., p.93).

I would hypothesise that youth unemployment may have changed this picture, creating a new kind of polarisation among young people. On the one hand, there will be more working class young people determined to seize, if they can, a secure and, if possible, highly paid job regardless of its unpleasantness. Within this group will be people like Des and Arthur with enough qualifications to enable them to obtain a position 'with prospects' and among whom going to university will come to have decreasing attraction because 'unemployment and inflation in all Western countries seem to be encouraging a scramble by able young people for whatever jobs are going' (Stevens 1978). On the other hand, there will be young people like Harry whose work record is so poor that they may have little possibility of redeeming it even if they find work about which they feel so enthusiastic that they will stick to it. Present social arrangements may require a large number of dropouts like Harry, for, as Heilbroner (1974, p.236) suggests, 'the smooth running of postindustrial society may hinge, even more than that of industrial society, on the presence of that "secondary" labour force (the drop-outs, casual labour-market participants, or exploited minorities) who continue to be available for picking the fruit, the digging of ditches, the sweeping of floors, the washing of dishes'.

I revisited Arthur in August 1981. He had recently married and was living not far from Littlehampton in a house on mortgage which was modern and attractive. Like Des, he had been working steadily for a British corporation, and enjoying promotions. He said that he was now earning £6000 a year, and his wife a similar salary. The Unit and, no doubt, the escapades which preceeded it, seemed to him something that happened 'long long ago'. He was very pleased to have a steady job at a time of high unemployment. He had hopes of further promotion and towards this end he was studying part time for a diploma in accountancy. He considered the A level subjects he was expected to take at the Unit had been quite irrelevant to his career. In regard to the history of policy in the Unit, Arthur's biography is particularly ironic, for at the end of the third year, in reviewing the poor academic efforts of Ava and Arthur, Ron and Stafford decided not to accept any further teenage clients.

F. REHABILITATION AND OTHER OUTCOMES IN THE CASES STUDIED

Among other points which come out of our case studies are the very varied interconnections between crime, punishment and rehabilitation, as the figure below illustrates. Let us relate each of the paths in the figure to the material in our case studies. In so doing, it may be useful to consider the extent to which the decisions behind the directions which clients took were, on the one hand, calculative, and, on the other hand, normative. A calculative act, or failure to act, is one which takes place or is avoided because of its effects on the actor. A normative act, or failure to act, is one which takes place or is avoided because of the moral sentiments which it evokes, regardless of its effects on the actor.

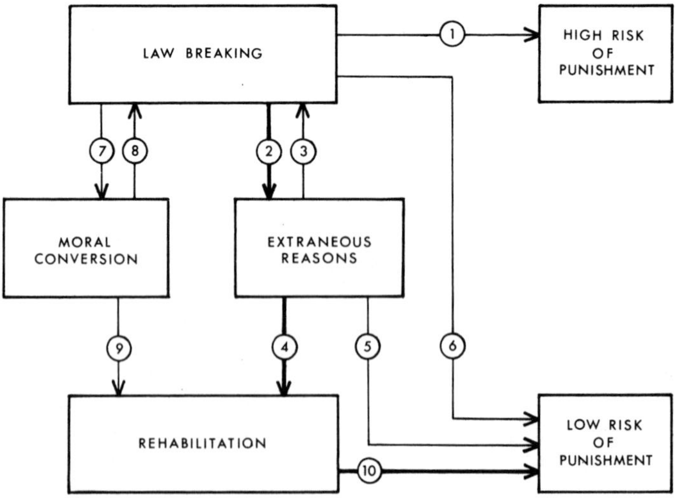

PATHWAYS TO CRIME, PUNISHMENT AND REHABILITATION

1. This was a well trodden path taken by the many clients who found themselves in a situation of such great stress that they sought release even at the price of a high risk of punishment. This strategy tended to contain a hybrid of calculative and normative components. Many clients who did not rehabilitate seem to have felt such an intolerable level of moral obligation to the Unit that they considered that any means of escape which was out of character would have been regarded as unseemly or unacceptable. Some of these clients dashed down this path when their underlying impulse for punishment was unhappily stimulated as appears to have been the case, for example, with Ellis.

2. Here the client modified his behaviour because of the effects breach of the law might have on his commitments, whether these consisted of education (Leo), education and political involvement (Adam), a career (Des and Arthur) or even the freedom involved in drifting (Harry). This path might be described as one of Beckerian normality, though, strictly speaking, Becker's theory of normality entails the particular conjuction of path 2 with paths 4 and 10.

3. This path going the opposite way involves breaking the law regardless, or even because of, one's commitments. For example, Geoff broke the law in obtaining cocaine in order to be able to fulfil his second HND job assignment.

4. Here the calculative need to modify one's behaviour leads to lowering significantly one's rate of reoffending. Adam, Des, Harry and Arthur all took this path.

5. This path might be called one of Mackian normality, after Mack (1972), who studied highly criminal, 'able' individuals who regularly broke the law as an intrinsic part of their lifestyle in spite of various commitments, which, indeed, obligated them to take various measures to ensure protection from the police. Following such a direction is represented in our case studies by Leo. It may be hypothesised that path 5 will be preferred to path 4 when the illegal act constitutes a central, essential and unambiguous element in one's personality or values.

6. This is a path taken by individuals who break laws in order to avoid breaking other laws which might result in a high risk of punishment. Thus, when Des felt a strong impulse to steal lest people in Brixton and elsewhere 'feel sorry for' or 'sympathise with' his poverty, he tended to light a cigarette of cannabis as his customary way of relaxation and coping with tension. This path is also one taken by individuals who commit the offence of bribing the police in order to avoid punishment for other offences.

All the above routes are highly calculative in motivation. We may now turn to normative pathways:

7. This was a passage taken by Ava, who developed a moral revulsion to her delinquency, drugtaking, regarding it as 'juvenile', an epithet which she tended to apply to any kind of behaviour for which she felt little esteem.

8. Moving in this opposite direction is represented by Adam during his imprisonment. His sense of moral repugnance towards the social order was such that, not permitted any political outlet, or even unenlightened in the structure of political systems or in political history, his strong sentiments led to violent, and other illegal, acts which required great moral courage.

The remaining lines in the diagram are the consequences of other lines. Thus, path 7 will normally lead to path 9, and paths 4 and 9 will normally lead to path 10.

The extent to which the various pathways between crime, punishment and rehabilitation entail or exclude taking other pathways in the system in the actor's future might be an interesting programme for further research.

NOTES

[1] 'The reality of the educational side was that never at any time during my primary school attendance did I ever want to do well at my lessons for some very simple reasons. From Primary school there were two schools that the kids in my class could go to after qualifying exams. One was St Bonaventura's (Bonny's) a Secondary school, and the other was Holyrood, which we called the toffy school. Now my aim from the minute I went into primary school was to attend Bonny's, as that was where my older brothers and other kids from my street had gone so I had already made up my mind that this was where I was going. This meant that there was no incentive for me to go anywhere else and anyway going to Holyrood meant the expenses of paying for a uniform so there was no way this could happen. Therefore, it was Bonny's for me. Expenses aside, the dominating factor that made me always want to go there was that everyone in my street went to Bonny's. Bonny's was for our kind and I knew I'd be happier there. I can still remember the day when they read out the results of the qualifying exams, with Smelly and I nearly crapping our breeks, no doubt he did, in case we passed with a high mark and were sent to Holyrood. So idiots that we were, we rejoiced in failing the exams' (Boyle 1977, pp.20-1).

[2] '... the only way I was able to live with myself was not to succumb, not to allow the screws to do what they wanted with me. No, by far the best way was to fight them, even if I lost, and suffered the pain that went with it. One important thing I noticed was

that I was getting stronger after each incident. If it can't kill you it can only strengthen you. If I continued to gather strength then the system would be the eventual loser' (Boyle 1977, p.174).

[3] 'This was a period in my life when I reflected on my whole being. Self-analysis became a daily habit as I was trying to find out more about myself and to come to some understanding of where I had come from and where I was going ... now I was beginning to put it all together for the first time in my life. Day after day I lay in this cell thinking, thinking, thinking' (Boyle 1977, pp.190-1).

[4] 'I was now doing physical exercises in my cell with an intensity that I hadn't shown before. I came to the conclusion that from now on the confrontation would be fierce and bloody, and therefore I should be prepared both at physical and mental level' (Boyle 1977, p.179).

[5] Robert Allerton, who, from his childhood, responded to violence by authority in the same uncompromising manner as Adam (Parker and Allerton 1962), once received an invitation by a prison instructor in English to live for a time in her house upon his release so that he could have the amenities for developing his manifest skills as a writer. Allerton (ibid., p.130) remarks that 'it was my impression - and maybe I am wrong - that all she wanted to do was to keep me as her little lap-dog and tour me around, showing off her great he-man criminal to her friends'. Allerton regarded the offer as an insidious exchange, insulting to a person like himself who refused to be subordinated or used in any way in the pursuit of his goals.

[6] 'You don't feel you're forgotten in prison somehow, not so much as you are in a [mental] hospital. There you feel that nobody knows you; they're all sick people, a lot of them just walk around all day and they don't talk. Everyone talks here, you've got a lot of friends ... besides to be in a mental hospital you have to be silly, and I don't think I am silly, not all that silly anyway' (Parker 1969, p.200).

PART III

RESULTS OF THE ANALYSIS AND POLICY IMPLICATIONS

> It is still uncertain what the hostels are trying to do (Sinclair 1971, p.143).

> 'Do you like to come here and teach this class? I bet if these students had their wishes they'd be somewhere else, maybe out stealing, instead of sitting in this dumpy room. But they do it because it gets them something else they want' (Chambliss ed. 1972, p.x).

10 The Unit as a People Product Organisation

Some attempt at classification is essential if we are to grope to the discovery of what organisations do with their clients. Once such functions are studied they can then be investigated further to find out how they interrelate.

The aim of classifying what a people product organisation does, however, is not the unearthing of 'latent functions' which are only of academic interest. The aim is also to extract 'certain sensitizing concepts which may be of direct help to social policy formulators and planners. Surely part of the model's potential utility lies in its ability to alert policymakers to certain realities concerning the implementation phenomena' (Regier 1979, p.151).

Such sociological input, moreover, may be increasingly desired by policy implementors, overwhelmed as they so often are by quotidian problems which deprive them of an overall vision of what they are achieving. Former project staff at the Unit, for example, increasingly came to regard 'rehabilitation' not as a sensitising concept but as a senseless one. Thus, in an Interim Report to NACRO in 1975, Ron wrote of his clients that 'all of them make use of project staff from time to time - as parent substitute, as someone to argue with, to act as tutor, to arrange something, to provide money and advice'. In so far as this day-to-day contact satisfies need it probably contributes to rehabilitation'. In July 1980, however, Ron told me that he now regards the notion of rehabilitation as utterly misleading and confusing.

Rehabilitation, however, was in no way the only phenomenon about which the Unit had no clear conception. I have cited statements by Ron where the purposes of his policies, in particular control, were clearly stated. Such explicitness, however, was decidedly exceptional. It was much more common for staff to express vague notions, such as 'work on behalf of students', since efforts to maintain bureaucratic routine often took precedence over careful concern for what effects on clients were intended or probable. Moreover, even when control was stated as an aim, it was never clear whether it was desirable in itself or whether it was considered to have any relationship to changing the client's behaviour, and, if so, what kind of relationship, positive or negative, desirable or undesirable. The present chapter, therefore, discusses the functions which the Unit performed and their interrelationship.

A. PROCESSING PEOPLE

Processing clients was one of the main tasks which the Unit executed on their behalf. It processed them for the courts, places of tertiary education, jobs and psychiatric clinics. Most secretarial work consisted of letters and reports processing clients. Such processing, moreover, was carried out with great zeal. Testimonials to places of tertiary education, for example, were probably presented with greater attention to details of the client's promising qualities than similar documents sent on behalf of many of their pupils by headmasters and headmistresses.

Processing people is a marked feature of developed societies because the greater the restrictions on educational and other opportunities the smaller the supply of top people. The fewer the top people the greater their power and wealth. The greater their power and wealth the greater the need for a large number and variety of middle people to mediate between their clients and top people or, in most cases, other middle people of higher rank. The sociologist who spends much time in the company of offenders observes this pyramidal social arrangement at its most vivid whenever he finds himself observing a court, with its structured inequality between the seated, pinnacled ranks of judgment and the people standing in the dock below them. The languages spoken by judges and the judged are both forms of English, but otherwise have little in common. As Lewis and Hughman (1975, p.147) put it:

> Inevitably the doctrine of judicial isolation, together with a background of social privilege common to the majority inhibits them [judges] in gaining a high degree of personal understanding. In court, the physical distance between bench and dock is no more than a few yards, but the gulf which separates judge and defendant is enormous and bridged only by the speech of an advocate, himself probably as remote from his client as the judge ...

Parker (1963, p.145) captures the ritual terror, social distance and heightened bilingualism of the courts when he puts into words the thoughts of Charles Smith, a habitual prisoner who had served twenty-six years for nonviolent property offences whose total value came to £180:

> We face each other across the court, you in your majestic regalia of Law, and I in the grimy suit

> of crime. Behind you is society, on whose behalf you function, and which supports you in what you do. Behind me is an indefensible record, and a lifetime barren even of minor success. The gulf in sympathy and understanding between us is so vast, so deep, that communication is impossible. Yet you always ask me if I have anything to say.
>
> There is nothing I could think of that should be said. And even if I could I would never know how to express it.

In the judicial domain of our society, advisers in tricks of communication sometimes turn up, but, alas, often on the late side and often lacking complete expertise. After the nonviolent rapist, Andrew Brown, had been handed four life sentences in a single hearing, he reflected:

> Well, what I mean is, I didn't know the words you see, and that's what made it go badly with me in front of the judge. When they read out the charges to me I said what I shouldn't have done, I said 'Yes I fucked her. Yes I fucked her. Yes I fucked her,' and all like that, each one all the way through. Afterwards the screw said to me he said 'You shouldn't have said that, boy, that's not the way to talk ... What you should have said is "Yes, I had an intercourse with her"' ... I think that made it go bad for me. If I'd been better-spoken I might have got off lighter (Parker 1969, p.208).

One of the arts of the Unit was the supply on behalf of unacceptable people of acceptable speeches. These were articulated by members of staff more persuasively, in my estimation, than by legal aid barristers with whom they shared middle to upper class accent, vocabulary and form of argument.

Courts, colleges and companies were the main institutions for which the Unit processed its clients. There were, however, all sorts of other agencies which could at any time call for such activity by the Unit. For example, in January 1977, Ian took up part time employment with a firm producing office equipment. He worked two days and then, slight and slender in build, he quit because 'I was treated like a slave. The money was quite inadequate for the dirty, heavy work they gave me to do'. Since he left 'voluntarily', his unemployment benefit was considerably reduced. Ron helped him to draft an appeal letter, which was typed. Ron then added one of his own in which he thus wrote of a man who, although always plebeian in expression, was nevertheless one of the most linguistically direct of my informants: 'I'm writing this letter to say that he has set out his case in writing at my suggestion because I am afraid he may not have presented it very well verbally ...'.

Merton (1940, p.561), in writing about bureaucracy, states that 'the generality of the rules requires the constant use of categorization, whereby individual problems and cases are classified on the basis of designated criteria and are treated accordingly ... The structure is one which approaches the complete elimination of personalized relationships and of nonrational criteria (hostility, anxiety, affectual involvement, etc.)'. But (in the USA, where many officials obtain their position by ballot) 'a measure of flexibility is attained by electing higher functionaries' (ibid.). Letters from the Unit, often beginning with the announcement, 'NACRO-Education is a Home Office sponsored project helping ex-offenders to rehabilitate themselves through education', often secured 'a measure of flexibility', as with Ian's problem with his unemployment benefit. Abercrombie and Hill's (1976, p.416) statement that 'patronage exists where institutions are weak' must be qualified by the fact that patronage is also used to counteract institutions, such as local offices of government departments, which are strong in relation to the ordinary citizen.

In relation to the subject of our research, the vital question of concern is the extent to which the processing function of the Unit, particularly when directed towards easing the opening of the gates of educational institutions for ex-offenders, was valuable or otherwise in their rehabilitation. As we review our case studies we find that in some cases processing was useful in achieving this aim, whereas, in other cases, used in isolation from catering for clients' other needs, it was inappropriate. Thus, the presentation of Adam to scholarly experts as a person whom they might consider worthy of their attention because of the fairly well defined knowledge he determinedly wished to gain a mastery of seems to have been of benefit to him in organising his intellectual enquiries, and connected activities, so as to exclude his previous way of life. Similarly, in Leo's case, the Unit's pertinacity obtained a university place for him and increased his commitment to formal education. Without such processing he might have spent a long period after his release unemployed, studying linguistic theory and higher mathematics in individual seclusion, in a state of bitterness even greater than the one in which I last saw him, and in a mode of existence not much more glamorous than prison. Indeed, even after his degree, he ruminated, 'After you've served a sentence of four years, committing any kind of offence [such as stealing] which will get you three months is hardly worth bothering about'.

In so many other cases, by contrast, the processing of ex-offenders appears to have been extremely wanton. The consequences appear to have been so disastrous that it would not be amiss to turn our attention again to one of the most notable cases. We may recall the way in which Ken's overcommitment was contained within the 'supportive' school environment, thus enabling him to achieve impressive GCE success. But he, like other overcommitted students, now regards the letters of praise with which he was furnished before going to university as having turned out to be of no help to him at all when it came to coping with the university environment into which he had been processed, even though he, again like so many others, is inclined to blame himself, thus exacerbating his sense of lack of worth. As he wrote to Ron from university while awaiting trial,'*Whatever the court imposes on me will be secondary to the punishment of the recrimination my mind imposes on me*'.

B. CONTROLLING PEOPLE

'Hostels are not custodial institutions as such, but represent a compromise between custodial sentences and supervision in the community' (Brody 1976, p.17). As earlier discussed, the control element expanded greatly in the Unit's short experimental period. As Ron put it in the third year:

> Obviously the tutorial system of this year has made a big difference ... they are now under our general control. We can find out straight away why they haven't gone to a particular class. I think it makes them feel more secure to feel under our general control. When they seem tired in the morning we always ask, 'What were you up to last night?'. We are much more intimately connected with them at all levels now. The totality of the situation has changed.

As already indicated, the students were as aware as the staff of the way in which the tutorial relationship could operate as a channel for information to 'the office' and used for the purpose of 'general control'. As a fourth year student told the press:

> Within the group there was no open intention to commit crime - you didn't know who was going to tell the office. It kept everyone silently in check (Cambridge Evening News, 23/6/80, p.17).

The Unit was by no means alone, as a 'voluntary' rehabilitation hostel, in developing devices for controlling its clients. For example, the staff of Hargrave House on one page (Sugden and Skinner n.d., p.59-60) condemns counselling methods but, on the next page, introduces us to a binding licensing argreement for its tenants replete with many clauses and with penalties. Similarly, it is said that prison officers can gain more information about one prisoner from another in open prisons than in closed ones.

Moreover, staff was aware of the extent to which activities which escaped its control could be controlled in a more conventional way more effectively than in open society. Elaborating on the obvious, Stafford pointed out that:

> An important point is that education and rehabilitation are so intertwined. If you are a recidivist then before long you are going to be removed by the police because this is the first place they are going to look, so that chances of breaking the law and escaping are small, so that education is bound to be interrupted (cf. Sinclair and Snow 1971, p.70).

As the amount of control increased, the Unit inevitably took on many of the characteristics of prison. Geoff's notion that 'the Unit is just like prison rather than a way out of prison', and his supporting argument that the tutorials constituted a 'therapy rap' to which he had been heavily subjected in prison, were very important ideas to him in resolving his distressing indecisiveness. But it was also an observation which increasingly fitted the facts. As control increased many clients reacted to it in typically inmate ways. By the fifth year, when so many 'hard core' offenders were accepted, violence and other expressions of status competition between students; physical threats to staff; and the vandalism of doors, floors, walls, ceilings, beds, windows and other parts of the residential scenery made the penal equation very pronounced. Moreover, members of staff themselves could hardly fail to perceive the very diminished gap which had developed between the regime of the Unit and prison. Their perception, however, was often equivocal. Thus, in the fifth year, a junior member of staff was commissioned to produce a booklet about the Unit designed to encourage favourable attitudes in the Home Office and other funding agencies. His manuscript was too outspoken on sensitive issues and was suppressed by his superiors. This ban was particularly ironic because he also tried to highlight features of normality and freedom in the hostel. When he did so, however, he tended to receive hostile criticism for his superficiality. For example, when he wrote that 'a residential worker would ... turn the run down house in Cambridge into an institution, another more subtle kind of prison', one of the author's senior colleagues responded to his observation with the marginal comment: 'Very simplistic. It is an institution'. (In the sixth year, however, the regional organiser of NACRO wrote to a concerned local resident the longstanding formula that a residential worker would turn the hostel into an institution!)

As events clearly showed, however, the existence of forces of control, whether within or coming from outside the Unit, by no means meant that they were effective, still less that they necessarily had any rehabilitative value. Much seemed to depend, as with all the Unit's functions, on the meanings which clients attached, and the attitudes with which they reacted, to control. Ian, for example, seems to have accommodated very readily to a controlled environment, as he had so often in the past, for example, by refusing, during one of his sentences, to be removed from a closed to an open prison. Ian did not reoffend when he was in Cambridge, as against when he was in Manchester, and it is possible that the atmosphere of control - as well as commitment, however unstable, to professional career goals while in Cambridge - might account for the difference.

By contrast, Harry seems to have reacted in precisely the opposite fashion. Control may have been a green light for him merrily to kick over the traces. A dropout does not positively respond with zeal to forces which would hold him in, even if failure to do so involves the risk of reconviction in a heavily policed town.

It has come to be honestly recognised that people who respond to control by changing their accustomed behaviour once they have left the controlled environment are decidedly in the minority. If this were not the case then prisons would merely be little jails instead of the multi-storey fortresses against the freedom of the outside world which they are, constantly expanding in size and number, and largely populated by offenders repeatedly returning through 'the revolving door'. Even among the minority the sequence of control leading to changed behaviour seems to be varied and idiosyncratic. Adam saw prison control as part of a wider system of political control which he wished to smash, and he therefore abandoned criminal behaviour which had led to prison in the past lest it upset his unusual plans. Leo responded by increasing the concealment of his offences from the police. According to Harry, incarceration in a Detention Centre was 'a deterrent'. As we have seen, after leaving the Unit, he took the idea of 'rehabilitation' as reformation seriously and reasoned that if he could offend so often while being rehabilitated how much more likely was he to do so in ordinary life, and thus court arrest, which would interfere with what he considered to be a free and easy lifestyle, if he did not mend his ways. As against these three cases, however, must be set the many cases of individuals who reoffended soon after release from prison or the Unit, regardless of whether or not they had also offended while at these institutions.

How to convert control into rehabilitative change for the multitude of recidivists is a problem which I do not think anybody has solved. Cornish and Clarke (1975) studied two groups of delinquents subjected to different programmes in a penal school, one called 'training' and the other called 'treatment'. No difference was found in the later behaviour of the two populations. The authors wistfully remark, 'It is possible, however, that such programmes may be more successful in maintaining any behavioural changes they are able to bring about in the residential setting if, in some way, the offender can take his institutional environment (or salient aspects of it) with him when he leaves' (ibid., p.49). This logical deduction has the appearance of sound advice, but I cannot think of any systematic way in which it can be translated into action in a liberal democracy. What is more likely and, indeed, so often the case, is for the offender to gravitate back to other residential, institutional settings, of which prison, with its salient aspect of control, is one of the most prominent. Moreover, I can descry, in our sample, only two cases - Ava, with the antipathy she developed towards drugtaking, and Harry, with his deduction of how prone to lawbreaking he might be even 'in ordinary life' - in which clients rehabilitated by taking behavioural changes brought about (or, rather, initiated) in the residential setting with them when they left. Again, however, such cases seem fleeting and certainly follow no regular pattern. It is certainly difficult to see how the social processes involved in such cases can be developed into a systematic and coherent programme.

The question may be asked, therefore, if there was nowhere that clients could take salient aspects of the Unit's environment, apart from prison, were there no environments, such as universities or polytechnics, which the Unit might have tried to change in some way in order to make them congenial to highly institutionalised undergraduates? The question is important, because the Unit's clients of its third and later years who went on to higher education but failed to graduate did not have particularly violent dispositions or pose any great threat to society.

C. MOBILISING PEOPLE

The Unit, unlike its parent body, NACRO (Griffiths 1975, pp.689-90; Fitzgerald 1977, pp.146 & 195), did not perform any significant mobilising function. It processed clients into other organisations but it did not, either itself, or in concert with other bodies, attempt to make any alterations in such organisations before its clients reached them. In the case of Ken, the Unit emphasised how well he had performed but it did not point out to his future mentors the kind of problems he had not yet learned to face. No provision was made either for continuity in the university setting of features of the Unit's environment or, alternatively, for special help with methods of learning which are appropriate to a university setting. Only after it was too late to put matters right did Ron appreciate the stark contrast between the educational environment of the Unit and that of the university which Ken went to:

> While he was here, he showed himself to be capable of immensely hard work, to have a quick mind, and a demeanour ... very responsive to the regime and staff at this project, which perhaps led us to press him too hard, to overdirect him. His career at university was disastrous ... failure at university was the major contributory factor leading to the cheque card theft ... He says he stole the cheque card quite deliberately to relieve the tension ... He misses the close contact with teachers that he had here (emphases mine).

Some rehabilitative organisations, by contrast, make it one of their principles to mobilise and educate people in charge of other organisations to make attitudinal and other changes appropriate for the reception of ex-offenders. For example:

> The small staff at Apex make regular visits to an increasing number of employers to discuss doubts and fears, to persuade employers to take on ex-offenders ... By mid 1977 the bank of potential employers stands at 1000. Knowledge of an offender's offence and background gives many employers the opportunity to exercise tolerance and gives special assistance in overcoming problems which may not arise from work but certainly affect performance (Hinton 1977, p.29).

If Ken's mentors at university had been alerted to his problems and had prepared some line of action to help him to cope with them then he may have rehabilitated, just as he kept out of crime most of the time he was connected with the Unit. Such an outcome would have been a significant breakthrough, for rehabilitation projects do not normally rehabilitate many of their clients in any well organised way. One of the reasons they are unable to do so may be that they tend to work in isolation from other institutions with which clients interact. It cannot be very surprising, therefore, that such projects tend to fail as soon as their clients go through the transition from a project to more conventional institutions in society.

D. CHANGING PEOPLE

In considering the extent to which the Unit changed clients,

I have naturally been mainly concerned with the extent to which it rehabilitated clients or, alternatively, exacerbated their recidivist tendencies. It may be noted in passing, however, that such effects are not the only ones which a rehabilitation project may produce. To take one example, chosen because it has a bearing on the habitual assumption that a rehabilitation project needs to be residentially based, Ava, for a long period after she had left the Unit, talked of a change in a recess of her mind in the form of nightmares of embarrassment:

> All the time I was in the Unit I didn't have any confidence in myself at all. I even have dreams about it now - giving your address to people, like giving your address for library books. I got a real complex about it ... I don't think the Unit helped.

In our analysis, we have picked out individual cases, showing positive and negative effects of the Unit in terms of rehabilitation. In this way, we have tried to avoid the problem whereby 'averaging over dissimilar members of a sample can give meaningless results; effects for one person may cancel out effects for another, when the two are arbitrarily combined and averaged ... sometimes we simply have to keep our eyes open and look carefully at individual cases' (Eysenck 1976, p.9). It is much more common, however, in conventional evaluations to concentrate on the statistical analysis of global aggregates. It may be of interest, therefore, to view the Unit in the context of studies which are concerned with the performance 'on the whole' of rehabilitation projects.

I have examined material from America (Bailey 1966, Lohman et al. 1967, Lerman 1968, Kirby 1970, Johnston et al. eds. 1970, Empey and Lubeck 1971, Robison and Smith 1971, Logan 1972, Reckless and Dinitz 1972, Doleschal and Klapmuts 1973, Hirschi 1975, and Lipton et al. 1975); from Britain (Mannheim and Wilkins 1955, Hood and Sparks 1970, Bottoms and McClintock 1973, and Soothill 1974); from Scandinavia (Uusitalo 1968, Anttila 1971, and Christie 1971); and from Yugoslavia (Vodopivec 1974). None of this literature is able to show any valid and statistically significant effect in rehabilitating offenders. This conclusion holds regardless of whether the projects concerned presented themselves as punitive or therapeutic. The same finding applies both to programmes which deal with the offender for his offence, as well as those which cater for him after he has been dealt with, such as after-care hostels. Faring no better are programmes which deal with the offender years <u>before</u> he commits any offence, as with the Cambridge-Somerville Youth Study (McCord and McCord 1959), where an experimental group of 250 boys was matched against a control group and for a period of six years provided with counselling, special academic tutoring, introductions to youth organisations and, in some cases, psychotherapy.

In short, 'rehabilitative programmes - whether involving psychiatric treatment, counselling, casework or intensive contact and special attention, in custodial or non-custodial settings - have no predictably beneficial effect' (Brody 1976, p.37).

Millham et al. (1978, p.161) note how rehabilitation projects tend to change their high minded aims once failure to rehabilitate more than a handful of offenders, and, even in these cases, through unintended and unpredictable mechanisms, becomes evident.

A 'Report on the NACRO Education Meeting held on Monday, 28 March 1978 at the Royal Commonwealth Society', one of several such meetings held each year, and attended by all the Unit's full time teaching staff, expressed its change in goal in the idiom of 'good influence' (though without going so far as to claim in so many words that it had ever achieved it):

> Experimental projects such as the Cambridge Project ... could not claim any special rehabilitative value. The aim was to exert a good influence ...

Interestingly, the notion of good influence occurs in other studies of rehabilitation projects. For example, a report on a 'detached' worker sent by the National Association of Youth Clubs in a missionary endeavour to organise the 'unattached' youths of 'Seagate' states:

> Because the group had become proficient ... in amateur dramatics it could not automatically be assumed that ... the group would necessarily have changed ... one of the group was placed on probation for three years for stealing electrical equipment worth over £300. Other members were at various times found guilty ... In spite of this there were some definite improvements which could be traced back to the worker's influence (Morse 1965, p.60).

By the summer of 1978, the good influence claimed by NACRO became substantially attenuated. As Ron put it:

> I've used the idea that I can influence people, but the problem is that we hope, but we don't assume, that the influence we're giving is a good one ... All the students who come to us are rather like unknown plants: we don't know if they need to be in the sun or the shade or warm conditions or cold conditions ... we are not trying to claim that the influence is good ... it is not a thing that I would assume.

In a memorandum of the project dated 30 January 1979, 'influence' disappears completely, and the role of the Unit is presented in even more attenuated, and almost syllogistic, terms:

> The student needs ... to ... adjust to new demands. Hence the idea of the Unit as an intermediate stage between the penal system and one or other of the systems of normal life. Hence the term "Intermediate Education".

In the Unit's ideology, therefore, there was an uneasy slide of words and confidence downhill from 'rehabilitation' to 'good influence' to 'influence' to 'intermediate education'. This last term has a reassuring tone. One thinks of other intermediate steps, such as, for example, a traffic island. The island makes it easier to cross the road. Indeed, very few people dash back from the island to their starting point, or remain hopelessly stranded, or assume that the island automatically ensures safe passage beyond. But analogues of such actions could be found in the Unit. Moreover, the Unit's programme could be regarded not as a 'stage between' but as an 'interface institution' (Hunt and Hunt 1967) which came between the penal system and systems of normal life (whatever these are) by interposing schooling, which, as we have seen, could hardly claim to have prepared clients for anything definite.

E. SERVING PEOPLE

A project which does not rehabilitate ex-offenders may, nevertheless, justifiably claim encouragement and support because it offers service to people in other ways. Indeed, there has been at least one agency, the Newham Alternative Project, which rejected the notion of rehabilitation from the start, on the grounds that 'it is naive to expect most "offenders" to mend their ways or take seriously any effort by the establishment to reform/punish/deter them' (Dronfield 1980, p.42). Instead, NAP claimed to make life easier for offenders during times, however short, outside prison. It also claimed to serve the needs of the 'community':

> The project served as an information centre for the locality on lots of occasions. We displayed information on our windows about the Claimants Union, legal surgeries, NAP, exhibitions, events, and so on ... Although the borough had several specialist help agencies (e.g., a very good Citizens Advice Bureau), people often found it easier to drop into a centre which they passed every day, and which was informal in the extreme ... Some of the neighbours called in often, either for a chat, or to borrow things, and some of the children used NAP as somewhere to go after school (ibid., pp.34-5).

In our case studies, only Leo stands out as having received from the Unit significant service which he might not have obtained in any other way. It came mainly in the form of hard cash, which enabled him to travel for university interviews. The Unit also provided him with free telephone calls to universities. However, as Parkinson (1970) points out, material assistance is often derided by social workers on the grounds that it does not answer to people's 'real' needs even at the right time when it is needed, and, indeed, in the altercation between Ron and Ken over a loan for a down payment for renting a flat discussed earlier, the supposed need of the client to be tutored or counselled can be seen doing battle with his financial needs.

As NACRO-Education became more directly educational its other forms of service suffered. Thus, Ron wrote in his first annual report, 'If study turns out to be the wrong thing, something else is tried ... If they fail to make progress in their studies we work out an alternative'. And, indeed, as we saw in Percy's case, clients sometimes worked out alternatives for themselves, and even caused the people running the Unit to remark on the educational elements in such alternatives, even though the latter did not constitute formal, syllabus or classroom education. Nobody denied that Percy's activities were not in accordance with the educational ideal, for example, that 'young people ... must be able to formulate their own needs, organise their own learning, knowing when and how to find it' (Youth-aid 1979, pp.2-3).

By the time the Unit had established itself as a school, however, such unprogrammed, spontaneous flowering of independent curiosity and talent was not allowed to breathe for long. For example, Ozzie, a fourth year student, had passed an A level in prison, where he had also become an artist. His prison welfare officer had told him that under the aegis of NACRO he would be free to continue with study or with art or with a combination of both. The Management Committee selected Ozzie because Ron considered him low risk. The committee also considered, however, that Ozzie's educational performance was likely to be unimpressive. When this forecast turned out to be right, Ozzie put his studies aside and turned his room into a studio. This honest but flagrant rejection of the Unit's educational programme resulted in the staff making Ozzie feel unwanted. He said that he heard that Stafford, for example, maligned him in tutorials with other students by referring to him as an 'evil genius' - as Roth (1972, p.849), in a study of the control of hospital patients, points out, 'the negative evaluation of patients is strongest when they combine an undeserving character with illegitimate demands'. Ozzie felt aggrieved, and considered that staff could have increased amicable relations between other students and himself by saying, 'Look, you are studying, he is painting. It's the same thing. What you are conveying - he does it with colours, you do it with a pencil'. Strikingly, Ozzie appears to have been virtually the only <u>undercommitted</u> student who felt mounting interpersonal stress, became increasingly alcoholic, reoffended and returned to prison. Had he, like other undercommitted students, such as Arthur, adopted a policy of situational adjustment by unwillingly sitting through some classes in the school, giving excuses for absence from others and bided his time till he could find accommodation where he could do his own thing (a possibility not open to Arthur, who, as earlier discussed, was a judicial detainee in the Unit) such early and sudden recidivism may not have happened. On the other hand, my impression from his subsequent letters from prison, and from my visit to him there, is that, returned to that institution, he was now fairly free to expand his artistic and other abilities.

If the Unit had not become set on developing a school, and if it had not persisted with a hostel as an expedient measure for obtaining a grant from the Home Office to help finance the school, then it would have had time to provide other services for clients, of which the most important was probably working at assisting them to obtain suitable accommodation as soon as possible after their release from custody. In this way, the Unit could have become an efficient centre for advice on educational, housing and other problems instead of maintaining a hostel and a school of very dubious rehabilitative value. Unfortunately, at the Unit, the opportunity of alternative accommodation for clients as a reason for their moving out was usually accorded low priority by staff. By contrast, an intimation of the appreciation which clients may have felt for assistance in obtaining accommodation other than in a hostel for fellow ex-offenders is given in an essay which Ben wrote after the summer of 1975, when the Tech happened to have spare housing which it was able to offer to the Unit's students while Ron was on leave:

> *The Unit is too isolated, too protective. This was not apparent to me until we moved out of the Unit for the summer and into an everyday student house. The change in atmosphere was really refreshing. There is more individuality, more privacy, and yet it seems a closer community. One of the factors which helps to achieve this is the regular appearance of some of the guys' chicks* [many of whom, no doubt, would have been disinclined regularly to appear at a hostel for ex-offenders].

11 Education and Rehabilitation

In this chapter, I focus on the questions thrown up by the research concerning the relationship between education and rehabilitation. It is important to emphasise from the start, however, that it has not been part of my brief to question directly the basic cultural assumptions within these areas. It has not been my concern why people are punished for using some drugs, such as cannabis, but not others, such as alcohol. Nor have I speculated about the reasons for the criminalisation within a certain age range of homosexual behaviour, which in other cultures would provoke quite a different reaction, such as amusement or a matter of fact acceptance of it as a form of erotic life well within the range of behavioural diversity. Problems like these belong mainly to the realm of the anthropologist, with his ability to regard cultural values, including those in his own society, as exotic, rather than as part of the natural order of things. Similarly exotic are many of the fundamental values on which our educational system is based. For example:

> The United States is becoming more and more of a "credential society", a kind of pseudo-meritocracy in which a person is judged by his credentials - his high school or college diploma - rather than his performance on the job. These tendencies have been aggravated by the various campaigns to persuade youngsters to finish high school ... The fact that there seems to be little correlation with people's performance on the job and either the amount of education they have had or the marks they have received does not help the young man who has been turned down on the grounds of insufficient education before he can demonstrate his competence or before he can develop that competence (Silberman 1973, p.68).

The 'pseudo-meritocracy' of western society is probably closely connected with the traditional wisdom that formal education is a cure for all our social ills. This naive faith was formulated by the Cambridge Evening News (23/6/80, p.17), in spite of all the information it had gathered on the Unit since its foundation, in the following terms: 'Crime is mostly committed by the educationally deprived.

Provide criminals with an education and they will cease to commit crime'.

Tied up with such premisses are other basic cultural assumptions such as that learning is principally for young people, for 'educationally deprived' is a term which is not usually applied to older people.

Again, I abnegate the task of directly addressing myself to explaining these various cultural axioms. My main concern is the analysis of the way they manifested themselves in the Unit. Any questioning of such axioms which occurs as a result of the research may be regarded as an intellectual bonus.

A. EDUCATIONAL DISCONTINUITY

NACRO has run a variety of projects. A researcher connected with one of them concerned with ex-offenders' housing needs has appropriately pointed out:

> It would be rash to proceed to a reconviction study before having established precisely what was being done at the project and what was being achieved in terms of resettlement. If one of the assumptions underlying such a project is that by assisting offenders to become resettled in the community by meeting their housing and other needs reduces their likelihood of their re-offending, then it is first necessary to determine the extent to which such needs are <u>actually</u> met (Crow 1979, pp.3-4; emphasis his).

What applies to housing needs also applies to educational needs. It is my contention that by and large educational needs of students at the Unit were not actually met. Ben's essay, cited at the end of the last chapter, may again be consulted to see the way in which educational needs were defined by a student:

> *Educationally speaking I believe it would be well worth the time, effort and finances to set up some sort of ... course which offered no qualifications but <u>instead prepared students</u> with a fairly wide field of knowledge <u>for further education</u>. I think that the chase for 'A' levels is not as acceptable to mature students as it is to those coming straight from school* (emphases mine).

We have seen how the Unit failed to prepare its students for further education. Moreover, only at the beginning of 1979, when the Unit as an educational institution was coming to an end, was it recognised, in 'Proposals for the Future of the Cambridge Educational Unit' which never got off the ground, that '"O" and "A" level work had proved limiting'.

It was rare for students to express their frustrations as directly as Ben had in his essay. Indeed, Ben himself, in the first year, found an alternative outlet one night, after overindulgence in drink, in smashing several windows in the Unit. The following morning, the residents pleaded ignorance about who the culprit might be. It was clear, however, that somebody would 'grass' before long, and Ben came forward to own up. Ron praised this act of disclosure as one of courage, and told him that we all go through bad patches. But Ben did not come to the Unit to learn how much courage he had. He had already learnt in prison its limited extent only too well. Ron's attempt to display empathy was of little use to Ben. As Geoff remarked after he received a similarly patronising gesture from a psychiatric social worker, 'He's always going on about how he smokes pot. But that don't bother me. His job is to help me to get off dope'. Similarly, by vandalising the hostel, Ben was expressing what he dared not express in words, that he needed help in getting off his unrelaxed study habits, as well as in dealing with an educational 'chase' with which he could not cope.

By the time the Unit turned itself into a school, the problem of lack of preparation for higher learning became even worse. The problem was never confronted, in spite of the fact that it is well known in educational psychology that the transition from one mode of education to another can create maladjustment. As a teacher using progressive methods observed of pupils who had been schooled in traditional methods (Mitchell 1972, p.100):

> When they moved up to my class they obviously missed the props which the authoritarian regime had provided ... they were unable to show initiative - broken pencils caused consternation and they needed permission before they made a move. These children had remembered what they had been taught but were unable to use that knowledge except within the context in which it had been learned; they lacked confidence to progress ... Their written work was presented beautifully but lacked originality; they had acquired some knowledge but had not yet learned what is, to my mind, the most important factor in junior education - learning how to learn.

The ex-prisoners in the Unit's school by no means 'missed the props which the authoritarian regime provided'. Indeed, in the school, adaptation was reinforced to props of rigid rules and procedures. Once such props were removed, clients entering university who had anxiously relied on them felt crippled. Feeling such a state of debility caused Ken to write to Ron on 20 January 1978:

> *Thinking about Jim's journey to University next year although he is reading different subjects*

he may suffer similar problems and as long as it doesn't interfere with his work it may be best to wean him of his dependency on the Unit and perhaps force him into situations which he will have to face next year. If nothing else they may give you an early warning as to how he may perform at University. I'm not sure but I'd hate him to suffer this.

This wise advice from one for whom intermediate education was intermediate between prison and prison went unheeded and the personal crises of students of the Unit's fourth year who went on to become undergraduates were not averted. Twelve months after Ken's letter, Jim was tried for highly imprisonable offences and, although not imprisoned, dropped out of formal education.

What may seem very curious is that Ron was not unaware of the educational needs of such students, for, in his plea to the court on behalf of Ken on 3 July 1978, Ron wrote:

> University had been "everything" for him yet when he went up he felt ... the perpetual quandary of not knowing what was expected of him socially, of never knowing how to act ... I would add that I know of several other cases of offenders dropping out of university for the same reason.

Unfortunately, so committed were Ron and other members of the Unit's staff to schooling that they devoted no time or attention to teaching any student 'what would be expected of him socially' or 'knowing how to act' in the future.

B. EDUCATIONAL CONTINUITY

If the assessment in the previous section has any accuracy, that clients of mature years who were subjected to schooling (either in the Unit or in prison) were not able to cope with discontinuity when they went to university, then it seems possible that the converse should also hold, that clients of mature years who went on to university and successfully graduated were not subjected to schooling. This hypothesis, indeed, turns out to be so, as the cases of the three clients who fall into this category, Adam, Leo and Gene, show. None of these graduates went to classes in prison or at the Unit.

In prison, Adam was offered the opportunity, which he rejected, of attending classes in various disciplines. He possessed an important component which is still part of British higher education, that of being able to work independently and follow one's own interests. Putting this ability into practice before and after release served as a useful preparation for study at university level. Upon entry into formal education at that level he was situationally well adjusted, and, because other people's approval, disapproval or expectations were irrelevant to his goals, he never became overcommitted.

Leo's position was similar. He studied in prison not in order to compete but simply because 'there was nothing else to do', a predicament not unlike the one which he faced when he came out of prison. His private reading was of his own choice and multidisciplinary. He took exams in a nonchalant and detached way. At university, there was little to prevent him from studying in a similar way and with similar success.

Gene served a comparatively short sentence for an offence whose circumstances seemed unlikely to recur (his wife had deserted him, leaving debts in his name, and he forged her signature in selling the house which they had bought together). He studied in prison by correspondence. When he later became a student at the Tech and then university he continued mainly to rely on his own resources. At the end of his first year at university, he wrote to Ron that 'it seems that I'm in my natural environment'.

All these students had their motivations for avoiding prison classes. Adam, as discussed earlier, despised the inmates who attended them as collaborators with authority. Leo kept to himself because many criminals regarded him as worse than a criminal and he regarded himself as better than a criminal. Similarly, Gene considered himself not a criminal but as someone who had made an error of judgment, and, therefore, dissociated himself from other prisoners. Indeed, he maintained a similar relationship with his co-residents in the Unit. Most of the Unit's residents tended to keep their distance from each other but at least admitted that they had something in common with each other as ex-cons, for whom crime and prison had been significant parts of their lives. Gene, who lived in the Unit longer than any other resident, considered that he had nothing whatsoever in common with any of the other students, apart from having happened to have been in prison.

Regardless, however, of the individual reasons for these students avoiding schooling in prison they all pursued their education there in an autonomous, noncompetitive and mainly informal way. None of them regarded himself as a person of little worth and none of them felt the need to compete for status in prison classrooms or in any other way. Their continued progress in education after coming out of prison could only expand their feeling of self-esteem. They stand as models of what could have been achieved with the Unit's other clients, if the latter had been encouraged to read books of their own choice, if they had been allowed to proceed at their own pace, if they had been discouraged from seeking to compete, and if staff, instead of adopting the traditional role of disciplinarians, had adopted the role of consultants to their clients on such educational problems as how to obtain reading material on subjects of their interest and ability. If, in short, education had been presented to such clients as an art thriving on freedom, individuality and cooperation, and on everything that is authentically different from prison, then they may have begun the process of ceasing to think of themselves as failures, which, in turn, is surely one of the most essential conditions for success.

C. EDUCATION AND HIDDEN TALENT

Neither Adam nor Leo nor Gene would have gained an interest in continuing their education if they had not happened to go to prison. Writing about education for adults, a director of the National Extension College points out that 'there has always been a part-time adult route' (Freeman 1976, p.5) but it is a 'tough route' (ibid). As a result, 'there are millions of underachievers in the UK' (ibid.). It is a sad commentary on our society that, released from tough obstacles in the outside world, many people who are locked up find, to their surprise, that the prison route is one of the main routes whereby 'underachievers' can become achievers.

Douglas (1964, p.127) says that 'in recent discussions there has been a tendency to assume that there is only a limited number of persons who can benefit from higher education and that there is a clearly defined "pool of talent" on which to draw for university places. It is clear from the present study that the pump is badly leaking at the points of secondary selection and school leaving'.

I consider that this statement is probably becoming more the case today than at the time of Douglas's study. But, in addition, we are much more aware today that education has been affected not only by leaks in the years up to school leaving but also by a tremendous lack of returning inflow in the years after school leaving. If opportunities for higher education are restricted mainly to people who have not had any urge to get out of the classroom for a few years then the result is a state of affairs which is 'bad for a country which, at a time of the greatest technological and social changes that the world has ever known, depends as few others on the development of the abilities of <u>all</u> its citizens, and on many and diverse kinds of ability' (Mauger 1972, p.131). If there is hidden talent among people who go to prison then there is also likely to be some among people who do not. On the same day as the Unit officially opened there was a letter in <u>The Daily Mail</u> from a woman who was studying in her spare time with the object of gaining university entrance. She complained of the cost of textbooks and of Adult Education courses which her endeavours were imposing on her family. Why, she asked, were law-abiding people like herself denied financial assistance whilst prisoners were provided with education free of charge? Although Adam, Leo and Gene are not under attack by the way she poses her question since unlike many other prisoners they made minimal use of financial assistance earmarked for education the main thrust of her argument seems to me unassailable.

D. EDUCATIONAL BARRIERS TO TALENT

New technology is rapidly creating a culture and society of such complexity that, as argued above, it requires the tapping of the most diverse kinds of intellectual talent, however hidden they may presently be.

The same new technology, however, is also introducing into our lives a simplicity which can free the world of learning from traditional priorities. With an inexpensive wristlet calculator, for example, the present emphasis on universal numerical skills beyond a minimal level becomes something of an anachronism, as Leach indicated at a time when one needed pockets for such instruments. Liberated from the curricular priority of mathematics people who have little interest in it, without needing to rebel against it and thus create a mental block which may last them the rest of their lives, can turn to other educational pursuits which are more to their liking. Moreover, various jobs can now be filled by people particularly chosen because of their demonstrable, though less quantifiable, qualities of personality, rather than because of qualifications of an academic kind. But this too rarely happens. Society's treatment of Ian is a highly illustrative example.

Ian was completely committed to an honourable profession, nursing, even at a humble level. He possessed abilities for the job and was willing to advance his abilities on the job. But he was excluded because he was not very clever at algebra and geometry. Facing the challenge of mastering such abstruseness in a limited time he became overcommitted, then undercommitted, then overcommitted, and so on, until he lost all commitment to symbolic equations. Now that he is spending a long period behind bars, the prison route revives his hope of gaining required qualifications. The state is now paying more for his upkeep than if he had been allowed to use not only his training in basic nursing but also his charm, friendly manner, compassion, zeal and keenness to render help in comfortably decarcerating recuperating patients from hospital. Meanwhile, in the job market for nursing on which scarcity of demand has been imposed by the instrument of increasing requirements for qualifications, people who are more academically minded than Ian but who may lack many of his qualities are permitted to enter. When Becker (1963, p.27), in discussing 'extraneous reasons' for people's conventional behaviour, says that 'the middle-class youth must not quit school, because his occupational future depends on receiving a certain amount of schooling' he is not stating a truism; he is implying that 'a certain amount of schooling' may be largely extraneous to one's occupational future. The operative words, however, are 'middle class', for working class youths may indeed quit school because they have not been disciplined or conditioned to an easy acceptance of such extraneousness.

The use of the educational system to deny, confuse or frustrate the inner aspirations of lower working class young people is serious enough. But this mechanism may be regarded as even more grave when the system operates to generate delinquency, a tendency which is far from obscure. As Glasser (1976, p.385) observes:

> In the high schools in depressed areas, I have found that as few as 5 percent of the students believe that they are successful. I don't think those who now consider themselves failures came to school feeling that way. They learned they were failures as they moved through school. Once they feel they're failures, they reinforce this belief by doing nothing or by resorting to delinquency. Then we threaten or punish, which reinforces their failure.

The diploma disease intensifies. If we turn back to The Jack-Roller we find that Shaw (1930) demonstrates that part of the rehabilitation of 'Stanley' consisted of his obtaining a job as a salesman, in which he took pride and for which he was temperamentally well suited. But imagine if he had had to take a cluster of O levels followed by a diploma in salesmanship! Would this form of certificatitis have more adequately prepared him for salesmanship and rehabilitation than whatever form of informal socialisation had enabled him to be successful at his occupation?

The hollowness of the myth that any kind of responsible position requires academic qualifications was demonstrated in Britain in 1980 when the suggestion was widely broadcast that the unemployed should volunteer for all kinds of unpaid work in the social services. Nobody in power so much as whispered the possibility that academic qualifications might be necessary for such positions. It seems that the question of paper qualifications arises only when working people wish to be paid for working.

The abuse of learning, whereby 'schooling is among other things a process for the manufacture of underdogs' (Galtung 1975, p.550) is not only a matter of politics but also of academic ethics. One of the ways of opposing this abuse is for academicians to refuse to disclose a young person's academic attainments unless a potential employer can show that proficiency in subjects studied is necessary for the job being offered. Such a policy may turn out to be very far from foolproof but it may generate a questioning of the cherished assumption that a school certificate, degree or whatever improves the mind in some general way so that it can then be applied to all sorts of unrelated fields of life. It is a version of that theory upon which the Unit was based. Discussion of the extent of its validity will be summed up in our concluding chapter.

12 Conclusion

This final chapter has two objectives. Firstly, we shall compare Becker's commitment theory of deviancy and normality with a practical project we have studied for making deviant people 'normal'. Secondly, we shall compare the analytical approach I have adopted, partly inspired by Becker, with the approach that other researchers have taken in studying residential institutions for the rehabilitation of offenders through education. I would not have had the need to produce the analytical tools used in this study if I had considered that more serviceable ones were in the academic storehouse.

A. EXPLAINING REHABILITATION

In order to examine the factors making for rehabilitation or continued recidivism, it may be useful to collect our case studies, coded according to meanings, attitudes and functions, in a table. Clients who failed to rehabilitate are listed on the left and those who rehabilitated on the right:

BEN:	1X↑;PP	ADAM:	1;PP,PS
LEO:	1↑;PP,PS	AVA:	1Y,2,3↓;PCo,PCh
JACK:	1X→Y,3;PCh	DES:	1X→3,2;PCo,PP
KEN:	1X↑;PP,PCo	HARRY:	1Y,3;PP,PCo,PCh
IAN:	1Y↔X,2,3;PP,PCo	ARTHUR:	1Y,2;PP,PCo,PCh
ELLIS:	1X↑;PP,PCo		
GEOFF:	1X→Y,3;PP,PS		

By scrutinising this table the following generalisations may be formulated:

1. If we were to consider Becker's theory in its primitive form then it will not stand up to the evidence deriving from the project studied, for so many of the clients who failed to rehabilitate were more than committed - they were overcommitted. The evidence, however, calls for a clear division of the attitude of commitment according to its level. I do not think there is anything abstruse

about the notion of different levels of commitment, even though they may go unnoticed by the casual observer. The situation is analogous to certain other forms of behaviour. Eating, for example, can be straightforwardly observed. Keener observation, however, may detect signs of overeating. Overcommitment may be as common as overeating - and certainly as common as overdrinking!

2. Our case studies provide only one case at all compatible with Becker's unaltered theory of commitment, that of Adam. As argued earlier, had the project been a very different one, so that it developed in its clients a 'normal' level of commitment to education, then, I consider, it may have produced many more cases of commitment to education leading to rehabilitation. Moreover, that Adam's biography is so extraordinary is most instructive, for it indicates that project policies were so misconceived, and administered so counterproductively, that only an extraordinarily determined client could extricate himself from its entanglements which were unhelpful and make full use of whatever features of the Unit which were helpful in enabling him to fulfil his commitment to education and rehabilitate.

3. Only if the definition of rehabilitation is altered to include avoiding reconviction might we have a second case of commitment leading to rehabilitation, that of Leo. I have, however, opposed stretching the meaning of rehabilitation in this way, in spite of the frequency with which it is done in other studies. I have argued that a proper understanding of the complex relationships between crime, punishment and rehabilitation is possible only if, on the one hand, the concept of rehabilitation and, on the other hand, avoidance of reconviction are analytically kept strictly separate.

4. No factor is more closely associated with failure to rehabilitate than overcommitment to the educational programme. This finding is both tragic and ironic, because it implies that so many of the Unit's clients were more anxious than the ordinary person to succeed in education, more sensitive to possible obstacles, more embarrassed about failure, and so on. Moreover, tragedy and irony are amplified by the Unit's failure to reduce any client's overcommitment to a normal level of commitment to education. Indeed, in three of our seven cases of continued recidivism, those of Ben, Ken and Ellis, according to staff's own retrospective comments, the clients concerned were subjected to undue pressure, so that their overcommitment actually increased. Furthermore, reversion from overcommitment to undercommitment, as in the cases of Jack and Geoff, or oscillation between these extremes, as in the case of Ian, in no way helped matters. Such attitude changes, on the contrary, were associated with feelings on the part of these clients that all their efforts had been and/or would be of no avail, and resulted in a sense of heightened failure, lowered self-worth, heavier guilt, desperation, inability to see alternatives to crime, etc. Overcommitment occurs in six out of our seven cases of continued recidivism,

and in only one out of five cases of rehabilitation, that of Des. Even this one case is a borderline, in that an accustomed urge to steal was calmed by continued, if not increased, use of cannabis.

5. Striking in our findings is that three out of our five cases of rehabilitation are associated with undercommitment to the Unit's academic programme. By means of excuses, pretence and other forms of situational adjustment such clients were able to avoid the pressure which the staff attempted to impose on them. The situation may have been very different if, as our discussion of the fourth year client, Ozzie, indicates, such clients had not been prepared to prevaricate in order to avoid the stress contingent on being pressurised.

6. Similarly striking is the proportion of cases in the rehabilitation column, compared to those in the recidivist column, in which the Unit was perceived not only as a staging post but also as a resort. It seems that, for some clients, temporary removal from their accustomed environment may have had a rehabilitative influence. This finding is one which probation officers, and students of probation work, may wish to note. It is also important to the theoretical sociologist with his interest in the common phenomenon whereby people seek 'a kind of moratorium in which a broad and unspecialised ... commitment can be maintained' (Becker and Carper 1956, p.290; see also Cohen and Taylor 1976).

7. The perception of the Unit as a colony does not produce any definite, overall pattern among our cases studies. Much seems to have depended on the way in which the Unit was perceived as a colony.

8. None of the functions of the Unit was intrinsically either positive or negative with respect to rehabilitation. The processing of Des, whereby he was authoritatively recommended to a potential employer who had a job with prospects to offer which Des became committed to, for example, seems to have had a rehabilitatively positive effect. Against such a sequence, however, must be set cases like those of Ben, Ken and Ellis, processed into the disaster areas of subsequent educational programmes to which they transported their overcommitment, and the case of Geoff, processed as an opiate addict especially deserving of methadone medication, but neither able to withdraw from it nor able to come to terms with his self-conscious inability.

The processing of clients by means of testimonials to the courts in judicial proceedings remains ambiguous in rehabilitative terms since no judicial sanction has either a predictably rehabilitative or a predictably recidivising effect (Brody 1976).

Our conclusion about the intrinsically indeterminate properties of processing also applies to the Unit's control function. On the one hand, control seems to have worsened the careers of overcommitted clients, whereas undercommitted clients, as discussed above, seem to have found techniques of avoiding its stressful effects. Moreover, we have the unique case of Harry, for whom control seems to have been rehabilitatively positive. As we may recall, he reasoned that if he could offend so easily under the control of a rehabilitative outfit he had better stop doing so after leaving the Unit (with its routine processing of clients for the courts) if he was to make absolutely sure that he did not take any risk of suffering the greater control, so threatening to the value he placed on maximising liberty and pleasure, of imprisonment.

9. Finally, it seems clear that in itself knowledge is not virtue; education in itself is not rehabilitative. That commitment to education is rehabilitative has not, however, been disproved in this study, even though any notion that overcommitment to education is rehabilitative most certainly has been disproved. Moreover, nothing in our research indicates that commitment to education is any more rehabilitative than commitment to any other line of action, whether the latter be a happy marriage, a career requiring minimal qualifications before employment, or contributing to wars of liberation in southern Africa.

B. PREVIOUS STUDIES OF REGIMES WITH RESEMBLANCES TO THE UNIT

Space allows for consideration of only two other approaches which have been used in studying residential centres for the education of people who have offended. For each approach I have chosen what I hope is one of the best examples. Both have their merits and, indeed, involve types of analysis which may suffice for regimes significantly different from the Unit. Both examples, however, also have shortcomings.

Inmate interactions Polsky's (1962) study of 'Cottage Six' at Hollymeade, an institution for delinquent boys, is a classic in the field of group dynamics, demonstrating how, for example, in different settings within the institution, the boys form a 'subculture', based on a pecking order, for collective activities. Such a phenomenon probably occurs in a range of organisations, though it was rare in the Unit, where, as in other after-care hostels, the more typical feeling was 'I don't want to spend two years in the nick with a lot of cons and then the next two years with a lot of ex-cons' (Sinclair and Snow 1971, p.93). Various reasons for the difference suggest themselves, of which the adolescent age of the Cottage Six residents may possibly be one. The reader has the impression, however, that Polsky may have put too much of an exclusive emphasis on inmate interactions for he goes so far as to embrace a dogma that 'for the sociologist, the critical observation unit is an interpersonal act in an institutional context' (ibid., p.53). Interpersonal acts are important, but one wonders why they are so 'critical' as, for example, to leave little room in analysis for discussion of the boys' backgrounds or their intended careers.

Polsky's main thesis is that the subculture of the boys is mainly delinquent (although there are strong indications that it is also used for constructive purposes) and, therefore, subverts the therapy that the boys receive. Since Polsky is exclusively concerned with arguing this thesis it is unfortunate that he fails to refer us to any evidence, or even to entertain any doubt, that therapy would have rehabilitative effects if a delinquent subculture were absent or if, say, a subculture of good behaviour while in the institution were present instead.

Having made the assumption of the rehabilitative value of therapy, however, Polsky confuses us at the end of the book by a disclaimer to the effect that 'no attempt ... based on this small sample is made to relate the social experience at Hollymeade to community adjustment. This epilogue merely highlights the direction taken by the boys two years after discharge' (ibid., p.185). Why Polsky makes no such attempt is unclear. One would have thought, for example, that the smallness of the sample would encourage him to make such an attempt, for it seems hard to see how any researcher can tackle a large sample before he has gained insights and developed hypotheses from a study in depth of a small sample. Confusion is further confounded by indications that, two years on, the former delinquents at Cottage Six seem to have done rather well! For seventeen out of twenty-six are stated to be 'community-adjusted' rather than deviant. The former term is used to embrace several variables, including ability to 'maintain themselves in the familial environment' (ibid.). This variable is particularly important because problems in the familial environment were one of the main factors which brought the boys to Cottage Six in the first place. In the present monograph's terminology, there appears to be a distinct possibility that Cottage Six served as a resort enabling the boys to behave differently when they returned home.

An underlying difficulty in Polsky's study appears to be a total confusion concerning the difference between the concept of control and the concept of change. Polsky tells us, for example, that 'the professional staff are pre-occupied with changing individual boys' values and personality structures' (ibid., p.170). But is this the case? In a preface by Jerome Goldsmith, whom I take to be a senior member of the professional staff, we are told that 'the unit administrator emphasizes therapeutic management of these children'. But there is surely a difference between 'management', however therapeutically it is ideologically presented, and changing people's values and personality structures. Even the simple fact that 'children' is used by custodians (see also p.125) of boys who are well into adolescence, on the border of manhood and even preparing for such avocations as army paratrooper (ibid., p.160) seems to indicate that the regime was as concerned with management and subordinating forms of control as with change.

However, in his new preface to the book (1977), Polsky seems to be vaguely moving in the direction of recognising the difference between the control and change functions. For, in reappraising his analysis, he suggests that control may heighten delinquency: 'I would now contend ... that the more powerful administration within the institution not only accommodates to, but systematically fosters the emergence of peer-subsystems ... the residents will be sufficiently ingenious to evolve deviant structures for circumventing authoritarian controls' (ibid., p.9). In this new preface, however, Polsky does not make clear what these controls consisted of, apart from a slight implication that they may be connected with therapy, which he now refers to as counselling. We can only suppose that such authoritarian controls were related to new policies of which Polsky had approved fifteen years previously (1962, pp.176-8). 'Changing the basic unit of treatment from the individual boy to the entire cottage and "move" the clinic into it' (ibid.) heads the list. The reader may see a resemblance between this policy change and the movement of a school into the Unit in Cambridge.

The boys' perspective I consider that the confusions in Polsky's analysis stem from the fact that he has so far been unable to bring himself completely to recognise that the received wisdom that therapy is rehabilitative is not unquestionable truth but merely a proposition which calls for empirical investigation. Polsky, however, is not the only researcher in this sociological field of enquiry to work with presuppositions. Indeed, Gill's (1974) study of an approved school obliges us with an unsupported dogma which is virtually the opposite of Polsky's, namely, that if the environment of a residential regime is different from the offender's normal environment any rehabilitative effects of the former are destined to remain in the past as soon as the resident returns to the latter (ibid., ch.9). Interestingly, just as Polsky's dogma seems to derive from adopting the stance of, and identifying with, management for most of the period of his research so Gill's dogma seems to derive from an exclusive preoccupation with 'the boys' perspective' (Gill 1975, p.121). Gill's main conclusion is that the boy in an approved school 'considers it to be an interlude in the real business of living' (ibid., p.145). But it is very difficult to interpret the significance of this conclusion, for there is no reason to regard the boys' perspective as the last word on the matter. Gill, however, seems to consider it unnecessary to follow up the boys into 'the real business of living' to see what effect, if any, their 'interlude' had on them. As a result, we are left once again with a study of a regime for the education of residentially aggregated offenders without any coherent attempt at evaluation. Boys at approved schools are boys who have been convicted, and we now know that boys who have been convicted <u>in fact</u> have a greater tendency to reoffend than boys who have escaped conviction (e.g., West and Farrington 1977, p.128). It would, therefore, have been useful to know if the form of treatment which convicted boys receive, such as the experience of approved school, is responsible for the difference and, if so, how.

In the present study, I have, along with Gill, avoided the way in which 'in traditional theory the deviant is not a man like other men ... thought to have nothing to say which could make sense to reasonable and conforming men' (Pearson 1975, p.205). In addition, in a relentless endeavour to maintain a professionally independent stance, I have evinced the perspective of the caretakers of the deviant. Listening carefully to what 'both sides' had to tell me was of immeasurable value in contributing to the task of fashioning concepts which would be useful in evaluating the project researched. The task has not been an easy one, for I can think of few other areas of sociology where Mills's (1959, p.226) statement that 'the problems of social science, when adequately formulated, must include troubles and issues, both biography and history, and the range of their intricate relations' is more applicable. At the end of the task, I hope that the conceptual tools fashioned with effort in the course of this study may be found useful by other researchers in reaping a plentiful intellectual yield.

Appendices

A A Brochure about the Project

Designed and Printed by L & T Press Ltd, Luton

NACRO pilot project

NACRO · Education

Educational Opportunities for Offenders

For care of offenders and the prevention of crime

NACRO-Education

The Problem

The Prison Department has an improving record of providing educational facilities for prisoners which can lead to recognised academic, technical and professional qualifications. Unfortunately, however, many prisoners do not complete courses of education because their sentence ends and the pressures of life outside are not conducive to study. Other prisoners serving short-term sentences do not have the opportunity to begin such courses. Similarly there are few educational opportunities for offenders serving non-custodial sentences.

There is unfortunately no provision for the offender who wants to continue studies begun during his sentence, or to break back into formal education in the hope of gaining a qualification. The problems facing an offender in search of education may include: a background of educational failure; consequent lack of the qualifications needed to secure places on further and higher education courses; little realistic hope of obtaining a maintenance grant; ignorance of the range of possibilities he might consider; lack of advice; homelessness or an unsatisfactory home background; lack of confidence; and a fear that at the end the desired job may not be obtainable anyway. Any combination of these problems can contribute to the high drop-out rate after discharge which so often frustrates the good work done in prison.

The Project

NACRO-Education was set up in May 1974 as an experiment to help offenders overcome these difficulties, obtain basic, further or higher education and gain qualifications. The Project is funded for the experimental period by the Home Office and charitable trusts.

The Project falls into two parts. The first, a National Education Advisory Service, is concerned to assess a potential student's needs, provide information, work out educational "propositions" for each person, and press applications for places and grants. In the first three years it has handled 450 cases. Placements have been arranged for students to do full-time courses at universities, polytechnics, government training schemes, teacher training colleges, technical colleges, schools of art, residential adult colleges, colleges of further education and horticultural colleges. These placements have involved educational establishments throughout the whole of England and Wales.

The second part, a student group in Cambridge, is based in a residential unit which can accommodate 10 students. So far 45 people have lived at the Unit.

How it Works

Anyone over 17, male or female, who has been recently released from a penal institution, expects to be released within a reasonably short-time, or is serving a non-custodial sentence, can apply to NACRO-Education. Although recent involvement in education is clearly an advantage, no exams need to have been passed to apply to the Project. Application forms are available through education and welfare officers in prisons and borstals, probation officers, and from the Project in Cambridge.

Applicants receive advice and counselling to help them choose the most appropriate course and method of study. The course placement service helps students to find places on existing courses and to obtain grants for that purpose.

Students at the residential unit are gradually enabled to gain confidence in themselves, to become better able to cope with stress and criticism and to plan ahead. They each have their own study bedroom and cater for themselves, and there are no residential staff. A few students at the unit attend the Cambridgeshire College of Arts and Technology, but most take part in 'O' and 'A' level courses run at the unit. Teaching is done in small groups, and each student has a weekly tutorial with one of the Education Officers when his progress and prospects and any problems can be discussed. Cultural, sporting and community service activities are also arranged.

The address of the national advisory service is:-

NACRO-Education,
P.O. Box 100,
1 Elizabeth Way,
Cambridge.
Tel: Cambridge (0223) 55968

Local services have been set up in Wiltshire and Greater Manchester to give advice and support. Enquiries in these areas should be addressed to:-

Mr William Hall	Mr David Haley
Assistant Chief Probation Officer	2 High Lane,
County Hall,	Chorlton-cum-Hardy,
TROWBRIDGE, Wilts.	MANCHESTER M21.
Trowbridge (02214) 3641 ext. 3651	*Manchester (061) 881 2007*

B Instructions on the Unit's Notice Board

"NACRO-Education"

<u>NOTICE TO ALL TEACHERS AND STUDENTS</u>

I have become concerned this week that the academic work of the project may be slipping below the standards necessary if good examination results are to be obtained.

The main problems seem to be:

(a) Poor class attendances

(b) Unsatisfactory output of written work

(c) Student anxiety over progress - particularly syllabus coverage

(d) Student anxiety that notes and marked written work, to be used for revision, are not accumulating fast enough.

Could I remind students that they are expected to maintain a satisfactory level of attendance. The minimum that I regard as satisfactory is 85%. If students have to miss a class they must see the teacher concerned and give their reasons, and must do what is necessary to catch up on the work they have missed.

I am asking three things of the teachers:

(1) to produce a summary of their plans for their courses, to be published so that students can see how their subjects are going to be developed,

(2) to give me a mark for each student every two weeks so that progress can be recorded,

(3) to advise classes specifically about note keeping and organising their work with a view to revision.

We now have 27 clear teaching weeks before the exams.

Ron

22.10.77

Bibliography

Abercrombie, N. and Hill, S., 'Paternalism and Patronage', British Journal of Sociology, vol.27, 1976, pp.413-29.

Anttila, I., 'Conservative and Radical Criminal Policy in the Nordic Countries', Scandinavian Studies in Criminology, vol.3, 1971, pp.9-22.

Bailey, W.C., 'An evaluation of 100 Studies in Correctional Outcome', in Johnston, N. et al. (eds), The Sociology of Punishment and Corrections, Wiley, London 1970.

Barnes, J.A., Social Networks, Addison-Wesley, Reading, Massachusetts 1972.

Bazalgette, J., School Life and Work Life: a Study of Transition in the Inner City, Hutchinson, London 1978.

Bean, P., Rehabilitation and Deviance, Routledge and Kegan Paul, London 1976.

Becker, H.S., 'The Career of the Chicago Public School Teacher', American Journal of Sociology, vol.57, 1952, pp.473-7.

Becker, H.S., 'Notes on the Concept of Commitment', American Journal of Sociology, vol.66, 1960, pp.32-40.

Becker, H.S., Outsiders: Studies in the Sociology of Deviance, Collier-Macmillan, New York 1963, Revised Edition 1973.

Becker, H.S., 'Personal Change in Adult Life', Sociometry, vol.27, 1964, pp.40-53.

Becker, H.S. and Carper, J.W., 'The Development of Identification with an Occupation', American Journal of Sociology, vol.61, 1956, pp.289-98.

Becker, H.S. and Strauss, A., 'Careers, Personality and Adult Socialization', American Journal of Sociology, vol.62, 1956, pp.253-63.

Becker, H.S. et al., Boys in White: Student Culture in Medical School, University of Chicago Press, Chicago 1961.

Beech, H.R. and Liddell, A., 'Decision-Making, Mood States and Ritualistic Behaviour among Obsessional Patients', in Beech, H.R. (ed), Obsessional States, Methuen, London 1974.

Biko, S., I Write what I Like, Heinemann, London 1978.

Bogdan, R., Being Different: the Autobiography of Jane Fry, Wiley, New York 1974.

Bottomley, K., Review of Bakal, Y., 'Closing Correctional Institutions', British Journal of Criminology, vol.14, 1974, pp.193-5.

Bottoms, A.E. and McClintock, F.M., Criminals Coming of Age, Heinemann, London, 1973.

Boyle, J., A Sense of Freedom, Pan Books, London 1977.

Briggs, D., In Place of Prison, Maurice Temple Smith, London

1975.
Brody, S., The Effectiveness of Sentencing, Home Office Research Study, 35, HMSO, London 1976.
Burroughs, W., Junky, Penguin Books, Harmondsworth 1977 [originally published as Junkie under the pen-name of Lee, W., 1953].
Calder, R., Man and the Cosmos: the Nature of Science Today, Penguin Books, Harmondsworth 1968.
Carter, M., 'Teenage Workers: a Second Chance at 18?', in Brannen, P. (ed), Entering the World of Work: Some Sociological Perspectives, HMSO, London 1975.
Chambliss, W. (ed), Box Man: a Professional Thief's Journey, Harper and Row, New York 1972.
Christie, N., 'Scandinavian Criminology Facing the 1970s', Scandinavian Studies in Criminology, vol.3, 1971, pp.121-145.
Cicourel, A. and Kitsuse, J.I., 'The Social Organization of the High School and Deviant Adolescent Careers', in Rubington, E. and Weinberg, M. (eds), Deviance: the Interactionist Perspective, Collier-Macmillan, London 1968.
Cloward, R. and Ohlin, L., Delinquency and Opportunity: a Theory of Delinquent Gangs, Free Press, New York 1960.
Cohen, A.K., Delinquent Boys: the Culture of the Gang, Free Press, Glencoe, Illinois 1955.
Cohen, S. and Taylor, L., Escape Attempts, Penguin Books, Harmondsworth 1976.
Cornish, D.B. and Clarke, R.V.G., Residential Treatment and its Effects on Delinquency, Home Office Research Study, 32, HMSO, London 1975.
Corrigan, P., Schooling the Smash Street Kids, Macmillan, London 1979.
Cressey, D., Other People's Money: the Social Psychology of Embezzlement, Free Press, Glencoe, Illinois 1953.
Croft, J., Crime and the Community, Home Office Research Study, 50, HMSO, London 1979.
Crow, I., Back into Society: a Report on the 134 Project's Attempts to Resettle Discharged Prisoners, NACRO, London 1979.
Curtis, D., Dartmoor to Cambridge: the Autobiography of a Prison Graduate, Hodder and Stoughton, London 1973a.
Curtis, D., 'Curtis Suggests College', Frontsheet, 1973b, pp.6-7.
Curtis, D., 'New College', Frontsheet, 1974, p.5.
Davies, M., Prisoners of Society: Attitudes and After-Care, Routledge and Kegan Paul, London 1974a.
Davies, M., 'The Persistent Offender', in Morris, A. (ed), The Lawbreakers, BBC, London 1974b.
Devlin, K., Sentencing Offenders in the Magistrates' Courts, Sweet and Maxwell, London 1970.
Dodd, D., 'Police and Thieves on the Streets of Brixton', New Society, 16th March 1978, pp.598-600.
Dole, V.P., Nyaswander, M.E. and Warner, A., 'Successful Treatment of 750 Addicts', Journal of the American Medical Association, vol.206, 1968, pp.2708-14.
Dole, V.P. and Nyaswander, M.E., 'Methadone Maintenance

Treatment: a Ten-Year Perspective', Journal of the American Medical Association, vol.235, 1976, pp.2117-9.
Doleschal, E. and Klapmuts, N., 'Toward a New Criminology', Crime and Delinquency Literature, vol.5, 1973, pp.607-26.
Douglas, J.W.B., The Home and the School: a Study of Ability and Attainment in the Primary School, MacGibbon and Kee, London 1964.
Downes, D.M., The Delinquent Solution, Routledge and Kegan Paul, London 1966.
Dronfield, L., Outside Chance: the Story of the Newham Alternative Project, RAP, London 1980.
Durkheim, E., The Rules of Sociological Method, Free Press, New York 1964.
Eckstein, S., 'The Irony of Organization: Resource and Regulatory', British Journal of Sociology, vol.27, 1976, pp.150-63.
Elliott, D., 'Delinquency, School Attendance and Dropout', Social Problems, vol.13, 1966, pp.307-13.
Elliott, D. and Voss, H., Delinquency and Drop-Out, Heath, London 1974.
Emery, R.E. and Marholin, D., 'An Applied Behavior Analysis of Delinquency', American Psychologist, vol.32, 1977, pp.860-73.
Empey, R.E. and Lubeck, S.G., The Silverlake Experiment, Aldine, Chicago 1971.
Etzioni, A., Modern Organizations, Prentice Hall, Englewood Cliffs, New Jersey 1964.
Eysenck, H.J., Fact and Fiction in Psychology, Penguin Books, Harmondsworth 1965.
Eysenck, H.J., 'Introduction', in Eysenck, H.J. (ed), Case Studies in Behaviour Therapy, Routledge and Kegan Paul, London 1976.
Farrington, D., 'Explanations of Juvenile Delinquency', in Morris, A. (ed), The Lawbreakers, BBC, London 1974.
Farrington, D., 'Delinquent Behaviour Modification in the Natural Environment', British Journal of Criminology, vol.19, 1979, pp.353-72.
Fersch, E.A., Goldfine, P.E. and Vrabel, J., 'The Need for Sanctuary from the Community', International Journal of Offender Therapy and Comparative Criminology, vol. 22, 1978, pp.68-79.
Fitzgerald, M., Prisoners in Revolt, Penguin Books, Harmondsworth 1977.
Fitzgerald, M. and Sim, J., British Prisons, Blackwell, Oxford 1979.
Folkard, M.S., Smith, D.E. and Smith, D.D., IMPACT: Intensive Matched Probation and After-Care Treatment, vol.2, Home Office Research Study, 36, HMSO, London 1976.
Foucault, M., Discipline and Punish: the Birth of the Prison, Penguin Books, Harmondsworth 1977.
Freeman, R., Can Education Rehabilitate?, Typescript, NACRO European Conference 1976.
Frøysa, I., Oslo Education Project, Typescript, NACRO European Conference 1976.
Galtung, J., 'Schooling and Future Society', School Review, vol.83, 1975, pp.533-68.

Gaskell, J. and Utting, D., 'The "Hell on Earth" Known as Elizabeth Way', Cambridge Evening News, 14th July 1977, p.11.
Gath, D.H., Tennent, T.G. and Pidduck, R., 'Criminological Characteristics of Bright Delinquents', British Journal of Criminology, vol.11, 1971, pp.275-80.
Geddes, D., 'The Crammer Boom', New Society, 15th February 1979, pp.350-2.
Gill, O., Whitegate: an Approved School in Transition, Liverpool University Press, Liverpool 1974.
Gill, O., 'Residential Treatment for Young Offenders', in Mays, J.B. (ed), The Social Treatment of Young Offenders, Longman, London 1975.
Glasser, W., 'Roles, Goals and Failure', in Bassin, A. et al. (eds), The Reality Therapy Reader, Harper and Row, London 1976.
Glickman, M.J.A., 'Education and Work: an Anthropological View of the Transition Process', in Brannen, P. (ed), Entering the World of Work: Some Sociological Perspectives, HMSO, London 1975.
Goffman, E., Asylums: Essays on the Social Situation of Mental Patients and other Inmates, Penguin Books, Harmondsworth 1961.
Gold, M., 'Undetected Delinquent Behavior', Journal of Research into Crime and Delinquency, vol.3, 1966, pp.27-46.
Goody, J. (ed), The Developmental Cycle of Domestic Groups, Cambridge University Press, Cambridge 1958.
Gordon, G. and Morse, E.V., 'Evaluation Research', Annual Review of Sociology, vol.1, 1975, pp.21-42.
Green, A.W., 'The Middle-Class Male Child and Neurosis', American Sociological Review, vol.11, 1946, pp.31-41.
Griffiths, D., 'The Prison Reformers', New Society, 25th December 1975, pp.689-90.
Griffiths, W.A., After-Care Hostels - a Critique of the Family Model, NACRO Papers and Reprints, 5, 1970.
Halls, W.D., 'United Kingdom', The Encyclopedia of Education, Macmillan and Free Press 1971.
Hasenfeld, Y., 'People Processing Organizations: an Exchange Approach', American Sociological Review, vol.37, 1972, pp.256-63.
Heilbroner, R.L., 'Economic Problems of a "Postindustrial" Society', in Potter, D. and Sarre, P. (eds), Dimensions of Society, London, London University Press 1974.
Heim, A.W., AH4 Group Test of General Intelligence Manual, Revised Edition 1970.
Henry, S., The Hidden Economy: the Context and Control of Borderline Crime, Robertson, Oxford 1978.
Hinton, N., 'Schemes with Offenders', Aspectos, August 1977, pp.27-30.
Hirschi, T., 'Labelling Theory and Juvenile Delinquency: an Assessment of the Evidence', in Gove, W.R. (ed), The Labelling of Deviance, Wiley, London 1975.
HMSO, Report of the Departmental Committee on Prisons, C7702 [The Gladstone Report], London 1895.
HMSO, The Organisation of After-Care. Report of the Advisory

Council on the Treatment of Offenders, London 1963.
HMSO, People in Prison, England and Wales, Cmnd 4214, London 1969.
HMSO, Report of the Parole Board for 1975, London 1976.
HMSO, The Sentence of the Court: a Handbook for Courts on the Treatment of Offenders, 3rd Edition, London 1978.
Holborn, J., 'Casework with Short-Term Prisoners', in Some Male Offenders' Problems, Home Office Research Study, 28, London 1975.
Holt, J., How Children Fail, Penguin Books, Harmondsworth 1964.
Home Office, Parole: Your Questions Answered, HMSO, London 1976.
Hood, R., Sentencing in the Magistrates' Courts, Stevens, London 1962.
Hood, R. and Sparks, R., Key Issues in Criminology, Weidenfeld and Nicolson, London 1970.
Hunt, R. and Hunt, E., 'Education as an Interface Institution in Rural Mexico and the American Inner City', Midway, vol.8, 1967, pp.99-109.
Hutt, M., 'Undergraduates and their Problems', in Daiches, D. (ed), The Idea of a New University: an Experiment in Sussex, André Deutsch, London 1964.
Hymphrey, D. and May, D., 'Why the Prisons could Explode', NACRO Newsletter, February 1977, pp.7-9.
Irwin, J., The Felon, Prentice-Hall, Englewood Cliffs, New Jersey 1970.
Irwin, J. and Cressey, D.R., 'Thieves, Convicts and Inmate Culture', Social Problems, vol.10, 1962, pp.142-55.
Jackson, B., Starting School, Croom Helm, London 1979.
Jackson, B. and Marsden, D., Education and the Working Class, Routledge and Kegan Paul, London 1962.
Jacobs, J., 'On the VD Trail', New Society, 6th May 1979, pp.492-5.
Jesness, C.F., The Fricot Ranch Study, Research Report 47, California Youth Authority, Sacramento, California 1965.
Johnston, N. et al. (eds), The Sociology of Punishment and Corrections, Wiley, London 1970.
Kirby, B., Crofton House: Final Report, San Diego State College 1970.
Klare, H.J., People in Prison, Pitman, Belmont, California 1973.
Korving, M. and Davidson, J., Careers without O-Levels, BBC, London 1975.
Lawrie, J., The Marriage of Gor: the True Account of a White Girl's Life with a Black Man. Gollancz, London 1960.
Leach, E.R., Literacy be Damned, Unpublished Lecture 1977.
Lemert, E., Human Deviance, Social Problems, and Social Control, 2nd Edition, Prentice-Hall International, London 1972.
Lerman, P., 'Evaluation Studies of Institutions for Delinquents: Implications for Research and Social Policy', Social Work, vol.13, 1968, pp.55-64.
Levey, S., Work Placement Report: Summer 1976, Unpublished 1976.

Levitt, E.E., The Psychology of Anxiety, Paladin Books, London 1968.
Lewis, D. and Hughman, P., Just How Just?, Secker and Warburg, London 1975.
Lindesmith, A., Addiction and Opiates, Aldine, Chicago 1968.
Lipton, D. et al., The Effectiveness of Correctional Treatment: a Survey of Treatment Evaluation Studies, Praeger, London 1975.
Locke, M. and Pratt, J., A Guide to Learning after School, Penguin Books, Harmondsworth 1979.
Lofland, J., Deviance and Identity, Prentice-Hall, Englewood Cliffs, New Jersey 1969.
Logan, C.H., 'Evaluation Research in Crime and Delinquency: a Reappraisal', Journal of Criminal Law, Criminology, and Police Science, vol.63, 1972, pp.378-87.
Lohman, J.D. et al. The Intensive Supervision Caseload, The San Francisco Project, Research Report 11, School of Criminology, Berkeley, California 1967.
Lumkin, P., The APEX Specialist Employment Service for the Prisoner and Ex-Prisoner, Typescript, NACRO European Conference 1976.
Lunzer, E. and Gardner, K., The Effective Use of Reading, Heinemann, London 1979.
McCord, W. and McCord, J., Origins of Crime, Columbia University Press, New York 1959.
Mack, J., 'The Able Criminal', British Journal of Criminology, vol.15, 1972, pp.44-9.
McKinnon, J., Onward Industries Workshop, Typescript, NACRO European Conference 1976.
McVicar, J., McVicar by Himself, Revised Edition, Hutchinson, London 1979.
Mannheim, H., Comparative Criminology, Routledge and Kegan Paul, London 1965.
Mannheim, H., 'The Study of Crime', in Welford, A.T. (ed), Society: Problems and Methods of Study, Revised Edition, Routledge and Kegan Paul, London 1967.
Mannheim, H. and Wilkins, L., Prediction Methods in Relation to Borstal Training, HMSO, London 1955.
Matza, D., Becoming Deviant, Prentice-Hall, Englewood Cliffs, New Jersey 1969.
Mauger, P., 'Selection for Secondary Education', in Rubinstein, D. and Stoneman, C. (eds), Education for Democracy, Revised Edition, Penguin Books, Harmondsworth 1972.
Maurer, D., The Big Con, Pocket Books, New York 1949.
Mays, J.B., Growing Up in the City: a Study of Juvenile Delinquency in an Urban Neighbourhood, Liverpool University Press, Liverpool 1954.
Mays, J.B. (ed), The Social Treatment of Young Offenders, Longman, London 1975.
Mead, M., Culture and Commitment, Panther Books, London 1972.
Meisenhelder, T., 'An Exploratory Study of Exiting from Criminal Careers', Criminology, vol.15, 1977, pp.319-34.
Merton, R.K., 'Bureaucratic Structure and Personality', Social Forces, vol.18, 1940, pp.560-8.

Merton, R.K., Social Theory and Social Structure, Enlarged Edition, Collier-Macmillan 1968.
Miller, D., Growth to Freedom: the Psychosocial Treatment of Delinquent Youth, Tavistock, London 1964.
Miller, W., 'Lower Class Culture as a Generating Milieu of Gang Delinquency', Journal of Social Issues, vol.14, 1958, pp.5-19.
Millham, S. et al., 'Another Try: an Account of a New Careers Project for Borstal Trainees', in Tutt, N. (ed), Alternative Strategies for Coping with Crime, Blackwell, Oxford 1978.
Mills, C.W., The Sociological Imagination, Oxford University Press, Oxford 1959.
Mishan, E.J., The Costs of Economic Growth, Penguin Books, Harmondsworth 1969.
Mitchell, J., 'Freedom in the Junior School', in Rubinstein, D. and Stoneman, C. (eds), Education for Democracy, Revised Edition, Penguin Books, Harmondsworth 1972.
Morrison, A. and McIntyre, D., Schools and Socialization, Penguin Books, Harmondsworth 1971.
Morse, M., The Unattached, Penguin Books, Harmondsworth 1965.
Mott, J. and Hope, T., 'Alcohol and Crime', Home Office Research Unit Research Bulletin, vol.3, 1976, pp.28-31.
National Association for Mental Health, Why Delinquency? The Case for Operational Research, HMSO, London 1949.
New Society, 'What do Exams Mean?', 28th June 1979, p.777.
Osol, A. and Farrar, G., Jr., The Dispensary of the United States of America, 25th Edition, Lippincott, Philadelphia 1955.
Parker, T., The Unknown Citizen, Hutchinson, London 1963.
Parker, T., The Twisting Lane, Panther Books, London 1969.
Parker, T. and Allerton, R., The Courage of His Convictions, Hutchinson, London 1962.
Parkinson, G., 'I Give them Money', New Society, 5th February 1970, pp.220-1.
Pearson, G., The Deviant Imagination: Psychiatry, Social Work and Social Change, Macmillan, London 1975.
Pease, K. et al. Community Service Assessed in 1976, Home Office Research Study, 39, HMSO, London 1977a.
Pease, K. et al., 'The Development of a Scale of Offence Seriousness', International Journal of Criminology and Penology, vol.5, 1977b, pp.17-19.
Peryer, D. et al., Residential Care, NACRO, London n.d.
Pharmaceutical Codex, 11th Edition, Pharmaceutical Press, London 1979.
Phillips, M., 'Homes for Children', New Society, 10th March 1977, pp.493-4.
Plummer, K., Sexual Stigma: an Interactionist Account, Routledge and Kegan Paul, London 1975.
Polsky, H., Cottage Six: the Social System of Delinquent Boys in Residential Treatment, Russell Sage Foundation, New York 1962, with New Preface 1977.
Polsky, N., Private Communication, in Becker (1963, pp.171-2).
Probyn, W., Angel Face: the Making of a Criminal, Allen and Unwin 1977.

Radzinowicz, L., 'The Criminal in Society', Journal of the Royal Society of Arts, vol.112, 1964, pp.916-29.
Radzinowicz, L. and King, J., The Growth of Crime: the International Experience, Penguin Books, Harmondsworth 1977.
Raubolt, R. and Bratter, T., 'Treating the Methadone Addict', in Bassin, A. et al., The Reality Therapy Reader, Harper and Row, London 1976.
Ray, M., 'The Cycle of Abstinence and Relapse among Heroin Addicts', Social Problems, vol.9, 1961, pp.132-40.
Reckless, W., Six Boys in Trouble, Michigan University Press, Ann Arbor 1929.
Reckless, W. and Dinitz, S., The Prevention of Juvenile Delinquency: an Experiment, Ohio State University Press, Columbus 1972.
Regier, M., Social Policy in Action: Perspectives on the Implementation of Alcohol Reforms, Heath, Lexington, Massachusetts 1979.
Riesman, D., Faces in the Crowd, Yale University Press, London 1952.
Robison, J. and Smith, G., 'The Effectiveness of Correctional Programs', Crime and Delinquency, vol.17, 1971, pp.67-80.
Roth, J., 'Some Contingencies of the Moral Evaluation and Control of Clientele: the Case of the Hospital Emergency Service', American Journal of Sociology, vol.77, 1972, pp.839-56.
Sahlins, M., Stone Age Economics, Tavistock, London 1974.
Sampson, H. et al. 'The Mental Hospital and Marital Family Ties', Social Problems, vol.9, 1961, pp.141-55.
Sanford, N., 'The College Student in 1980', in Eurich, A. (ed), Campus 1980, Delacorte Press, New York 1968.
Sawdon, A. et al., Study of the Transition from School to Working Life, Youthaid, London 1979.
Schutz, A., 'The Stranger', American Journal of Sociology, vol.49, 1944, pp.499-507.
Scull, A.T., Decarceration: Community Treatment and the Deviant - a Radical View, Prentice-Hall, Englewood Cliffs, New Jersey 1977.
Shaw, C., The Jack-Roller: a Delinquent Boy's own Story, University of Chicago Press, London 1930, New Edition 1966.
Shaw, C., The Natural History of a Delinquent Career, Albert Saifer, Philadelphia 1931.
Shaw, C., Brothers in Crime, University of Chicago Press, Chicago 1938.
Silberman, C.E., Crisis in the Classroom, Wildwood House, London 1973.
Silberman, M., Care or Crime? - Alternatives to Delinquent Behaviour, Royal London Discharged Prisoners' Aid Society, London 1969.
Sinclair, I.A.C., Hostels for Probationers, Home Office Research Study, 6, HMSO, London 1971.
Sinclair, I.A.C. and Clarke, R.V.G., 'Acting-Out Behaviour and its Significance for the Residential Treatment of Delinquents', Journal of Child Psychology and Psychiatry, vol.14, 1973, pp.283-91.

Sinclair, I.A.C. and Snow, D., 'After-Care Hostels Receiving a Home Office Grant', in Explorations in After-Care, Home Office Research Study 9, HMSO, London 1971.
Smith, R., 'Culture and Structure in the Caribbean: some Recent Work on Family and Kinship Studies', Comparative Studies in Society and History, vol.6, 1963, pp.24-45.
Soothill, K., The Prisoner's Release, Allen and Unwin, London 1974.
Spradley, J., You Owe Yourself a Drunk: an Ethnography of Urban Nomads, Little, Brown and Co., Boston 1970.
Stevens, A., 'Worried Youngsters are Putting Jobs before Degrees', The Observer, 2nd July 1978, p.3.
Stevens, S.S., 'On the Theory of Scales of Measurement', in Liebermann, B. (ed), Contemporary Problems in Statistics: a Book of Readings in the Behavioral Sciences, Oxford University Press, New York 1971.
Sugden, G. and Skinner, L., The Pro's and the Ex-Cons: a Record of Our Experiences in Setting up the Hargrave House Project - and how we Feel about the Whole Question of Housing for Exprisoners. Hargrave House Project, London n.d.
Sutherland, E.H., The Professional Thief: by a Professional Thief, Chicago, University of Chicago Press 1937.
Taylor, L., 'Observing Delinquency', in Taylor, L. et al., Signs of Trouble: Aspects of Delinquency, BBC, London 1976.
Terkel, S., Working: People Talk about what they Do all Day and how they Feel about what they Do, Wildwood House, London 1975.
Thomas, D.A., Principles of Sentencing, Second Edition, Heinemann, London 1979.
Thomas, W.I. and Znaniecki, F., The Polish Peasant in Europe and America, Gorham Press, Boston 1918-20.
Thorpe, D., 'Intermediate Treatment', in Tutt, N. (ed), Alternative Strategies for Coping with Crime, Blackwell, Oxford 1978.
Thorvaldson, S.A., The Effects of Community Service on the Attitude of Offenders, unpublished PhD thesis, University of Cambridge 1978.
Tobias, J.J., Crime and Industrial Society in the Nineteenth Century, Penguin Books, Hardmondsworth 1967.
Tunstall, J. (ed), The Open University Opens, Routledge and Kegan Paul, London 1974.
Turner, M., Safe Lodging, Aldine, Chicago 1961.
Tutt, N., 'Introduction', in Tutt, N. (ed), Alternative Strategies for Coping with Crime, Blackwell, Oxford 1978.
Uusitalo, P., Prison and Labour Colony: a Comparison, Helsinki, 1968.
Van Den Haag, E., 'Snobbery', British Journal of Sociology, vol.7, 1956, pp.212-16.
Vanfossen, M.G., A Theoretical Model for the Analysis of Social Interaction Situations, unpublished PhD thesis, Emory University 1960.
Veness, T., School Leavers: Their Aspirations and Expectations, Methuen, London 1962.
Vodopivec, K., Maladjusted Youth: an Experiment in Rehabi-

litation, Heath, Lexington, Massachusetts 1974.
Wade, A. (ed), Martindale: the Extra Pharmacopoeia, Pharmaceutical Press, London 1977.
Walker, N., Crime and Punishment in Britain, Revised Edition, Edinburgh, Edinburgh University Press 1968.
Walker, N., Sentencing in a Rational Society, Allen Lane, London 1969.
Walster, E., 'The Temporal Sequence of Post-Decision Processes', in Festinger, L. et al. (eds), Conflict, Decision and Dissonance, Tavistock, London 1964.
Warner, L.W. and Abegglen, J.C., Big Business Leaders in America, Harper, New York 1955.
Weber, M., The Theory of Social and Economic Organization, Parsons, T. (ed), Oxford, Oxford University Press, 1947.
West, D., The Young Offender, Penguin Books, Harmondsworth 1967.
West, D., 'Parole in England: an Introductory Explanation', in West, D. (ed), The Future of Parole: Commentaries on Systems in Britain and U.S.A., Duckworth, London 1972.
West, D. and Farrington, D., Who Becomes Delinquent?, Heinemann, London 1973.
West, D. and Farrington, D., The Delinquent Way of Life, Heinemann, London 1977.
Wheeler, S., 'The Structure of Formally Organized Socialization Settings', in Brim, O. and Wheeler, S., Socialization after Childhood, Wiley, New York 1966.
Willcock, H.D., Deterrents and Incentives to Crime among Boys and Young Men Aged 15-21 Years, HMSO, London 1974.
Williamson, H. 'Choosing to be a Delinquent', New Society, 9th November 1978, pp.333-5.
Willis, P., Learning to Labour: How Working Class Kids Get Working Class Jobs, Saxon House, Farnborough 1977.
Wootton, B., Crime and Penal Policy: Reflections on Fifty Years' Experience, Allen and Unwin, London 1978.
Wright, M. (ed), Uses of Criminological Literature, Butterworths, London 1974.
Yablonsky, L., 'Experiences with the Criminal Community', in Gouldner, A. and Miller, S. (eds), Applied Sociology: Opportunities and Problems, Collier-Macmillan, London 1965.
Yablonsky, L., 'An Analysis of the Hippie Movement', in Palmer, S. and Linsky, A. (eds), Rebellion and Retreat: Readings in the Forms and Processes of Deviance, Merrill, Columbus 1972.
Yeger, S., 'Weekend Junkies', New Society, 19th February 1970, pp.308-9.
Young, W.A., Community Service Orders, unpublished PhD thesis, University of Cambridge 1978.
Youthaid, Life is not an Academic Subject, Youthaid, London 1979.
Zald, M.N. and Denton, P., 'From Evangelism to General Service', Administrative Science Quarterly, vol.8, 1963, pp.214-34.

Index of Clients of the Unit

Each name is followed (in parenthesis) by the age at which the client came to the Unit and by the academic year(s) in which (s)he resided there. The year (s)he is classified as having spent most of his or her residence in the Unit is underlined.